T0212969

Lecture Notes of the Institute for Computer Sciences, Social Informatics and Telecommunications Engineering 193

More information about this series at http://www.springer.com/series/8197

Phan Cong Vinh · Le Tuan Anh
Nguyen Thi Thuy Loan
Waralak Vongdoiwang Siricharoen (Eds.)

Context-Aware Systems and Applications

5th International Conference, ICCASA 2016
Thu Dau Mot, Vietnam, November 24–25, 2016
Proceedings

Springer

Editors
Phan Cong Vinh
Nguyen Tat Thanh University
Ho Chi Minh City
Vietnam

Le Tuan Anh
Thu Dau Mot University
Thu Dau Mot City
Vietnam

Nguyen Thi Thuy Loan
Nguyen Tat Thanh University
Ho Chi Minh City
Vietnam

Waralak Vongdoiwang Sricharoen
University of the Thai Chamber
  of Commerce
Bangkok
Thailand

ISSN 1867-8211   ISSN 1867-822X (electronic)
Lecture Notes of the Institute for Computer Sciences, Social Informatics
and Telecommunications Engineering
ISBN 978-3-319-56356-5   ISBN 978-3-319-56357-2 (eBook)
DOI 10.1007/978-3-319-56357-2

Library of Congress Control Number: 2017936359

Printed on acid-free paper

This Springer imprint is published by Springer Nature
The registered company is Springer International Publishing AG
The registered company address is: Gewerbestrasse 11, 6330 Cham, Switzerland

Preface

ICCASA 2016, an international scientific conference for research in the field of context-aware computing and communication, was held during November 24–25, 2016, in Thu Dau Mot City, Vietnam. The aim of the conference is to provide an internationally respected forum for scientific research on the technologies and applications of context-aware computing and communication. This conference offered an excellent opportunity for researchers to discuss modern approaches and techniques for context-aware systems and their applications. The proceedings of ICCASA 2016 are published by Springer in the *Lecture Notes of the Institute for Computer Sciences, Social Informatics and Telecommunications Engineering* series (LNICST; indexed by DBLP, EI, Google Scholar, Scopus, Thomson ISI).

For this fifth edition, repeating the success of previous years, the Program Committee received submissions from ten countries and each paper was reviewed by at least three experts. We chose 20 papers after intensive discussions held among the Program Committee members. We appreciate the excellent reviews and lively discussions of the Program Committee members and external reviewers in the review process. This year we chose two prominent invited speakers: Dr. Sang Keon Lee from the National Infrastructure Research Division at Korea Research Institute for Human Settlements (KRIHS) in South Korea, and Dr. Waralak Vongdoiwang Siricharoen from the School of Science and Technology at the University of the Thai Chamber of Commerce (UTCC) in Thailand.

ICCASA 2016 was jointly organized by The European Alliance for Innovation (EAI), Thu Dau Mot University (TDMU), and Nguyen Tat Thanh University (NTTU). This conference could not have been possible without the strong support of the staff members of these three organizations. We would especially like to thank Prof. Imrich Chlamtac (University of Trento and Create-NET), Anna Horvathova (EAI), and Ivana Allen (EAI) for their great help in organizing the conference. We also appreciate the gentle guidance and help from Prof. Nguyen Manh Hung, Chairman and Rector of NTTU, and Prof. Nguyen Van Hiep, Rector of TDMU.

November 2016

Phan Cong Vinh
Le Tuan Anh
Nguyen Thi Thuy Loan
Waralak Vongdoiwang Siricharoen

Organization

Steering Committee

Imrich Chlamtac	CREATE-NET, Italy (Chair)
Phan Cong Vinh	Nguyen Tat Thanh University, Vietnam
Thanos Vasilakos	Kuwait University

Honorary General Chairs

Nguyen Van Hiep	Thu Dau Mot University, Vietnam
Nguyen Manh Hung	Nguyen Tat Thanh University, Vietnam

General Chair

Phan Cong Vinh	Nguyen Tat Thanh University, Vietnam

Technical Program Chairs

Le Tuan Anh	Thu Dau Mot University, Vietnam
Loan T.T. Nguyen	Nguyen Tat Thanh University, Vietnam

Technical Program Session or Track Chairs

Nguyen Dang Binh	Hue University of Science, Vietnam
Tran Vinh Phuoc	Thu Dau Mot University, Vietnam

Workshops Chair

Emil Vassev	University of Limerick, Ireland

Publications Chairs

Phan Cong Vinh	Nguyen Tat Thanh University, Vietnam
Hoang Manh Ha	Thu Dau Mot University, Vietnam

Marketing and Publicity Chair

Do Nguyen Anh Thu	Nguyen Tat Thanh University, Vietnam

Patron Sponsorship and Exhibits Chairs

Nguyen Thanh Tung   Hanoi Vietnam National University, Vietnam
Nguyen Thi Anh Tuyet   Thu Dau Mot University, Vietnam

Panels and Keynotes Chair

Vangalur Alagar   Concordia University, Canada

Demos and Tutorials Chair

Nguyen Thanh Binh   Ho Chi Minh City University of Technology, Vietnam

Posters Chair

Thai Thi Thanh Thao   Nguyen Tat Thanh University, Vietnam

Industry Forum Chair

Phan Ngoc Hoang   Ba Ria-Vung Tau University, Vietnam

Special Sessions Chair

Phan Cong Vinh   Nguyen Tat Thanh University, Vietnam

Local Arrangements Chairs

Lai Xuan Thanh   Binh Duong ICT, Vietnam
Hoang Trong Quyen   Thu Dau Mot University, Vietnam
Tran Van Trung   Thu Dau Mot University, Vietnam

Website Chair

Tran Thi Nhu Thuy   Nguyen Tat Thanh University, Vietnam

Conference Coordinator

Anna Horvathova   EAI (European Alliance for Innovation)

Technical Program Committee

Abdur Rakib   The University of Nottingham, UK
Amol Patwardhan   Louisiana State University, USA
Aniruddha Bhattacharjya   Narasaraopeta Engineering College, India
Areerat Songsakulwattana Rangsit University, Thailand
Asad Masood Khattak   Kyung Hee University, South Korea

Ashad Kabir	Swinburne University of Technology, Australia
Ashish Khare	University of Allahabad, India
Athar Sethi	Universiti Teknologi PETRONAS, Malaysia
Charu Gandhi	Jaypee Institute of Information Technology, India
Chien-Chih Yu	National ChengChi University, Taiwan
Chintan Bhatt	Charotar University of Science and Technology, India
David Sundaram	The University of Auckland, New Zealand
Dinh Duc Anh Vu	University of Information Technology, Vietnam
Duong Tuan Anh	Ho Chi Minh City University of Technology, Vietnam
Dzati Athiar Ramli	Universiti Sains Malaysia, Malaysia
François Siewe	De Montfort University, UK
Gabrielle Peko	The University of Auckland, New Zealand
Giacomo Cabri	University of Modena and Reggio Emilia, Italy
Govardhan Aliseri	Jawaharlal Nehru Technological University Hyderabad, India
Hoang Quang	Hue University of Sciences, Vietnam
Hoang Huu Hanh	Hue University, Vietnam
Huynh Quyet-Thang	Hanoi University of Science and Technology, Vietnam
Huynh Trung Hieu	Ho Chi Minh City University of Industry, Vietnam
Huynh Xuan Hiep	Can Tho University, Vietnam
Ichiro Satoh	National Institute of Informatics, Japan
Issam Damaj	The American University of Kuwait, Kuwait
Jamus Collier	University of Bremen, Germany
Krishna Asawa	Jaypee Institute of Information Technology, India
Kurt Geihs	University of Kassel, Germany
Le Manh	Van Hien University, Vietnam
Loan T.T. Nguyen	Nguyen Tat Thanh University, Vietnam
Ly Quoc Ngoc	Ho Chi Minh City University of Science, Vietnam
Manmeet Mahinderjit Singh	Universiti Sains Malaysia, Malaysia
Moeiz Miraoui	University of Quebec, Canada
Mubarak Mohammad	Concordia University, Canada
Muhammad Fahad Khan	Federal Urdu University of Arts, Science and Technology, Pakistan
Naseem Ibrahim	Albany State University, USA
Ngo Tan Vu Khanh	Oracle Co., Vietnam
Nguyen Quoc Huy	Saigon University, Vietnam
Nguyen Dang Binh	Hue University of Sciences, Vietnam
Nguyen Hong Phu	University of Luxembourg, Luxembourg
Nguyen Hung Cuong	Hanoi University of Science and Technology, Vietnam
Nguyen Kim Quoc	Nguyen Tat Thanh University, Vietnam
Nguyen Loc	Sunflower Soft Co., Vietnam
Nguyen Thanh Binh	Ho Chi Minh City University of Technology, Vietnam
Nguyen Thanh Phuong	Polytechnic University of Bari, Italy
Nguyen Tuan Dang	University of Information Technology, Vietnam
Ognjen Rudovic	Imperial College London, UK

Contents

Modelling and Reasoning About Context-Aware Agents over Heterogeneous Knowledge Sources

Hafiz Mahfooz Ul Haque, Abdur Rakib[✉], and Ijaz Uddin

School of Computer Science, The University of Nottingham,
Malaysia Campus, Semenyih, Malaysia
{khyx2hma,Abdur.Rakib,khyx4iui}@nottingham.edu.my

Abstract. This paper presents a conceptual framework and multi-agent model for context-aware decision support in dynamic smart environments based on heterogeneous knowledge sources. The framework relies on distributed ontologies and allows us to model context-aware agents which reason using rules that are derived from ontologies using the notion of multi-context systems. The use of the proposed framework is illustrated using a simple system developed from ontologies considering three different smart environment domains.

Keywords: Context-aware agents · Multi-context system · Defeasible reasoning · Ontology

1 Introduction

There is no doubt that with an increasing number of smart devices such as smartphones in use, the vast amounts of contextual data being generated has great influence on context-aware mobile computing research. Smartphones have a variety of embedded sensors that can be used to automate data collection and provide a platform to infer rich contextual data about users, including location, time, and environmental condition, among others. This is known as customized information according to the specific context. To be more precise, these sensors can be used to gather the contextual information of a user or to manipulate the context. Different notions of context have been studied across various fields of computer science and various physical and conceptual environmental aspects can be included in the notion of context [11]. Among others, Dey et al. [6] define a context-aware system as a system which uses context to provide relevant information and/or services to its user based on the user's tasks. The formal context modelling and reasoning about context is one of the fundamental research areas in context-aware computing. In the literature, various context modelling and reasoning approaches have been proposed, including ontology and rule-based approach [8,13,14]. In our previous work [13,14], we have developed formal logical frameworks and shown how context-aware systems can be modelled as multi-agent reasoning agents. A formal logical model allows us to capture a system's

© ICST Institute for Computer Sciences, Social Informatics and Telecommunications Engineering 2017
P. Cong Vinh et al. (Eds.): ICCASA 2016, LNICST 193, pp. 1–11, 2017.
DOI: 10.1007/978-3-319-56357-2_1

behaviour in a systematic and precise way. This is because a formal logic has simple unambiguous syntax and semantics, which also allows automated reasoning. Our approach to context modelling was based on a domain specific centralised ontology, which allows a formal representation of domain knowledge and advancing contextual knowledge sharing among the agents. However, in a real context-aware deployment setting, we can envisage a coalition of heterogeneous domains which need to mutually share/exchange context knowledge. This needs different modelling approach to deal with distributed context handling considering more than one domain. In this connection, the notion of multi-context systems has been used for interlinking different knowledge sources in order to enhance the expressive capabilities of heterogeneous systems. A multi-context system (MCS) includes a set of contexts and a set of inference rules that allows information to flow among different contexts [7]. In MCS, each context is defined as a self-contained knowledge source which includes the set of axioms and inference rules to model the system and perform local reasoning. Literature highlighted many definitions of multi-context systems (see e.g., [1,5]). In [5], Brewka et al. define multi-context system as a number of people, agents, databases etc. to describe the available information from a set of contexts and inference rules and specify the information flow among these contexts. In [1], Benslimane et al. have described ontology as a context, which is itself an independent self-contained knowledge source having a set of axioms and inference rules with its own reasoner to perform reasoning. In this work, we consider the concept of context in two levels. The first level is based on multi-context system to model heterogeneous systems similar to contextual ontologies studied by [1]. For the second level, we follow the approach proposed in our previous work [13,14], where a context is formally defined as a *(subject, predicate, object)* triple that states a fact about the subject where — the subject is an entity in the environment, the object is a value or another entity, and the predicate is a relationship between the subject and object. In this paper, we extend our previous work [13] by introducing a different modelling approach to deal with distributed context handling considering more than one domain. This approach is novel in a sense that context-aware agents use contextual information which are extracted from different knowledge sources.

The rest of the paper is organized as follows. In Sect. 2, we briefly review distributed description logics and related work. In Sect. 3, we contextualize ontologies using three domains to illustrate the central idea of our multi-context systems. In Sect. 4, we briefly describe a tool, *D-Onto-HCR*, which is developed to translate the semantic knowledge into Horn-clause rules which are used to model context-aware systems as multi-agent systems. In Sect. 5, we presents a conceptual framework for modelling context-aware reasoning agents using the MCS notion. In Sect. 6, we illustrate the use of the proposed framework using an example system and conclude in Sect. 7.

2 Background and Related Work

2.1 Distributed Description Logics

Recent developments in the field of semantic web have led to a renewed interest in the distributed knowledge bases [3,9,15]. A growing body of research realizes the significance of extending the OWL based formalisms by providing inter-ontology mappings through distributed description logics. Distributed description logic (DDL) is a formal logical framework which combines different description logics (DLs) knowledge bases to express heterogeneous information. A DDL is basically a generalization of the DL framework, which is designed to formalize multiple ontologies interconnected by semantic mappings [15]. One of the reasons for interconnecting ontologies is to preserve their own identity and specify their independence [9]. DDLs have introduced the notion of multiple ontologies with distributed reasoning where each local ontology has its own local knowledge base. Each local ontology knowledge base consists of TBox and ABox axioms. The correspondences of different ontology axioms is called inter-ontology axioms or bridge rules. Bridge rules map the TBox axioms of one ontology with the TBox axioms of other ontology in an implicit manner. In other words, distributed TBox expresses the semantic relations among local TBoxes via bridge rules. These bridge rules allow concepts of an ontology to subsume a concept from another ontology, and they express the semantic mappings among different ontologies. A bridge rule is an inter-ontology axiom having one of the following forms: $C_i \sqsubseteq_{\Rightarrow} D_j$; $C_i \sqsupseteq_{\Rightarrow} D_j$; where C_i, D_j are concepts of ontologies O_i and O_j respectively. A distributed DL knowledge base (DKB) is a set of different DL knowledge bases, expressed as a pair $\langle \mathfrak{T}, \mathfrak{A} \rangle$, which consists of distributed TBoxes and ABoxes. Let us assume we have a collection of DLs and each DL is represented by $\{\mathcal{DL}_i\}$, where $i \in I$ is an element of a non empty set of indexes used to identify ontologies.

A distributed TBox (DTBox) defines TBoxes $\{T_i\}_{i \in I}$ of all local DLs from their corresponding domain ontologies, and bridge rules between these TBoxes which are of the form $\mathfrak{B} = \{\mathfrak{b}_{ij}\}$ (which states a set of bridge rules $\mathfrak{B}$ from $\mathcal{DL}_i$ to $\mathcal{DL}_j$ and $\{\forall i, j(i \neq j) \in I\}$). So, DTBox is represented as $\mathfrak{T} = \langle \{T_i\}_{i \in I}, \mathfrak{B} \rangle$.

A distributed ABox (DABox) $\mathfrak{A} = \langle \{A_i\}_{i \in I}, \mathfrak{C} \rangle$ consists of ABoxes $\{A_i\}_{i \in I}$ of all local DLs from their corresponding domain ontologies, and a set of individuals that may either be partial or complete are of the form $\mathfrak{C} = \{\mathfrak{c}_{ij}\}$ which means the individuals corresponds from $\mathcal{DL}_i$ to $\mathcal{DL}_j$ and $\{\forall i, j(i \neq j) \in I\}$.

2.2 Related Work

There has been a renewed research interest in making multiple heterogeneous ontologies interoperate. For example, the work by [15] has introduced a system which can carry out reasoning services with multiple ontologies. The authors have discussed the reasoning problem in multiple ontologies interrelated with semantic mappings, where the results of local reasonings performed in single ontologies are combined via semantic mappings to reason over distributed ontologies. In [4], a framework is presented for multi-context reasoning systems, which allows combining arbitrary monotonic and nonmonotonic logics and non-monotonic bridge rules are used to specify the information flow among contexts. In [2], authors have proposed a distributed algorithm for query evaluation in a Multi-Context Systems framework based on defeasible logic. In their work, contexts are built using defeasible rules, and the proposed algorithm can determine for a given literal P whether P is (not) a logical conclusion of the Multi-Context Systems, or whether it cannot be proved that P is a logical conclusion. However, our purposed approach of reasoning is quite different in a sense that heterogeneous knowledge sources are translated into a set of Horn-clause rules, which are used to model context-aware non-monotonic rule-based agents.

3 Contextualizing Ontologies Using Multi-context System

In [13], we have shown how we use OWL 2 RL ontologies and Semantic Web Rule Language (SWRL) for context-modelling and rule-based reasoning that enables the construction of a formal context-aware system as a distributed non-monotonic rule-based agents. In this work, to model the systems, we extract heterogeneous contextual information from multiple ontologies with the intention of preserving the identity and independence of each specialized domain ontology. To model distributed domains for an example system, we develop three ontologies named as Smart Patient Care (O_{SPC}), Smart Home (O_{SHO}) and Smart Hospital (O_{SHP}) which have their corresponding DL knowledge bases as $\mathcal{DL}_{SPC}$, $\mathcal{DL}_{SHO}$ and $\mathcal{DL}_{SHP}$ respectively. We have discussed how we translate a DL ontology (OWL 2 RL) into a set of plain text Horn-clause rules in [13]. Additionally, we construct the bridge rules which are semantically mapped using distributed DL Knowledge bases. Figure 1 depicts the extracts of class hierarchies of three ontologies. Some of the bridge rules are given below:

$$O_{SPC} : Patient \sqsubseteq_{\rightarrow} O_{SHO} : AuthorizedPerson. \qquad (1)$$

$$O_{SPC} : Nurse \sqsubseteq_{\rightarrow} O_{SHO} : AuthorizedPerson. \qquad (2)$$

$$O_{SPC} : Nurse \sqsubseteq_{\rightarrow} O_{SHP} : ParamedicalStaff. \qquad (3)$$

$$O_{SPC} : CallAmbulance \sqsubseteq_{\rightarrow} O_{SHP} : AmbulatoryClinic. \quad (4)$$

Bridge rules 1 and 2 show the relationship between O_{SPC} and O_{SHO}, and rules 3 and 4 show the relationship between O_{SPC} and O_{SHP}. Rule 1 states that a Patient from Patient Care Ontology is an Authorized Person in the Smart Home. Rule 2 and 3 express that a Nurse from the Patient Care Ontology is an Authorized Person in the Smart Home and at the same time a Nurse is a Paramedical staff in the Smart Hospital. These rules can also be represented in first order form as follows:

$$Patient(?p) \mapsto AuthorizedPerson(?p) \qquad (1)$$

We model the context using ontologies (including bridge rules, OWL 2 RL and SWRL rules) and extract a set of Horn-clause rules from different ontologies

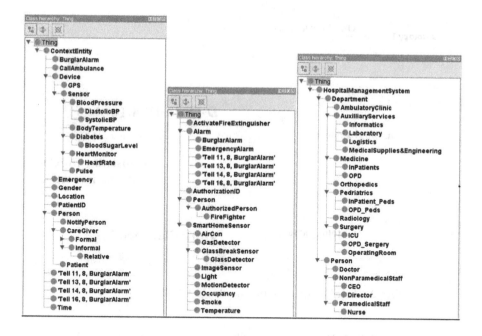

Fig. 1. Class hierarchy of smart environment ontologies

using the tool discussed in the next section. Each agent in the context-aware system has a program, consisting of these extracted Horn clause rules.

4   D-Onto-HCR

To extract the rules from different ontologies, we developed an OWL-API based translator, which takes ontologies as input and then translates the set of axioms (in OWL 2 RL and SWRL form) into a set of plain text Horn-clause rules. The design of the OWL API corresponds to the OWL 2 Structural Specification and this dynamic design model allows developers to provide flexible implementations for major components of the system. In OWL API, the names and hierarchies for the axioms, class expressions and entities correspond to the OWL structural specification. Indeed, there is a proximal one to one translation between OWL API model interfaces and the OWL 2 Structural Specification, implying that this becomes easier to correlate the high level OWL 2 specification with the design of the OWL-API [10]. To extract ontology axioms and facts, we use OWL-API to parse the ontology.

Protégé [12] ontology editor allows SWRL rules to be written in Horn-clause rule format but practically these rules are written in functional syntax which are in DL-Safe rule form. *D-Onto-HCR* translates DL-safe rules axioms into Horn-clause rules format. Additionally, this translator extracts concepts from different ontologies and maps them correspondingly in the from of bridge rules which are

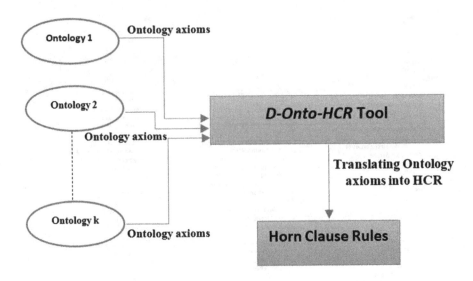

Fig. 2. Distributed semantic knowledge translation process

transformed in OWL 2 RL rule format. These rules are then translated into a set of plain text Horn-clause rules format. Figure 2 shows the distributed semantic knowledge translation process. Each ontology has an ontology IRI (International Resource Identifier) to identify ontology and their classes, properties and individuals. The translation process works as follows: (i) When the tool starts its execution, it loads all listed ontologies from the published source as an input in OWL/XML format; (ii) It uses OWL parser to parse the ontologies into OWL API objects which then extracts the set of TBox and ABox axioms; (iii) The set of TBox axioms are then translated into a set of plain text Horn clause rules; (v) ABox axioms and DL safe SWRL rules are already in the Horn-clause format; (vi) The bridge rules (inter-ontology axioms) are extracted from different ontologies and are also transformed into a set of Horn-clause rules. Multi-context system is a powerful framework for modelling different knowledge sources. Considering the reservations of keeping their own identity and independence as an independent system, the *D-Onto-HCR* tool transforms useful information from these knowledge sources (without making any alteration in ontologies) into a standardized format, i.e., Horn-clause rule format.

5   Multi-agent Model over Heterogeneous Knowledge Sources

We extend the logical framework presented in [13] by incorporating the notion of multi-context systems where rules are derived from heterogeneous semantic knowledge sources. The system consists of $n_{Ag}(\geq 1)$ individual agents $Ag = \{1, 2, ..., n_{Ag}\}$. Each agent $i \in A_g$ has a program, consisting of a finite set of strict, defeasible, and bridge rules, and a working memory, which contains facts. Each agent in the system is represented by a triple $(\Re, \mathcal{F}, \succ)$, where $\mathcal{F}$ is a finite set of facts contained in the working memory, $\Re = (\Re^s, \Re^d, \Re^{br})$ is a finite set of strict, defeasible, and bridge rules, and $\succ$ is a superiority relation on $\Re$. Strict rules $(\Re^s)$ are non-contradictory whereas defeasible rules $(\Re^d)$ can be defeated based on contrary evidence. Bridge rules $(\Re^{br})$ are non-contradictory rules which represent the distributed knowledge base concepts. In this framework, each context-aware agent is designed to solve a specific problem. Agents in the system acquire contextual information from domain specific ontologies (rules and facts of an agent can be derived from one or multiple ontologies), perform reasoning (based on the information they have in their knowledge bases), communicate with each other, and adapt the system behaviour accordingly. An example set of Horn-clause rules and facts are shown in Table 1. As system moves, the matching rules will be fired based on their predefined priorities which are set by the system designer. That is, a context-aware system composed of a set of rule-based agents, and firing of rules that infer new facts may determine context changes and represent overall behaviour of the system.

In this framework context-aware agents are modelled using different knowledge sources, where each of them has its own knowledge source and a reasoning strategy. For example, Fig. 3 shows that working memories of three agents contain facts (elements of ABox) from one ontology or multiple ontologies. Agent 1's working memory contains the contextual information C_{11}, C_{12}, C_{15}, and C_{17} which are instances of the Smart Home ontology and C_{22} which is an instance of the Smart Hospital ontology. The working memory of agent 2 has contextual information only from Smart Hospital ontology whereas the working memory of agent N contains the instances from all the ontologies. In a similar fashion bridge rules of an agent include concepts from multiple ontologies.

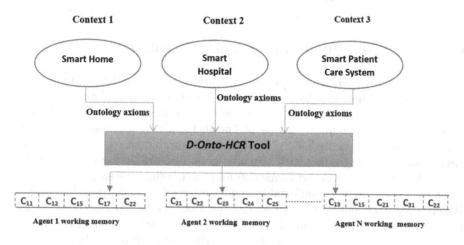

Fig. 3. MCS based context-awareness in the working memory of agent i

Table 1. Example rules for smart environment context-aware system

---

Agent 1: Home care

Initial facts: Person('John), AuthorizationID('P0001),
hasAuthorizationID('John, 'P0001), FireFighter('Simon)

R11: Person(?p), hasAuthorizationID(?p, ?aid), AuthorizationID(?aid) →
AuthorizedPerson(?p)

R12: FireFighter(?ff) ↦ AuthorizedPerson(?ff)

R13: Tell(3,1, NotifyPerson(?p, ?loc)) → NotifyPerson(?p, ?loc)

R14: NotifyPerson(?p, ?loc), FireFighter(?ff) → isRescuedBy(?p, ?ff)

Agent 2: Smoke detector

Initial facts: Smoke('True), hasNotifiedSmokeLocation('True, 'Kitchen)

R21: Smoke(?s), hasNotifiedSmokeLocation(?s, ?loc) ⇒ BurglarAlarm(?loc)

R22: Smoke(?s), hasNotifiedSmokeLocation(?s, ?loc) ⇒ ∼ BurglarAlarm(?loc)

R23: BurglarAlarm(?loc) → Tell(2, 3, BurglarAlarm(?loc))

Rule Priority: R21 ≻ R22

Agent 3: Emergency monitor

Initial facts: PersonWithinRange('John, 'Kitchen), isFireExtinguisherInstalled
('FEK01, 'Yes)

R31: Tell(2, 3, BurglarAlarm(?loc)) → BurglarAlarm(?loc)

R32: BurglarAlarm(?loc) → hasAlarmingSituation(?loc, 'Emergency)

R33: hasAlarmingSituation(?loc, 'Emergency), isFireExtinguisherInstalled
(?fe, 'Yes) → ActivateFireExtinguisher(?loc)

R34: hasAlarmingSituation(?loc, 'Emergency), PersonWithinRange(?p, ?loc) →
NotifyPerson(?p, ?loc)

R35: NotifyPerson(?p, ?loc) → Tell(3,1, NotifyPerson(?p, ?loc))

---

6   Case Study: Smart Environment Facilitator

We model a smart environment facilitator system considering three different and independent domains, namely Smart Home, Smart Hospital, and Smart Patient Care. The purpose is to model context-aware reasoning agents in healthcare environments which require sharing of knowledge across the domains, including data generated by embedded sensors and wearable smart badges in that environments, while dealing with semantic heterogeneity that exists across the knowledge sources. The Smart Home ontology models the assisted living environment with user-friendly, comfortable and security related facilities. The Smart Hospital ontology models medical services provided to the inpatient and outpatient care. The Smart Patient Care ontology models various devices connected with a patient which monitor the patient's vital information, including blood pressure, blood sugar, and heart rate. As we have already developed ontologies of these domains, to illustrate the use of the framework we consider a very simple

Table 2. Example reasoning steps of the smart environment system

	Home care (Agent 1)			Smoke detector (Agent 2)			Emergency monitor (Agent 3)		
#Steps	Memory Config.1	Action1	#Msg1	Memory Config.2	Action2	#Msg2	Memory Config.3	Action3	#Msg3
0	{Person('John), AuthorizationID('P0001), hasAuthorizationID('John,'P0001), FireFighter('Simon), —}	—	0	{Smoke('True), hasNotifiedSmokeLocation('True,'Kitchen), —}	—	0	{PersonWithinRange('John,'Kitchen), isFireExtinguisherInstalled('FEK01,'Yes), —}	—	0
1	{Person('John), AuthorizationID('P0001), hasAuthorizationID('John,'P0001), FireFighter('Simon), AuthorizedPerson('Simon)}	Rule (R11)	0	{Smoke('True), hasNotifiedSmokeLocation('True,'Kitchen), BurglarAlarm('Kitchen)}	Rule (R21)	0	{PersonWithinRange('John,'Kitchen), isFireExtinguisherInstalled('FEK01,'Yes), —}	Idle	0
2	{Person('John), AuthorizationID('P0001), hasAuthorizationID('John,'P0001), FireFighter('Simon), AuthorizedPerson('Simon)}	Rule (R12)	0	{Smoke('True), hasNotifiedSmokeLocation('True,'Kitchen), Tell(2,3,BurglarAlarm('Kitchen))}	Rule (R23)	0	{PersonWithinRange('John,'Kitchen), isFireExtinguisherInstalled('FEK01,'Yes), —}	Idle	0
3	{Person('John), AuthorizationID('P0001), hasAuthorizationID('John,'P0001), FireFighter('Simon), AuthorizedPerson('Simon)}	Idle	0	{Smoke('True), hasNotifiedSmokeLocation('True,'Kitchen), Tell(2,3,BurglarAlarm('Kitchen))}	Idle	0	{PersonWithinRange('John,'Kitchen), isFireExtinguisherInstalled('FEK01,'Yes), Tell(2,3,BurglarAlarm('Kitchen)), —}	Copy	1
4	{Person('John), AuthorizationID('P0001), hasAuthorizationID('John,'P0001), FireFighter('Simon), AuthorizedPerson('Simon)}	Idle	0	{Smoke('True), hasNotifiedSmokeLocation('True,'Kitchen), Tell(2,3,BurglarAlarm('Kitchen))}	Idle	0	{PersonWithinRange('John,'Kitchen), isFireExtinguisherInstalled('FEK01,'Yes), Tell(2,3,BurglarAlarm('Kitchen)), BurglarAlarm('Kitchen)}	Rule (R31)	1
5	{Person('John), AuthorizationID('P0001), hasAuthorizationID('John,'P0001), FireFighter('Simon), AuthorizedPerson('Simon)}	Idle	0	{Smoke('True), hasNotifiedSmokeLocation('True,'Kitchen), Tell(2,3,BurglarAlarm('Kitchen))}	Idle	0	{PersonWithinRange('John,'Kitchen), isFireExtinguisherInstalled('FEK01,'Yes), Tell(2,3,BurglarAlarm('Kitchen))}	Rule (R32)	1
6	{Person('John), AuthorizationID('P0001), hasAuthorizationID('John,'P0001), FireFighter('Simon), AuthorizedPerson('Simon)}	Idle	0	{Smoke('True), hasNotifiedSmokeLocation('True,'Kitchen), Tell(2,3,BurglarAlarm('Kitchen))}	Idle	0	{PersonWithinRange('John,'Kitchen), isFireExtinguisherInstalled('FEK01,'Yes), hasAlarmingSituation('Kitchen,'Emergency)}	Rule (R33)	1
7	{Person('John), AuthorizationID('P0001), hasAuthorizationID('John,'P0001), FireFighter('Simon), AuthorizedPerson('Simon)}	Idle	0	{Smoke('True), hasNotifiedSmokeLocation('True,'Kitchen), Tell(2,3,BurglarAlarm('Kitchen))}	Idle	0	{PersonWithinRange('John,'Kitchen), isFireExtinguisherInstalled('FEK01,'Yes), ActivateFireExtinguisher('Kitchen), hasAlarmingSituation('Kitchen,'Emergency)}	Rule (R34)	1
8	{Person('John), AuthorizationID('P0001), hasAuthorizationID('John,'P0001), FireFighter('Simon), AuthorizedPerson('Simon)}	Idle	0	{Smoke('True), hasNotifiedSmokeLocation('True,'Kitchen), Tell(2,3,BurglarAlarm('Kitchen))}	Idle	0	{PersonWithinRange('John,'Kitchen), isFireExtinguisherInstalled('FEK01,'Yes), NotifyPerson('John,'Kitchen), hasAlarmingSituation('Kitchen,'Emergency)}	Rule (R35)	1
9	{Person('John), AuthorizationID('P0001), hasAuthorizationID('John,'P0001), FireFighter('Simon), Tell(3,1,NotifyPerson('John,'Kitchen))}	Copy	1	{Smoke('True), hasNotifiedSmokeLocation('True,'Kitchen), Tell(2,3,BurglarAlarm('Kitchen))}	Idle	0	{PersonWithinRange('John,'Kitchen), isFireExtinguisherInstalled('FEK01,'Yes), Tell(3,1,NotifyPerson('John,'Kitchen)), hasAlarmingSituation('Kitchen,'Emergency)}	Idle	1
10	{Person('John), AuthorizationID('P0001), hasAuthorizationID('John,'P0001), FireFighter('Simon), NotifyPerson('John,'Kitchen)}	Rule (R13)	1	{Smoke('True), hasNotifiedSmokeLocation('True,'Kitchen), Tell(2,3,BurglarAlarm('Kitchen))}	Idle	0	{PersonWithinRange('John,'Kitchen), isFireExtinguisherInstalled('FEK01,'Yes), Tell(3,1,NotifyPerson('John,'Kitchen)), hasAlarmingSituation('Kitchen,'Emergency)}	Idle	1
11	{Person('John), AuthorizationID('P0001), hasAuthorizationID('John,'P0001), FireFighter('Simon), isRescuedBy('John,'Simon)}	Rule (R14)	1	{Smoke('True), hasNotifiedSmokeLocation('True,'Kitchen), Tell(2,3,BurglarAlarm('Kitchen))}	Idle	0	{PersonWithinRange('John,'Kitchen), isFireExtinguisherInstalled('FEK01,'Yes), Tell(3,1,NotifyPerson('John,'Kitchen)), hasAlarmingSituation('Kitchen,'Emergency)}	Idle	1

example scenario which includes three agents. As shown in Table 1, each agent has a set of facts and a set of Horn-clause rules. In Table 2, we have shown example reasoning steps to demonstrate how the system generates the specified goals within n time steps and interaction is performed between agents by exchanging messages using *Copy* action [13]. The agents are resource-bounded in terms of the computational time, communication, and space in memory that it consumes [13]. The semantics of the agents' language is based on transition systems and follow the approach of [13]. We view the process of producing new contexts from existing contexts as a sequence of states of an agent, starting from an initial state, and producing the next state by one of the following actions: **Rule:** firing a matching rule instance in the current state (possibly overwriting a context from the previous configuration due to space bound and conflicting contexts appearing in the memory); **Copy:** if agent i has an $Ask(i, j, P)$ (or a $Tell(i, j, P)$) in its current state, then agent j can copy it to its next state provided j's communication counter has not exceeded communication counter threshold value (possibly overwriting a context from the previous configuration due to space bound and conflicting contexts appearing in the memory); and **Idle:** which leaves its configuration unchanged.

As we see the structure of the table, the left most column represents the time step, the rest each three columns *Memory config.*, *Action*, and *#Msg* are assigned for each of the agents which represent the newly inferred contextual information, an appropriate action performed by an agent in a particular step to make a transition from one configuration (state) to another, and the number of messages exchanged respectively. In the column *Memory config.*, the left side of the vertical bar ($|$) is known as static memory which holds the set of initial facts while the right side (known as dynamic memory) shows the newly derived/communicated contextual information. The size of static memory is determined by the set of initial facts, and the size of dynamic memory is set by the system designer considering minimal memory units required to achieve the desired goals. At the initial configuration, the dynamic memory size of agent 1 and agent 2 is 1 unit while the dynamic memory size of agent 3 is 2 units. However, if we reduce these memory units, the system would not be able to produce a desired goal, e.g., a resident in the smart home is rescued by a fire fighter in case of an emergency alarming situation is reported in the kitchen (i.e., the context $isRescuedBy('John,'Simon)$ appearing in the working memory of one of the agents in the system).

7   Conclusion and Future Work

In this paper, we present a context-aware multi-agent model using the notion of multi-context systems. The proposed framework considers distributed description logic approach to suitably model the core notion of multi-context systems using semantic knowledge sharing. In future work, we aim to develop an optimized Android based application incorporating multi-context system with the specialized domain ontologies having their own conceptualization structure and reasoning strategy.

References

1. Benslimane, D., Arara, A., Falquet, G., Maamar, Z., Thiran, P., Gargouri, F.: Contextual ontologies. In: Yakhno, T., Neuhold, E.J. (eds.) ADVIS 2006. LNCS, vol. 4243, pp. 168–176. Springer, Heidelberg (2006). doi:10.1007/11890393_18
2. Bikakis, A., Antoniou, G., Hasapis, P.: Strategies for contextual reasoning with conflicts in ambient intelligence. Knowl. Inf. Syst. **27**(1), 45–84 (2011)
3. Borgida, A., Serafini, L.: Distributed description logics: directed domain corre- spondences in federated information sources. In: Meersman, R., Tari, Z. (eds.) OTM 2002. LNCS, vol. 2519, pp. 36–53. Springer, Heidelberg (2002). doi:10.1007/ 3-540-36124-3_3
4. Brewka, G., Eiter, T.: Equilibria in heterogeneous nonmonotonic multi-context systems. In: Proceedings of the Twenty-Second AAAI Conference on Artificial Intelligence, pp. 385–390. AAAI Press (2007)
5. Brewka, G., Roelofsen, F., Serafini, L.: Contextual default reasoning. In: Proceed- ings of the 20th International Joint Conference on Artifical Intelligence, pp. 268– 273 (2007)
6. Dey, A.K.: Understanding and using context. Pers. Ubiquit. Comput. **5**(1), 4–7 (2001). doi:10.1007/s007790170019
7. Eiter, T., Fink, M., Schüller, P., Weinzierl, A.: Finding explanations of inconsis- tency in multi-context systems. Artif. Intell. **216**, 233–274 (2014)
8. Esposito, A., Tarricone, L., Zappatore, M., Catarinucci, L., Colella, R.: A frame- work for context-aware home-health monitoring. IJAACS **3**(1), 75–91 (2010)
9. Grau, B.C., Parsia, B., Sirin, E.: Working with multiple ontologies on the semantic web. In: McIlraith, S.A., Plexousakis, D., Harmelen, F. (eds.) ISWC 2004. LNCS, vol. 3298, pp. 620–634. Springer, Heidelberg (2004). doi:10.1007/ 978-3-540-30475-3_43
10. Horridge, M., Bechhofer, S.: The OWL API: a Java API for OWL ontologies. Semant. Web **2**(1), 11–21 (2011)
11. Lieberman, H., Selker, T.: Out of context: computer systems that adapt to, and learn from, context. IBM Syst. J. **39**(3–4), 617–632 (2000)
12. Protégé: The Protégé ontology editor and knowledge-base framework (Version 4.1), July 2011. http://protege.stanford.edu/
13. Rakib, A., Haque, H.M.U.: A logic for context-aware non-monotonic reason- ing agents. In: Gelbukh, A., Espinoza, F.C., Galicia-Haro, S.N. (eds.) MICAI 2014. LNCS (LNAI), vol. 8856, pp. 453–471. Springer, Cham (2014). doi:10.1007/ 978-3-319-13647-9_41
14. Rakib, A., Ul Haque, H.M., Faruqui, R.U.: A temporal description logic for resource-bounded rule-based context-aware agents. In: Vinh, P.C., Alagar, V., Vassev, E., Khare, A. (eds.) ICCASA 2013. LNICSSITE, vol. 128, pp. 3–14. Springer, Cham (2014). doi:10.1007/978-3-319-05939-6_1
15. Serafini, L., Tamilin, A.: DRAGO: distributed reasoning architecture for the semantic web. In: Gómez-Pérez, A., Euzenat, J. (eds.) ESWC 2005. LNCS, vol. 3532, pp. 361–376. Springer, Heidelberg (2005). doi:10.1007/11431053_25

Context-Based Project Management

Ammar Alsaig[1,2(✉)], Alaa Alsaig[1,2], and Mubarak Mohammad[1,2]

[1] Concordia University, Montreal, Canada
aasaig@uqu.edu.sa, mubarak.sami@gmail.com
[2] Jeddah University, Jeddah, Kingdom of Saudi Arabia
aalsaig@uj.edu.sa

Abstract. Context-based computing has become an integral part of the software infrastructure of modern society. Better software are made adaptive to suit the surrounding environment. Context-based applications best fit into environments that undergo constant and frequent changes. Temperature management, Time management, GPS are just few examples where context-awareness becomes inevitable. Project Management is another domain that requires constant monitoring. The current tools of project management handle data gathering, plotting, and organizing, but requires high-level of human intervention to analyze data and integrate it. To the extent of our knowledge there is no efforts to introduce context awareness to project management domain. In this work, we introduce context and formally model project context using FCA. Additionally, we provide the results of the full implementation of our approach on a real-world software project. We show that our approach can formally answer queries that traditional tools could not answer. Also, we introduce a brief comparison between our approach and traditional project management software. Finally, we show that our approach can improve project management tools and minimize the effort spent by project managers.

Keywords: Context · Project management system · Model · Formal concept analysis FCA · Lattice tree

1 Introduction

Projects and project management are part of every organization or company lives. Since businesses are evolving the requirements related to project management is increasing. That is, project management is not only about time management, team communication, or task tracking, there are, however, other requirements are needed to enhance the management of projects such as task correlation and dynamic update when a change occurs. The context of projects includes important information to enhance accuracy and efficiency of software management tools. By knowing the context of a specific task, the estimation of needed time to complete a specific task and other related tasks will be clearer to the team. Hence, better management and results. The Context-awareness and context-based applications is one of the essential method used recently to enhance most the current systems. Context-awareness plays an important role in Ubiquitous computing [4], cloud computing [5], mobile applications [6], cyber physical systems [7] and others.

© ICST Institute for Computer Sciences, Social Informatics and Telecommunications Engineering 2017
P. Cong Vinh et al. (Eds.): ICCASA 2016, LNICST 193, pp. 12–21, 2017.
DOI: 10.1007/978-3-319-56357-2_2

Therefore, in this paper, we introduce context to the field of project management. Our goal is to make better project management tools by introducing the notion of context using formal data modeling.

There are two essential components of project management: service requester (client), who define requirements, and service providers (vendors) who should execute the project with respect to the defined requirements by client [3]. Project Managers, who work for service vendors, aim to achieve the best balance between Time, Cost and Quality that can fulfill the service requester needs and maximize the profit (minimize the cost) for service vendors. We refer to client requirements and vendor data as *Project Context*. The high dependency of project context components is illustrated in (Fig. 1). The balance between different components of project management depends on how well project managers are aware of the relationships between different data components within project context. Project managers often need to reconsider their decision regarding the trade-offs they need to commit during the development. Thus, questions like, what's the effect of an absence of certain resources assigned to a project? What are the relations between resources and risks? Or what are relations between tasks and risks? are examples of many other questions that need ready answers for project managers to make their decisions.

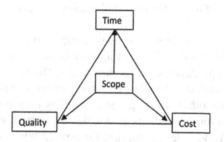

Fig. 1. Main components of projects

Project context is highly changeable. It is often redefined or updated during the project life cycle. This reflects changes also in the relations among data components of project context, which makes it challenging for project managers to follow as the project evolves. In many cases, project managers lose track of project changes which drive projects to failure. The current project management systems/tools such as Microsoft project management [7], redmine [9], and SAP project management [8] to name few, focus on the different area of project such as time management, cost management, resource management, risk management. etc. These tools work as an organizer of project data. However, when it comes to relationships within the data itself, these tools need a human analyst/project manager to put things together and to watch out for emerging risks as the project context changes [16]. In [10], the authors introduced a survey on IT project tools. It is mentioned that one of the strong reasons of projects failure is "*Not Having a System in Place for Approving and Tracking Changes*". In the same reference, the suggested solution for this problem should be "*Having a clear process that must be followed is the best way to ensure the pertinent details – how much it will cost, why it is necessary, the impact on the overall project – are known before the change is approved. It's also extremely effective for auditing performance during and after project completion".*

Therefore, we propose a formal approach to monitor the changes in project management context and keep track of the emerging relationships between its main components. We start from categorizing and classifying project data, formally modeling the data using FCA-lattice, and providing a full implementation of our approach.

2 Literature Review

In [11], a comparative study is done on twenty project management tools to view their features and summarize them. In the study, none of the mentioned software was characterized with the ability to show the interconnection between one task and another. That is, the change in one task could be tracked by the available software but not the affected tasks by these changes.

Adding the features of tracking the changes and building the dependencies among tasks using programming languages is possible as XPSuite did in their research [12]. However, it is not based on theoretical and formal methods. Formalism is required to provide an authorized definition for the relationships that exist among tasks within a specific project.

Some researchers work to define the relationship among organizations [13]. The relationship between an organization and another is based on sharing the work on specific tasks and the dependencies among these tasks. The research [13] suggesting to build a complete platform that is shared by all participating companies to have the ability to track tasks and notify others about progress that has been done on specific tasks. However, the definition for the methods used to define the relationship is not provided. This keeps the need to provide a definition for how to build relationship formally. Moreover, defining a class object in project management software that build the relationship among tasks is advantageous. This is because it gives the ability to define relationships among other objects or classes of the software.

According to [15], the writer introduced SMIT, which is a project management software that is able to plan and re-plan tasks within a project. That is, SMIT structured the tasks in hierarchy tree that is built on the relationship and dependencies among objects, attributes, and tasks. This is to give the ability to SMIT to plan or re-plan again whenever some changes that happen during project life cycle. SMIT is a great work and has very powerful features. However, the relationships among tasks were not defined formally. That is, SMIT software is not intelligent enough to realize the interconnection between tasks. The relationship was based on input given by the user, however, SMIT software is not aware of it. In our research, we introduced a software that is intelligent enough to build relationship between existing tasks or added tasks during project life cycle. These relationships are built using theoretical formula (FCA) that does build the connections among object based on context information.

3 Data of Project Management

There are three types of project data categorized by its source: client, vendor, and project managers. In addition, there is also data that dynamically emerge and develop during the project life cycle. Thus, we classify context project data into the following:

(A) Relations Context: This data represents the relationships among the entities and components of project context. It is domain dependent. Also, it is considered as the connection between each data component. For example, the link or relation between a task, to whom it is assigned and what risks are related to it, is defined in the Relations Context. The explanation of relationships among project data is out of the scope of this paper. Interested readers can refer to the following few examples of project management references [1–3] for more information.

(B) Client Context: It can also be called "input data". This data is the information based on which the project is initiated. In most cases, it defines the scope of the project, time frame and available budget. In some cases, some of this information is left open to be defined by service vendor, which means service vendor can trade-off on this open specification. For example, if the time-frame is left open for service vendor, service vendor can enhance quality, and minimize cost by extending the period of development and by assigning less resources to work on the project.

(C) Vendor Context: data that is defined by project manager of service Vendors. It includes the expected times of deliverables, the resources assigned on the project, the cost of these resources, and the risks associated with the project. This data can be updated later on when project context changes. For example, client during the project development decreases the time frame of the project. Project managers should consult the project plan, check the available resources, and review the costs and risks to know the effect of this decrease on the project context.

4 Modeling Data

In this section we introduce Formal Concept Analysis (FCA). Also, we model each data entity introduced in previous section using FCA.

4.1 Formal Concept Analysis (FCA)

FCA is a formal approach that defines relations between different data entities. In [17], they define FCA as *"a method mainly used for the analysis of data, i.e. for deriving implicit relationships between objects described through a set of attributes on the one hand and these attributes on the other. The data are structured into units which are formal abstractions of concepts of human thought, allowing meaningful comprehensible interpretation (Ganter & Wille, 1999)"*.

Because our focus is to capture and keep track of relationships within project context, we rely on FCA to formally define these relations. Therefore, our first class object in the model is FCA lattice. That is, all types of relations are represented as FCA lattice. This means that all data entities we have in our model will be based on objects and attributes.

4.2   Relations Context

This type of data defines the different relationships between the data entities of both Vendor Context and Client Context. The relationships in Relations Context are illustrated in (Fig. 2(A), (B)). The relations defined in the Figure are not exhaustive, many other components can appear in both Vendor and Client Context. Nonetheless, all information can be represented as shown in (Figs. 2 and 3). These relations are defined as FCA lattice. Thus, some relations can be inferred. For example, there is a relationship between resources and risks through requirements. The explanation of how this data is used in the system will be discussed in the implementation section.

	task	time	resource	cost	risk	resource-percent
task		X	X		X	X
time	X					
resource	X			X		X
cost			X			
risk	X					
resource-percent	X		X			

(A)

	Time Frame	Requriement	Budget
Scope	X	X	
Resources	X	X	X
Cost		X	X
Time	X		

(B)

Fig. 2. (A) Relations context for vendor context, (B) Relations context for vendor/client contexts

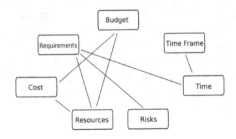

Fig. 3. Example of relations context relations between provider context

4.3   Client Context

Client Context is defined by the service requester. It includes all client requirement and specifications for the project. This includes but not limited to, time frame, budget, requirements and any other specifications regarding the project. In our model, Client Context consist of data entities. For example, time frame is an entity, budget is a different entity, and requirements list is another entity and so on. The relationship between those entities is defined in the Relations Context.

4.4   Vendor Context

Vendor Context is similar to Client Context. However, it is defined by the project executing team. In fact, it is the responsibility of project managers. The entities in this context includes but not limited to, project plan, cost, and resources...etc. Like Client Context, the interrelations between different data entities are defined in the Relations Context.

5 Implementation Tools

The main theoretical method on which our implementation is based is the FCA-lattice method. Through its formally well-defined functions and concepts, the implemented program initiates the project and updates its context as the requirements change. In our implementation we use python as the main programming tool. Details of both theoretical method and programming tools are going to be discussed in this section.

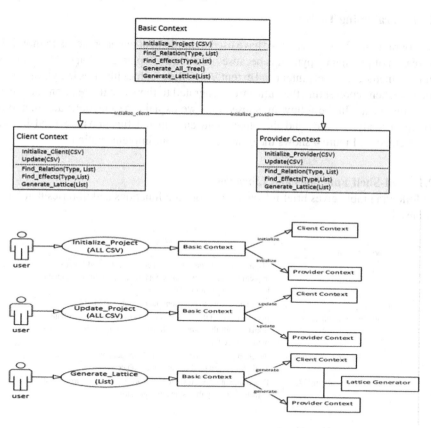

Fig. 4. Main classes in our implementation and general use cases

5.1 FCA Functions

The two formal functions used to find relations between objects and attributes are intention and extension functions. These two functions are formally defined as:

Extent and Intent Formula

Concepts Extent = Ext (X, Y, I) = {A ∈ 2x ∣ (A, B) ∈ B (X, Y, I) for some B}

Concepts Intent = Int (X, Y, I) = {B ∈ 2y ∣ (A, B) ∈ B (X, Y, I) for some A} [6]

The extent function returns all attributes that are shared by input object(s), where the intent function returns all objects that are shared by input attribute(s). For example, if Relations Context links a task with four resources, the extent function on that tasks gives back the four resources, while the intent of the four resources returns back this task Based on those two functions, our program can find all attributes shared by list of objects or all objects that are shared by list of attributes.

5.2 Programming Tools

The programming language that we have used to implement our approach is Python 2.7. The reason of picking up python is because of its ready implementation of FCA and its main two methods, namely intent and extent. Also, the graphics libraries in Python come in handy when representing the lattice tree generated to represent the relations between data components. In the following subsections we explain the functions and methods used from ready libraries and the other main customized functions we used in our implementation. Figure 4 shows the basic classes in our implementation.

5.2.1 Off-Shelf Functions and Libraries

The following table gives brief information about the functions and libraries that have been used as.

Library/function	Details
Concept	The main FCA library that has a component called Context that implements both intent and extent function in addition to graphic library to represent the lattice tree
Graphviz	The main library to represent the relations in pdf/png file
Context.FromFile(filename)	Function to read the FCA relations between objects/attributes from CSV file there are other function to define the context inline in the source file
Context.intension('objects')	Function that takes object/list of objects and returns list of attributes shared by the same object/objects
Context.extension('attributes')	Function that takes attribute/list of attributes and returns list of objects shared by the same attribute/attributes

5.2.2 Customized Functions

The following gives brief information about the functions and libraries that we have implemented (Table 1).

5.2.3 Case Study and Test Cases

We have deployed our program on a real software Enterprise Resource Planning (ERP) project. This project includes 260 tasks, 9 resources, 20 risks, and had to be implemented

Table 1. Implemented information of function and libraries

Library/function	Details
Initialize_Project(CSV) Initialize_Client(CSV) Initilaize_Vendor(CSV)	These three functions do the same thing. They are called only at the beginning of the project. They take as parameters all csv files that contain the relations between data components and the basic relationships
Update (type, updateQuery)	Similar to init functions but take either query (key value format) or a csv file that replaces another one
Find_effects(type, List)	This function will use either intension or extension formal FCA functions depending on the type argument. Type can be object or attribute. List should be list of objects or attributes
Find_Relations(type, List)	This function find all relations of an item/group of items (objects/attributes)
Generate_All_Tree() Generate_Lattice(List)	These functions are similar. One generate a lattice for all project, the other one does this for a specific subset of objects

in 7 months. We were able to model all project data using the above explained categorization. This data includes the initial data and the evolved data as project progressed. We were able to see the project from different point of view with the help of FCA extension and intension. The following brief test cases show some examples of this information. Figure 5 shows full lattice tree for the project plan.

Test Case: Find all risks associated with one resource.

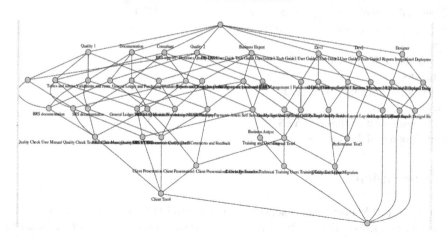

Fig. 5. Case study, FCA lattice generated from our program

- Result: our program shows all tasks associated with one resource, and shows all risks associated with these tasks.
- Test Case: Find the effects of updating requirements and resources
- Result: through the Relations Context and Vendor Context, system was able to find all relations shared by requirements and resources, and relations associated with resources and ones associated with requirements.
- Test Case: Find effects of Increase in resource cost per month
- Result: our program showed all tasks associated with that resource, and all risks.

6   Overall Observation

After full implementation of our approach on a real-world case study, we observed interesting findings. First, our approach does not only help in formalizing the relations among data entities but also to infer some relations based on the dependencies between data entities. Also, we were able to find any linked information to any piece of information in the project context which was not available with traditional PM tools. For example, finding assigned resources on a specific task, which risks linked to it, what is the time assigned to the task, and so on. This allows us to find the echo of any change in the project context. However, it is worth saying that our current implementation cannot replace the project management tools but can be deployed side by side to these tools to empower them and minimize the effort spent by project managers to update project context. We also give brief comparison table between our method and the standard project management tools in Table 2.

Table 2.   Context-based approach VS. Traditional tools

Criteria	Our method	Standard PM tools
Based on formal approach	YES	NO
Capture all types of relations	YES	NO
Easy update (no multiple places)	In Most cases	NO
Provide Gantt charts and other PM charts	NO	YES
Has easy-user friendly interface	NO	YES
can represent relationships in a figure between all data entities	YES	NO

7   Conclusion

Current Project Management practices need high-level human involvement to initiate and update projects as they evolve. Losing track of interrelations within project data due to frequent updates is one of the main causes of project failures. Our approach formally defines relations between different data entities. This keeps all relations captured along projects life cycle. This also provides easy update to project plan with clear view on effect on other part of the project. After implementing real world software project, we found that our approach was able to model all data of project successfully. Also, with the help of FCA intention and extension we were able to find any relationship that is direct or inferred from the project context. Finally, we have provided a brief comparison between our method and tradition project management tools. Although our method cannot replace traditional project management tools, it surely can strengthen the data integration, simplify context update and minimize human intervention.

References

1. Lewis, J.P.: Project Planning, Scheduling & Control, 4E. McGraw Hill, New York (2005). ISBN 978-0-07-146037-8
2. Newell, M.W., Grashina, M.N.: The Project Management Question and Answer Book, p. 8 (2004)
3. PMBOK, Third Edn., p. 165 (2004)
4. Weiser, M.: Some computer science issues in ubiquitous computing. Commun. ACM **36**(7), 75–84 (1993)
5. Mell, P., Grance, T.: The NIST definition of cloud computing (2011)
6. Charland, A., Leroux, B.: Mobile application development: web vs. native. Commun. ACM **54**(5), 49–53 (2011)
7. Baheti, R., Gill, H.: Cyber-physical systems. In: The Impact of Control Technology, vol. 12, pp. 161–166 (2011)
8. Lowery, G.: Managing Projects With Microsoft Project 4.0: For Windows and MacIntosh. Wiley, New York (1997)
9. Welti, N.: Successful SAP R/3 Implementation: Practical Management of ERP Projects. Addison-Wesley Longman Publishing Co. Inc., Boston (1999)
10. Lang, J., Davis, E.: Redmine-open source project management web-application (2010)
11. Schiff, J.L.: 12 common project management mistakes–and how to avoid them, 26 September 2012.   http://www.cio.com/article/2391872/project-management/12-common-project-management-mistakes–and-how-to-avoid-them.html. Accessed from CIO
12. Mishra, A., Mishra, D.: Software project management tools: a brief comparative view. ACM SIGSOFT Softw. Eng. Notes **38**(3), 1–4 (2013)
13. Angioni, M., Carboni, D., Melis, M., Pinna, S., Sanna, R., Soro, A.: XPSuite: tracking and managing XP projects in the IDE. In: Proceedings of the 2004 Workshop on Quantitative Techniques for Software Agile Process, pp. 46–52. ACM, November 2004
14. Aoyama, M., Yabuta, K., Kamimura, T., Inomata, S., Chiba, T., Niwa, T., Sakata, K.: A resource-oriented services platform for managing software supply chains and its experience. In: 2014 IEEE International Conference on Web Services (ICWS), pp. 598–605. IEEE, June 2014
15. Mihajlovic, Z., Velasevic, D.: Tracking software projects with the integrated version control in SMIT. ACM SIGSOFT Softw. Eng. Notes **26**(2), 38–43 (2001)
16. Munns, A.K., Bjeirmi, B.F.: The role of project management in achieving project success. Int. J. Project Manage. **14**(2), 81–87 (1996)
17. Cimiano, P., Hotho, A., Staab, S.: Learning concept hierarchies from text corpora using formal concept analysis. J. Artif. Intell. Res. (JAIR) **24**, 305–339 (2005)

Organisational Knowledge Sharing Using Social Networking Sites: Risks, Benefits and Barriers

Valeria Sadovykh[✉] and David Sundaram

Information Systems and Operations Management,
University of Auckland, Auckland, New Zealand
{v.sadovykh,d.sundaram}@auckland.ac.nz

Abstract. Augmented globalisation and the increased speed of operations in the business world have led to dramatic changes in organisational life; the traditional way of work is no longer competitive. It is assumed that an organisation that knows how to communicate and share knowledge quickly will always have an extra competitive advantage in comparison to others who do not participate in knowledge collaboration. Social Networking Sites (SNS) have created a new method of knowledge exchange and introduced new abilities for an organisation to share knowledge. This research investigates the role of SNS in organisational knowledge sharing through a review of concepts and theories from different disciplines. We explore and investigate how SNS are used to facilitate storage, access and knowledge sharing in organisational contexts. The research will conclude with the discussion on the risks, benefits and barriers to implementing SNS for knowledge sharing.

Keywords: Organisational knowledge sharing · Social networking sites · Knowledge exchange · Knowledge storage and access · Knowledge sharing tools

1 Introduction

"If only we knew what we know" is a refrain that has echoed across centuries, cultures, organisations and day-to-day affairs. The problem could be to do with the creation of knowledge, its acquisition and codification; the communication of knowledge; timeliness in the sharing of knowledge; the usage of appropriate knowledge in an appropriate context or the lack of process and systems to support knowledge sharing. In the current competitive business environment, organisations need to be adaptive in the face of change and uncertain events. The way forward to adaptability involves communication and the sharing of knowledge. According to Davenport and Prusak [7], in a rapidly globalised world the firm can survive only by improved communication. Knowledge sharing (KS) helps organisations quickly respond to changing market conditions by collaboration between organisational units, its partners, suppliers, and outsiders in the organisational sphere [20]. When an organisation has a 'sense' of what is going on in the network, with competitors or outside the organisational environment, they can sense future events and analyse them by their enriched knowledge base.

© ICST Institute for Computer Sciences, Social Informatics and Telecommunications Engineering 2017
P. Cong Vinh et al. (Eds.): ICCASA 2016, LNICST 193, pp. 22–31, 2017.
DOI: 10.1007/978-3-319-56357-2_3

1.1 Practical Problems

Despite accelerated technological improvements, some organisations are still not willing to share their own practices, but even if they are willing to participate in knowledge-sharing activities, they do not know, when or where, nor how to make it efficient and safe. The correct use of shared knowledge is also a question for the researchers: How to share your knowledge in a safe environment? How can we ensure that the knowledge we receive from the sender is high quality knowledge? What systems and innovations are available to support such knowledge sharing in organisations? These problems become even more magnified when we consider SNS as mechanisms, tools, and technologies for the creation, storage, refinement, and dissemination of knowledge.

1.2 Research Objectives and Process

Our research was motivated by the practical problem that most organisations share knowledge in an inadequate manner. We first identified practical problems that beset organisations that could be overcome through knowledge sharing. Then, practical problems motivated us to propose research questions which in turn help us to identify research problems and a research process to overcome it. In this paper we will investigate the new emergent technologies, such as SNS which are currently in use for social and business purposes, as well as explore the role of SNS and their application in organisational knowledge sharing.

To investigate the knowledge-sharing process in an organisational environment, we will study technological features, which can be used in the context of knowledge sharing within organisational walls as well as for external business use. We will review how SNS are used to facilitate storage and access to knowledge in organisations, empowering knowledge workers to achieve a sustainable level of knowledge sharing. We will also discuss the issues and requirements of SNS as one of the perspectives of successful KS.

Sect. 2 provides recommendations on the technological aspects which organisations need to be aware of for knowledge management and sharing. Then we will introduce the concept of social networking sites and its functionalities for knowledge-sharing which are currently being recognised as essential to any business (Sect. 3). We will also discuss the potential risks and benefits of using SNS for organisational knowledge sharing, as well as possible barriers that organisations face for implementing SNS for knowledge sharing. We will conclude this paper with the summary of the undertaken research and potential contributions of the performed work for researchers and practitioners (Sect. 4).

2 Systems to Support Knowledge Sharing

With the emergent interest in organisational knowledge-sharing, research on information systems has started to introduce the concept of a particular class of information systems, defined as Knowledge Management Systems (KMS). The objective of KMS is to support the creation, transfer and sharing of knowledge in an organisation by the assistance of emergent systems and technologies. In this paper we present a review on the potential role of information systems which support knowledge sharing. Davenport and Prusak [8] mentioned that computers have created a new method of knowledge exchange and introduced new abilities for an organisation to use existing knowledge, stored in the minds of knowledge workers. Individual knowledge can be transferred to an electronic format and used by other individuals. The computer itself has little to do with knowledge work; its purpose is to store, retrieve, reuse and share knowledge.

Information systems in knowledge sharing research have opened a significant subject for discussion. Based on [19], Information and Communication Technologies (ICT) are the tools that offer different opportunities in the domain of knowledge sharing. For example, electronic communication offers fast collaboration across geographical and time boundaries. Alavi and Leidner [1] state that with the help of online directories in knowledge management, the search for relevant and recorded knowledge is more efficient; also, real time access to transactional and customer data give an opportunity for an organisation to stay on the edge of the current market and have high performance efficiency. That is why interest in IT is raised not only in the research area, but in the business environment as well. Organisations invest significant amounts of time and money in knowledge sharing systems, for the purpose of staying competitive. According to [6], many knowledge management initiatives rely on IT as an important enabler. Knowledge Management Systems (KMS) was developed for the support of knowledge management processes namely knowledge creation, storage, retrieval, transfer and sharing. Alavi and Leidner [1] identified three common applications used in knowledge sharing practices: first, coding, storing and sharing best practices; second, the creation of corporate knowledge directories for storage; and third, the creation of knowledge networks for sharing.

Coding, storing and sharing best practices – the principle of this application is to make available internal knowledge for knowledge worker use. Corporate knowledge directories - mapping of internal expertise, in one sense is based on a similar technological platform and performs similar actions. Internal expertise codified and mapped. It is of use to have real time information on demand and the search time decreased through knowledge being classified by its importance and subject. Knowledge networks are a system application which removes boundaries between time, destination and knowledge worker title. Knowledge workers or communities of practice can communicate in real time across geographical and time boundaries. Communication can be performed face-to-face, by text and/or video application. These types of 'no boundaries' communication facilitates opportunities for organisations to build and share collective knowledge.

Tiwana [18] identified two primary activities of KMS which are storage and communication. From the literature review, it has been identified that knowledge itself has no value for an organisation if it is not used in an appropriate manner [16]. To enable the process of knowledge accumulation, organisations seek to implement specifically designed IS to fulfil knowledge management needs. Benbya et al. [3] identified the following four categories of KMS: Content management tools provide applications for classifying, codifying and integrating knowledge from different sources. Knowledge-sharing tools are system applications tools which make more approachable the process of knowledge-sharing between organisations, organisation partners and knowledge workers. Knowledge search and retrieve systems provide search engines. General KMS are a variety of systems that provide assistance for decision making. KMS offer support in managing knowledge with a technology perspective. Table 1 summarises the implications for KMS. Each KMS tool or type is built in association with these five parameters.

Table 1. General requirement for Knowledge Management Systems

Engagement	Engage in knowledge sharing activities, support development of individual and organisational competencies
Access	Access to knowledge to provide effective search for relevant information
Safety	Safe use of information and knowledge to insure quality and privacy
Process	Link among sources of knowledge to create wider breadth and depth of knowledge flows
Object	Gathering, storing and transferring knowledge

There are specific categories of KMS that have been established as separate stand-alone applications, tools and systems that can be grouped under GDSS, CSCW, EMS and SNS. These systems are separate streams of KMS that have been rigorously studied and utilized across various industries and enterprises.

GDSS are group decision-support systems, combining communication, computing and decision-making technologies for improving work performance between the groups [10]. GDSS is a class of Electronic Meeting Systems (EMS). GDSS are used in knowledge management for supporting meetings and group work. The GDSS include "electronic messaging, local- and wide-area networks, teleconferencing, and storage and forwarding facilities. Computer technologies include multi-user operating systems, fourth generation languages, data bases, data analysis facilities, data storage and modification capabilities" [11, p. 590]. The GDSS is useful for knowledge creation and transfer process, as it eliminates barriers of communication, enables parallel communication, offering an effective way to collect and evaluate information. The limitation of GDSS in knowledge can be seen from several contextual factors; for example, user participation in group networks can be affected by the organisational management style and cultural environment.

Another type OF KMS is Computer Supported Cooperative Work (CSCW), CSCW is not a system application, but a design-orientated concept. The focus of CSCW is on contextual factors of cooperative work. Schmidt and Bannon [17] explain three factors on which CSCW concentrates. First is awareness of individuals where knowledge workers are aware of the fact of cooperative work and where knowledge-sharing activities can take place. Second, articulation work is where the work must somehow be divided between individuals who assemble in organisational units. Last is appropriation, which means an individual acceptance of technology, how the individual or groups adapts technology, or how the design of technologies is appropriate for the user. The success of CSCW systems depends on the design concept, where the current managerial practices are revised, and the social context of cooperative work between knowledge workers is then investigated. In addition, aspects like individual adaption to technology are also included in a design of CSCW.

EMS - Electronic meeting systems is another version of GDSS, also having the function of supporting group meetings. However, the difference between GDSS and EMS, is that it not only supports the decision-making process, but also focuses on communication. The GDSS is more old-fashioned and is not an efficient application for collaborative work between groups. EMS oversteps the GDSS boundaries of time and geography, by using technology like network computers and projected screens. Groups do not need to be in the same room at the same time to perform a collaborative communication. EMS is a combination of GDSS and CSCW. The EMS difference is in providing more than just decision making: it provides communication in real time, making idea generation, planning and problem structuring more possible. The distinctions between GDSS and CSCW combine into a single technology application to support electronic meetings.

The EMS plays an essential role in knowledge management as well as GDSS and CSCW. These three terms in knowledge-management systems were the first emergent applications in the workplace which took the knowledge management process to a different level. The important fact to note, however, is that these three applications are affected by the technological environment, organisational environment and context and user involvement. In addition, just the use of the application will not lead group members to make a better quality decision; it might support its process and save time and money, but it cannot replace human decision making. The last category can be named as a more integrated and innovative application for knowledge management. It integrates the difference in time and location by using modern applications like social networking systems.

3   Knowledge Sharing Using Social Networking Sites

In this section we explore how social networking sites (SNS) as a web technology are used to facilitate storage and access to knowledge in organisations, empowering knowledge workers to achieve a sustainable level of knowledge sharing. This will also discuss the issues and requirements of SNS as one of the perspectives of KS.

Experts say that social networking allows an organisation to open boundaries of communication and discover new knowledge inside an existing structure, or even re-used knowledge, by capturing knowledge in the organisation with enterprise tools. In recent research on knowledge management it is often mentioned that a strategy brings virtual communities of practice, enabled by online interactive technologies, into an organisational environment. The latest news from the ICT field suggests that virtual communities of practice are becoming a knowledge management tool of choice for any multinational corporation, where knowledge sharing is an essential role as well as adding a competitive advantage to the business. Enterprise social networking is becoming a popular topic in research. Boyd and Ellison [4] define social networking sites (SNS) as Web-based services that provide the ability for stakeholders to (1) build a public or semi-public profile, (2) share the connection with other users within a bounded system, and

(3) view and communicate with the list of connected users within a system. The nature of communication and connection can vary from site to site (p. 211).

Despite the recent fame of virtual communities of practice in organisations around the world, not much is discovered regarding the aspects of success or failures. As well as their effect on knowledge sharing, we hear only that social networking is a tool for sharing knowledge, but how it works, no one can explain. One of the factors which influence employees to use the virtual communities in an organisational environment is its ability to share knowledge, despite hierarchy structure, age, experience and geographical barriers. We also have to keep in mind that to achieve successful use of an enterprise social networking tool, the workforce needs to participate in these activities, which will include several consequences: loss of time by employees in the workplace as well as inadequate use of this shared knowledge.

3.1 Knowledge Sharing in Social Networking Sites (SNS)

The label of "social networking" systems are based on the technologies that are used as an extension for the social activities in the Web sphere. SNS is more about already established relationships in the offline social world that are taken further to online communications develop new connections [5].

SNS offers a set of tools and applications and these can be grouped based on the organisational business needs and purposes. Hinchcliffe [12] created the FLATE-NESSES, it is an extended version of SLATES (search, links, authoring, tags, extensions and signals) a mnemonic developed by [14, 15]. Hinchcliffe [12] argues that the SLATES acronym omits some necessary social, freeform, network-orientated and emergent aspects of SNS in a business context. First we define SLATES, is the acronym created by [14] and then the extended version FLATNESSES. SEARCH: the knowledge worker must be able to find required information by use of keywords and page navigators. Search function is one of the essentials of KMS. Search allows employees to reuse already developed best practice, make quick and better quality decisions, save time and resources. LINKS: are key indicators "those search engines use to assess the importance of content" [14, p. 34]. AUTHORITY: a knowledge worker has an opportunity to author information, experience, comment. TAGGING: an easy and useful application that allows the knowledge worker to categorise information, resulting in better search outcomes and facilitating better information and knowledge-sharing within groups. EXTENSIONS: follows an approach similar to tagging, but also combined with authoring and links, helpful in identifying a pattern of used knowledge in an organisation. SIGNALS: are used by a knowledge worker to identify when new information of interest is available in an enterprise. One of the examples of signals application is RSS where the knowledge worker can subscribe to any organisation information, updates and project activities. Hinchcliffe [12] adds four components to the original acronym of SLATES. FREFORM is a simple upfront structure that combines a variety of tools. The enterprise might start with the use of easy freeform tools like blogs and wikis. EMERGENCE architecture is where the organisations required more complicated and task orientated tools, which are most significant in terms of productivity and timeliness. SOCIAL - Enterprise 2.0 and Web 2.0, 3.0, and 4.0 are not only system applications, but also enables people to come together and collaborate. For example, wikis provide this possibility in a virtual format, where the individuals search, publish and share information and their knowledge with their networks. NETWORK-ORIENTATED concentrates on the content of an application, where it is fully web-orientated, addressable and reusable.

To conclude, most of the above tools, technologies, and applications have been designed for the purpose of engaging individuals, groups, communities of practice, and/or knowledge workers in knowledge accumulation activities, where knowledge can be easily transferred, stored, retrieved and shared.

3.2 Risks and Benefits of Knowledge Sharing Using SNS

Why are many organisations still not getting competitive advantage from SNS; why does implementation of SNS still fail? To understand the existence and performance of SNS in an organisation, we need to explore the potential benefits and risks factors which motivate and frighten organisations in implementing SNS and knowledge workers in using it. Dawson [9] provides a list of potential risks and benefits of implementing new emerging technologies for organizational KS (refer to Fig. 1).

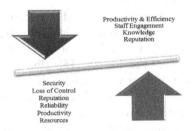

Fig. 1. Risks and benefits of using SNS for knowledge sharing

The first potential benefits which an organisation sees in SNS are productivity, efficiency and competitive advantage. Efficiency and productivity can be seen from the aspects of engagement and participation in knowledge-sharing communities. Faster access to knowledge and information resources allow employees to work more effectively, and personal efficiency can also rise, due to the reduction of unnecessary information and automatic email filters, to prevent excessive emails from disturbing employee productivity. Another important aspect regarding SNS is staff engagement by improved communication across an organisation. Geographical barriers are not a problem, as employees can collaborate with their co–workers any time by using SNS tools. Organisations who deploy SNS could also improve the learning process inside the enterprise, by easier access to content and learning resources. SNS can be used for commercial benefits, by bringing its performance, products, services, success stories and many other activities to the surface through Web 2.0, 3.0, and 4.0 technologies. It might increase the visibility of the organisation in its market by increasing brand awareness. Also by efficient use of SNS, an organisation might increase its customer satisfaction and service, allowing customers to be connected with experts and share their ideas. The SNS by itself does not require heavy investment or any training for the employees to start using it. Overall it can be called a cost effective technology solution [5].

Transparency of organisation by use of SNS can also bring its drawbacks, like loss of reputation or loss of control over employees and activities. Security, reputation, loss of control and privacy issues are four main risks facing an organisation when employing SNS. First of all, the security issue rise from the moment the organisation steps into network activities, it can suffer information loss, "confidential and competitive information can be leaked externally" [9]. Internal and external communication can affect the organisation's environment and its stability; employees might disturb it by inappropriate behaviour. SNS also brings the privacy issues to the surface; employees comments, activities, participation could be checked, watched, and controlled. This might lead to different organisational issues and disagreements between managers and employees. Transparency brings other essential risks. In the case of competitive advantage, the competitors, through the use of SNS tools, will be able to see what the organisations do and weaknesses that might provide an opportunity to build a competitive strategy. Even though SNS vendors promise a higher level of collaboration, the productivity loss can appear to be really expensive, by the use of internal and external social networking tools which might not always reflect the business outcomes; employees can waste their time and resources.

Overall, the dominant part of the reviewed literature emphasises the benefits of SNS, its usefulness in knowledge sharing, competitive advantage in market and collaboration inside and outside the organisational sphere. As we can see from our discussion, SNS have their own risks which might also offset their benefits. Risks and benefits are unique for every organisation. Therefore the organisation must offset the above, based on their business field, performance, environment and employees, before it goes ahead with the implementation process.

3.3 Barriers to Knowledge Sharing Using SNS

If SNS are to be used in organisations for knowledge management and knowledge-sharing, the enterprise will face changes in process, culture, environment and knowledge workers [13]. Changes are always difficult for an organisation. The organisation has to match SNS with its culture, environment, structure, communication climate, knowledge worker experience, age and interest [4, 9, 13]. For successful implementation and use of SNS, organisations are also required to build an open-minded and non-hierarchical environment for information and knowledge exchange [13]. Dawson [9] in his book "Implementing Enterprise 2.0" identified four common areas where the SNS might face complications in an implementation process (refer to Table 2). These are culture, executive attitudes, vested interest and design of initiative. In a similar pattern [2] describes culture, leadership, trust and supporting tools and technology as the common enablers of knowledge-sharing by SNS use in a workforce. Judging the similarity of the provided aspects, we assume that by stimulating a number of enablers we automatically remove the barriers. Leadership style or executive attitudes are also enablers that affect SNS implementation and the knowledge-sharing process. The more support the knowledge worker receives from their management, the less adaptation time will be needed for an organisation to utilise SNS benefits.

Table 2. Key barriers for knowledge sharing using SNS

Culture	Executive attitudes	Vested interests	Design of initiatives
• Strongly hierarchical • Risk averse • Lack of trust in employees • History of failure • Embedded habits	• Poor understanding of benefits and risks • Fear of loss control • Power of legal and risk functions	• Impact on existing investments • Impact on IT function • Loss of power	• Complex language • Technology focus rather than business • No solid business case • Complex initiatives

Vested interest and design of initiatives are mainly technological barriers, easy to change, but sometimes expensive. The main issues which can arise during the implementation process are that SNS might not collaborate well with already-existing IT investment and design and language might not generate positive responses from the knowledge worker. Another barrier is the motivational factor of employee participation in the knowledge-sharing networks, as well as their motivation to share their knowledge through SNS. The workforce is full of individuals, whose preferences may vary, which is why it is difficult to predict the individual factor affecting the implementation.

4   Conclusion

SNS are becoming an important pillar for actualising strategies and gaining competitive advantage through the sharing of knowledge. The social networking phenomenon has invaded not only our personal lives but also our organisational day-to-day work routine. SNS facilitate the interactions and conversations between people, resulting in the creation of virtual knowledge networks. Organisations need to accept that social software is a reality in today's always-on (24 × 7), on-demand, interactive, business and technological landscape. This leads to the physical and conceptual boundaries between the work world and personal world crumbling.

This research study has identified several problems regarding knowledge sharing process and systems in use. First, the technology advantage is not always a solution and second, the human factor will always triumph and must be examined more precisely for identifying its effects on knowledge sharing. Thus to build a strong communication flow, where knowledge can be shared easily, an organisation needs first to overcome the problem of understanding the participants, the context, environment and elements which contribute to knowledge-sharing practice.

This study was able to provide insights into the state of knowledge-sharing components and their importance to a process. We raised the issue of context and socioeconomic environment as well as motivation for the individuals who are the primary driver for knowledge sharing. Growing globalisation and rapidly changing environment, where multinational firms rely on knowledge workers with different cultural backgrounds, make us wonder how the individual context affects knowledge sharing and what could influence motivational factors for participation.

References

1. Alavi, M., Leidner, D.: Review: knowledge management and knowledge management systems: conceptual foundations and research issues. MIS Q. **25**(1), 107–136 (2001)
2. Ardichvili, A.: Learning and knowledge sharing in virtual communities of practice: motivators, barriers, and enablers. Adv. Developing Hum. Res. **10**(4), 541–554 (2008)
3. Benbya, H., Passiante, G., Belbaly, N.A.: Corporate portal: a tool for knowledge management synchronization. Int. J. Inf. Manag. **24**, 201–220 (2004)
4. Boyd, D.M., Ellison, N.B.: Social network sites: definition, history, and scholarship. J. Comput. Mediated Commun. **13**(1), 210–230 (2008)
5. Cook, N.: Enterprise 2.0: How Social Software will Change the Future of Work. Gower Publishing Ltd. (2008)
6. Cross, R., Parker, A., Prusak, L., Borgatti, S.P.: Knowing what we know: supporting knowledge creation and sharing in social networks. Organ. Dyn. **30**(2), 100–120 (2001)
7. Davenport, T., Prusak, L.: Working Knowledge: How Organizations Manage What They Know. Harvard Business School Press Books, Cambridge (1998)
8. Davenport, T., Prusak, L.: Working knowledge: how organizations manage what they know. Ubiquity **1**(24), 2 (2000)
9. Dawson, R.: Implementing Enterprise 2.0. Advanced Human Technologies, Sydney (2009)
10. DeLong, D.W., Fahey, L.: Diagnosing cultural barriers to knowledge managemnt. Acad. Manag. Executive **14**(4), 113–127 (2000)
11. DeSanctis, G., Gallupe, R.B.: A foundation for the study of group decision support systems. Manag. Sci. **33**(5), 589–609 (1987)
12. Hinchcliffe, D.: Enterprise Web 2.0. The state of Enterprise 2.0. (2007)
13. Kosonen, M., Kianto, A.: Applying wikis to managing knowledge - a socio-technical approach. Knowl. Process Manag. **16**(1), 23–29 (2009)
14. McAffe, A.P.: Enterprise 2.0: the dawn of emergent collaboration. MIT Sloan Manag. Rev. **47**(3), 21–28 (2006)
15. McAffe, A.: The business impact of IT. How to hit the enterprise 2.0. (2007, 2008)
16. Sadovykh, V., Sundaram, D.: If only we knew what we know organisational knowledge sharing–concepts and frameworks (2015)
17. Schmidt, K., Bannon, L.: Taking CSCW seriously. Comput. Support. Coop. Work **1**, 7–40 (1992)
18. Tiwana, A. (2000). The knowledge management toolkit. Upper Saddle River
19. Walsham, G.: Knowledge management: the benefits and limitations of computer systems. Eur. Manag. J. **19**(6), 599–608 (2001)
20. Warkentin, M., Bapna, R., Sugumaran, V.: E-knowledge networks for inter-organizational collaborative e-business. Logistics Inf. Manag. **14**, 149–163 (2001)

Context-Adaptive Business Networks

Jing Jing He, Elke Wolf, and David Sundaram[✉]

University of Auckland, 12 Grafton Road, Auckland, New Zealand
jji917@aucklanduni.ac.nz, {e.wolf,d.sundaram}@auckland.ac.nz

Abstract. Businesses are facing turbulences in an environment that includes social, political, technical and economic challenges. Traditional business networks lack the adaptability to rapidly reconfigure their strategy, people, structure, business processes, and systems to respond to such challenges. In this paper we analyse structures and limitations of traditional business networks (Sect. 2). Based on the literature on adaptive business networks (ABN) which have been discussed for about two decades (Sect. 3) we outline the most important conceptualisations of ABN. In order to emphasise the integrated perspective on the strategic, social, structural, business process, and information systems level - which we consider to be essential for adaptability - we create the term "Context-Adaptive Business Networks (CABN)" (Sect. 4). We discuss the necessary features of context-adaptability in more detail (Sect. 5) and conclude with suggestions how this context-adaptability can be achieved on all five levels (Sect. 6).

Keywords: Adaptability · Agility · Learning · Co-opetitive · Co-evolution · Context-adaptive business networks

1 Introduction

The information age has raised new challenges for business competitiveness. Customers in today's market are demanding better products and services at faster speeds and lower prices. Understanding customers' changes in needs and the ability to translate their needs into unique value-added products and service are vital in maintaining business competitiveness. Product life cycles and process execution times have reduced since the last century. Therefore, modern enterprises cannot survive as isolated and independent entities in this competitive environment.

Further, organisations have been facing increasing pressure to improve their financial performance and profitability. The speed with which an organisation can transform these to align with the uncertain environment is the key to survival.

These problems can be addressed by establishing both internal and external flexible environments which include a company's business partners, suppliers and customers. Organisations need real-time information from these stakeholders for fast decision-making in order to be adaptive to environmental changes. For this reason, many businesses are keen to create business networks to support the increased adaptiveness required in rapidly changing markets.

© ICST Institute for Computer Sciences, Social Informatics and Telecommunications Engineering 2017
P. Cong Vinh et al. (Eds.): ICCASA 2016, LNICST 193, pp. 32–41, 2017.
DOI: 10.1007/978-3-319-56357-2_4

In particular, the increased pressure is moving organisations towards adopting Adaptive Business Networks (ABNs). An ABN is a network formed by a group of adaptive organisations in which specifically selected business partners contribute their core competencies in order to meet changing customers' demands, competition and government regulations collaboratively.

In the following we analyse structures and limitations of traditional business networks (Sect. 2). Based on the literature on adaptive business networks (ABN) which have been discussed for about two decades (Sect. 3) we outline the most important conceptualisations of ABN. In order to emphasise the integrated perspective on the strategic, social, structural, business process, and information systems level - which we consider to be essential for adaptability - we create the term "Context-Adaptive Business Networks (CABN)" (Sect. 4). We discuss the necessary features of context-adaptability in more detail (Sect. 5) and conclude with suggestions how this context-adaptability can be achieved on all five levels (Sect. 6).

2   Traditional Business Networks – Structures and Limitations

The structure of a business network determines the relationships and functions of firms in the network. Vasara et al. [1] discuss two complementary measures of a network: density and centrality. Density refers to the measurement of the number of links (relationships) between the members in the network; it is the average intensity of contacts between actors maintained by a certain actor. Thus, in a high density network, the number of relationships is higher and the network has a higher interdependency level between members. Network centrality is described as the structural attribute of nodes in a network [1]. It measures the number of dominant nodes in the network.

In a traditional linear supply chain the originator of the network does not get any direct feedback from the last member in the chain. There is no circulation of information and the resources and information are directional. The controller of the network coordinates the business activities of the entire supply chain. This linear supply chain implies a high centralisation and low density type of network.

In an ego-centred (star-shaped) network, the network is fully concentrated. The only links to members are through the central actor of the network. The central actor has significant control over the multiple relationships with its business partners. This network has high centralisation and low density [1].

A hierarchical network is similar to an organisational structure which is characterised by a single commander. This type of business network has a high level of control and is effective for inter-organisational coordination of activities. The bureaucracy of this type of network results in ineffective communication and decision making, and therefore has low adaptability and is vulnerable to a turbulent environment, in which constant changes are needed to survive.

Heterarchy (Fig. 1) is different from all other network structures as it presents multiple loci of control. A heterarchical network includes interdependent and multiple lateral relationships between units and operates under decentralised decision making, mutual interest, shared responsibilities and distributed authorities, forming a virtual organisation to achieve a common goal. This network therefore has a large number of communication lines, and coordination is based on mutual agreements, contracts and trust. Control is weakened, which may allow the network to evolve into a community of organisations with characteristics of emergent and self-organised bodies. It also features collaboration, in which all the participants in the network feel equally motivated to contribute which, in turn, creates a high level of interactivity that promotes sharing of knowledge to improve overall performance. This network has high density and low centralisation features [2].

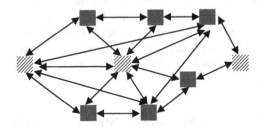

Fig. 1. Heterarchy (adapted from [2])

The key differences between a traditional supply chain and the modern adaptive network lie in their relationships, the level of involvement and the purpose of the network. A supply chain aims to deliver a product or service from supplier to customer and focuses on the relationship in a linear/sequential manner. In the adaptive network, the focus of the network is to combine the values from each business partner and ensure collaboration to deliver a product or service to their customers. The relationships in the network are multilateral. Each member has relationships with other members in the network and has equal responsibility towards the end customer's requirements.

In a rapidly changing business environment, traditional business networks lack the efficiency and effectiveness to achieve the necessary adaptability and agility. In traditional buyer-supplier relationships, the information flow and decision making are channeled through the customer service representative (CSR) and a purchasing agent from each company. Each company has its own separate divisions including marketing, management, transportation and planning. The CSR becomes the single connection for management, logistics and sales personnel in each of the companies who then communicate only indirectly. This effect is named the bow-tie effect and is deemed highly inefficient since this kind of relationship restricts information visibility and communication is ineffective [3].

The traditional supply chain is known for its "bullwhip effect". The bullwhip effect describes a phenomenon where orders to the suppliers tend to have larger variance than the order from the buyers [4]. The causes of the bullwhip effect have been identified to include order batching, price fluctuation and demand forecast updating. It leads to inefficient production and excessive inventory which reduce business performance. The bullwhip effect is a particular problem in the forecast-based supply chain. Therefore, it can be reduced by increasing the visibility of customers' demands.

A traditional business network structure typically consists of two layers: transaction and logistics. The logistics layer represents the management of relationships with partners involved in moving the goods to destinations, i.e. distributors, retailers and manufacturers. The transaction layer concerns the information and materials flow for production from the company's suppliers. Heck and Vervest [5] emphasise that the value of the traditional business network is a supply chain that has a long-term relationship with its partners, maintaining frequent information sharing with direct business partners, and having central control and decision making from the main company. However, this type of network lacks the adaptability to rapidly reconfigure its strategy, structure, social embedding, business process, and information systems in order to respond to environmental change, customer change or other new objectives. Adaptability should allow a quick 'pick, plug and play' of business partners to join the business and collaborate to achieve a new goal.

These limitations can best be addressed with a heterarchy network structure which implies less control and promotes collaboration between firms and offers the flexibility to face environmental challenges. The heterarchy network structure is the network structure closest to an ABN which will be discussed in the next section.

3   Concepts of Adaptive Business Networks

An ABN is defined as a network formed by a group of adaptive organisations in which the selected business partners contribute their competitive advantages to produce a product or service to satisfy customers' demands. The following table outlines selected important conceptualisations of ABNs from the literature over the past two decades in chronological order.

Concepts
Yusuf et al. [6]: Four key concepts for agile competition (competition based on core competence management, virtual enterprise formation, capability for re-configuration and knowledge-driven enterprise) result in a virtual enterprise that integrates the core competencies from a number of selected organisations that are able to respond quickly to market changes at low cost and with high quality
Haeckel [7]: The adaptive framework requires all steps of a Sense-Interpret-Decide-Act (SIDA) loop: sense, respond, plan and execute, as well as learning in between these processes
Christopher [8]: An agile supply chain is a business network with the four characteristics: virtual, market sensitive, process integration, and network based
Heinrich and Betts [3]: Adaptive business networks link companies to serve the customer who purchases the final product or service produced by the supply chain. Information within the network is communicated instantaneously and simultaneously to the companies that need it, eliminating the costly time delays that occur within the linear supply chain. Adaptability is achieved based on the capability to rapidly add and drop partners in respond to market condition changes, to adopt pervasive technology, develop standardised business processes, and be involved in continuous change to gain competitive advantage
Zhang et al. [9]: Important elements of an adaptive business network: Consistent action, technology enabled, continuous innovation, self-learning and self-regulation (Fig. 11).

Concepts
Organisations will develop self-organisation based on individual characteristics, network goals and interaction rules
Ivanov et al. [10]: Adaptability is the ability to change the behaviour of an organisation in order to achieve business goals in a changing environment. The business network is considered adaptive if it meets three requirements: It adapts to changes (1) in the business environment, (2) in the operations execution environment, and (3) in the internal structure of the network itself

4 Context-Adaptive Business Networks

As has been shown in the previous section, while many concepts of adaptability and ABNs discussed in the existing literature show certain common elements, there is no consistent reflection on all essential levels. Delporte-Vermeiren et al. [11] stress strategic, process, and technology aspects, Ford and Mousas [12] look at strategy, structure, and process, and Rittgen [13] focuses primarily on the process level.

We propose that an integrated perspective on five context levels is essential for business networks to be truly adaptive: the strategic, social, structural, business process, and information systems level. We specifically coin the term 'Context-Adaptive Business Networks' in order to emphasise the importance of all five context levels.

(1) **Strategic:** *Which common goal to pursue to cope with current changes?* The ability to quickly sense changes in the market and in customer requirements and combining the core competencies from business partners according to a common goal that guides the actions of business partners, e.g. achieving strategic advantages and sustainability by quickly adapting to environmental shifts. The emergent behaviour of self-organising and self-learning through complex interaction.

(2) **Social:** *Which business partners to select?* Selecting business partners and emphasising the dynamics of relationships between participants in the network, i.e. rapidly establishing and terminating relationships with identified organisations that are capable of providing the necessary skills and knowledge to fulfil a specific business need. When the specific customer requirement has been met, disconnection is also critical. In order for the network to be adaptive, the organisations participating in the network themselves must also be adaptive organisations.

(3) **Structural:** *How business partners relate to each other?* The structure of the network determines the flexibility and efficiency of change to support change in business strategies. The network requires a flexible structure that is dynamically aligned to a changing environment.

(4) **Business process:** *How business partners interact and collaborate?* Standardised business processes enable business partners to exchange information and knowledge rapidly for efficient decision making and consistent action. Thus, they allow for efficiency, flexibility, and agility in responding to change and ensure performance towards accomplishing the common goal.

(5) **Information systems:** *How the interaction is facilitated?* An ABN adopts IT solutions to support collaboration, adaptability and agility of business processes by using inter-organisational technologies, for instance BPM and ARIS. For

collaboration, the network may adopt IS or architecture to integrate the disparate process models into one integrated model. IS are needed to facilitate information sharing and real time decision making. For adaptability, pervasive technologies are required, that allow sensing of and response to changes in the market. Pervasive technologies can link with many incompatible technologies that support collaboration across organisational boundaries. Web Services are a type of pervasive technology that handle immense flows of data exchange within a network environment [3]. Agility can be supported by a flexible architecture to facilitate rapid change at strategy and business process levels.

5   Features of Context-Adaptive Business Networks

This section discusses key features that ABNs need in order for their members to collaborate effectively. These features include adaptability, agility, learning, coordination, cooperation and collaboration.

(1) **Adaptability:** Heck and Vervest [5] and Vervest et al. [14] describe adaptability as the ability of a network to quickly adapt to unexpected situations through 'pick, plug and play'. Pick, plug and play is the ability to quickly connect and disconnect business partners in the network which allows the network to respond to opportunities existing in the market. Pick refers to the establishment of a temporary connection with business partners to interoperate. This step includes the ability of the network to choose the appropriate partners such as suppliers, manufacturers and complementary organisations to contribute to the business's needs. Plug is the ability of the network to plug the business partner in to the system to start business operations rapidly and efficiently. Play is the business activities performed to meet specific situations. The concept of 'quick connect' refers to the ability to quickly select the appropriate business partners and establish the relationship to start business process interaction. The capability to 'quickly disconnect' is the ability to drop business partners from the network. From the business process dimension, organisations need to provide the capability and flexibility for managers to easily assemble and reassemble business processes to deliver changes in strategy. At the information system level, Heck and Vervest [5] suggested that modularity is required to allow for adaptability. Modularised systems allow for versatility, which is the ability of an organisation to produce a variety of products and services. Systems must be designed and redesigned to support the changes in business processes. Organisation structure must also be dynamic to cope with the frequent changes required by the organisation. New organisation structures may emerge as a result of change in strategy and business process.

(2) **Agility:** The ability to adapt is alone not sufficient, adaptation also needs to be rapid. Agility is the ability of the network to rapidly respond to changes in the market and customer demand [15]. Agility focuses on the speed of change and is described as the effectiveness and quickness of response to change and uncertainty. Lin et al. [15] state that an ABN requires responsiveness, competency, adaptability and quickness. Responsiveness is the ability to identify changes and react proactively; competency is the ability

to efficiently realise the network's goals; adaptability is the ability to change business processes to achieve goals; and quickness is the ability to reach the goal quickly. To achieve such agility, Lin et al., (2004) propose that the network requires collaborative relationships to form a competitive network, process integration to ensure systematic operation between business partners, and information integration to allow sharing of information and customer sensitivity so the network can read customer demand and respond. Hofman and Cecere [16] highlight another critical aspect of agility: high quality. The ability to respond to customers' requirements and to do so fast is still not sufficient, a quick response with poor quality does not qualify as agile. The goal of the network is to collaborate with other skilled companies to supply high quality customised products to their customers.

(3) Learning: Organisational learning is perceived as a critical factor for an organisation to gain competitive advantage, as it leads to improved performance, adaptability and innovation [17]. Argyris [18] describes learning as a process of detecting problems, and correcting the errors. The two types of learning, Single-loop learning (SLL) and Double-loop learning (DLL) have different influences on an organisation. SLL asks questions like "Are we doing things right?" which improves current operations by making corrections that often take the form of rules and policies at the operational level. DLL asks questions like "Are we doing the right things?" This involves questioning whether the rules or goals should be changed to correct the errors. DLL requires creativity, critical thinking and insight to comprehend the problems and propose the solutions to better achieve a goal. Nielsen's [19] triple-loop learning (TLL) involves creating new strategies for learning. TLL asks questions like "How do we decide what is right?" This involves discovering how previous actions have facilitated or inhibited learning. This 'learn how to learn' skill allows participants to better understand how to respond to changes in the environment. TLL therefore influences even higher levels of the organisation, involving a change in organisational goals and strategies. For participants to respond adaptively to the business environment, all three types of learning are needed. Smith and Young [17] suggest that learning in an organisation occurs at different levels including individual, group and the whole organisation. The purpose of learning is to create, capture and transfer knowledge throughout the organisation in order to respond adequately to changes in its environment. The individual's ability to innovate and be flexible is critical for them to transfer knowledge to new and unfamiliar situations. Rose-Anderssen et al. [20] describe three levels of learning to achieve knowledge transformation to produce innovation for an organisation. Knowledge transformation is about transforming the learning from past experiences, and creating new improvements and innovations. Reactive learning and adaptive learning create marginal improvement and expansive learning creates radical innovation, while knowledge transformation creates a learning community that produces a capability to "create the future." Expansive learning would provide an ABN the potential to gain the competitive advantage required to face uncertain business environments.

(4) Coordination, Cooperation, Collaboration, and Co-opetition: Business networks can typically fall into three categories: coordinated, cooperative and collaborative networks. Coordinated networks are often directed by a controller. The coordinator ensures that the activities performed by participants in the network are meeting predefined goals. Coordinated networks rely on high volumes of transactions distributed across the supply chain. Prevention of disruptions and economic scales are the keys that provide efficiency and competitive advantage in the network [21]. Supply chains are often coordinated networks. A cooperative network is seen as a collective activity in which two or more participants act together to achieve their shared collective goal (end, purpose) [22]. This definition of cooperation highlights (1) cooperation in the full sense involving a collective goal and (2) a collective goal requires participants to cooperate to achieve the goal. Such collective action does not mean joint actions. Dillenbourg et al. [23] note that in cooperation, the labour is divided among participants for an activity where each participant is responsible for only a portion of the problem solving. The tasks in a cooperative network are divided into independent subtasks (hierarchically). Participants interact by sharing complementary knowledge, resources, and thus leveraging for mutual benefit [24]. A collaborative network is led by an orchestrator who poses the vision for the network and organises through influence. There is no controller dominating the network; members are equal in status and share the benefits equally. When the network performance increases, everyone benefits. Each organisation belongs to the network because of its expertise and is equally motivated to participate and contribute to the network. The network is built and maintained by trust and joint venturing, and managing relationships is critical to achieving adaptability in a collaborative network. The requirements are largely undefined in the network, which allows members in the network to deal with more complex problems and explore and develop more opportunities through their dynamic interactivity. An ABN is therefore a collaborative network rather than a coordinated network, in which the goal is to merge expertise from various disciplines to drive innovation and promote network development. The other key difference between an ABN and a supply chain is that the all members of the network are liable for the end product produced for their customers. Collaboration drives innovation: this comes from the sharing of ideas among individuals or groups which creates knowledge and therefore continuous innovation. Innovation can be achieved within the firm, through collaboration among employees or groups. Co-opetitive Network - In today's complex business environment, traditional approaches to competitiveness no longer apply. Porter [25] and Brandenburger and Nalebuff [26] mostly view business success as either competition or cooperation. The complex business landscape has shifted towards competitive strategies focusing on interdependence between firms that are characterised by the simultaneous presence of cooperation and competition at various levels, i.e., within-firm and inter-firm [27]. Cooperation and competition merge together to form a new kind of strategic advantage: Dagnino and Rocco [27] named this the 'co-opetitive system of value creation'. The value created can be classified into either economic value (i.e. revenue increase) or knowledge value (growth of knowledge). Co-opetition can occur at the macro level (relationships between firms across industry), and the meso level (between competitors, suppliers, and customers within the same industry). Dagnino [27] also suggests that co-opetition is about 'incomplete interest and goal congruence' concerning firms' interdependence. The term co-opetition is used to embrace the firm, its customers, suppliers, competitors and complementors.

(5) Co-evolution: The ABN as a complex business environment has been described as a business ecosystem - complex, self-organising, emergent and co-evolving - enabling adaptation to the changing environment [28]. Co-evolution is a key concept for business ecosystems, and interdependence is the key concept in co-evolution. Interdependence indicates that participants in a network both influence and are influenced by the network. The leadership participant influences the co-evolutionary process. The ecosystem is complex as it consists of many self-organised organisations. The relationships between these self-organised organisations are interrelated and interconnected within the network. Wycisk et al. [29] describe self-organisation as a result of autonomous inter-action within the network, for instance, there is no controller that controls the operations. It has decentralised decision making, i.e. decisions are made in accordance with the impact of interrelationships with other organisations. Innovation and emergence are closely linked with self-organisation. Without an internal or external controller, organ-isations manage themselves. Pattern and structure arise from the interaction of the component organisations. The network as a whole adapts to its changing environment through being emergent, self-organising and co-evolutionary.

6   Conclusions

We find that many conceptualisations of ABN fall short on certain layers and coin the term 'context-adaptive business networks' in order to specifically emphasise the impor-tance of the five context levels: strategic, social, structural, business processes, infor-mation systems. To respond to changing environments, participants require flexible organisational structures, business processes, and technologies. The concept of adapt-ability requires the network to quickly connect and drop partners and to establish connections. Apart from this type of modularized approach the participants of CABN need to be agile and learning organisations. Not just SLL, but DLL and TLL need to be a way of life both for the participants as well as the CABN as a whole. Co-operation, co-ordination, collaboration, and co-opetition are vital modalities and strategies for CABN but one of the key capabilities is their ability to co-evolve with their ecosystem and the world.

References

1. Vasara, P., Krebs, V., et al.: Arachne-adaptive network strategy in a business environment. Comput. Ind. **50**(2), 127–140 (2002). Elservier Science B.V.
2. Todeva, E.: Business Networks: Strategy and Structure. Routledge, New York (2006)
3. Heinrich, C., Betts, B.: Adapt or die: transformating your supply chain into an adaptive business network. The University of Auckland library database (2003)
4. Lee, H.L., Padmannabhan, V., et al.: The Bullwhip effect in supply chains. Sloan Manage. Rev. **38**(3), 93–102 (1997)
5. Heck, E.B., Vervest, P.: Smart business networks: how the network wins. Commun. ACM **50**(5), 28–37 (2007)
6. Yusuf, Y.Y., Sahardi, M., Gunasekaran, A.: Agile manufacturing: the drivers, concepts and attributes. Int. J. Prod. Econ. **62**(1), 33–43 (1999)

7. Haeckel, S.H.: Adaptive Enterprise: Creating and Leading Sense-and-Respond Organisations. Harvard Business School Press, Boston (1999)
8. Christopher, M.: The agile supply chain: competing in volatile markets. Ind. Mark. Manage. **29**(1), 9 (2000)
9. Zhang, J., Junqin, X., et al.: Complex adaptive supply chain network: the state of Art. QingDao University (2009)
10. Ivanov, D., Sokolov, B., et al.: A multi-structural framework for adaptive supply chain planning and operations control with structure dynamic considerations. Eur. J. Oper. Res. **200**(2), 12 (2010)
11. Delporte-Vermeiren, D., Vervest, P., et al.: In search of margin for business networks: the european patent office. Eur. Manag. J. **22**(2), 167 (2004)
12. Ford, D., Mouzas, S.: Is there any hope? the idea of strategy in business networks. Australas. Market. J. **16**(1), 15 (2008)
13. Rittgen, R.: A contract-based architecture for business networks. Int. J. Electron. Commer. **12**(4), 31 (2008)
14. Vervest, P., Preiss, K., et al.: The emergence of smart business networks. J. Inf. Technol. **19**(4), 6 (2004)
15. Lin, C.T., Chu, H., et al.: Agility index in the supply chain. Int. J. Prod. Econ. **46**(23), 285–299 (2004)
16. Hofman, D., Cecere, L.: The agile supply chain. Supply Chain Manage. Rev. **9**(8), 2 (2005)
17. Smith, S., Young, A.: Adapting to change: becoming a learning organisation as a relief and development agency. IEEE Trans. Prof. Commun. **52**(4), 329–345 (2009)
18. Argyris, C.: Double loop learning in organisation. Harvard Bus. Rev. **55**(5), 11 (1977)
19. Nielsen, R.P.: Woolman's "I am We" triple-loop action-learning: origin and application in organisation ethics. J. Appl. Behav. Sci. **29**(1), 117–138 (1993)
20. Rose-Anderssen, C., Baldwin, S.J., et al.: Knowledge transformation, learning and changes giving competitive advantage in aerospace. Emerg. Complex. Organ. **11**(2), 15 (2009)
21. Word, J.: Business Network Transformation. Jossey-Bass, San Francisco (2009)
22. Tuomela, R.: Cooperation: A Philosophical Study. Kluwer Academic Publishers, Dordrecth (2000)
23. Dillenbourg, P., Baker, M., et al.: The Evolution of Research on Collaborative Learning. Elsevier, Oxford (1996)
24. Osarenkhoe, A.: A coopetition strategy- a study of inter-firm dynamics between competition and cooperation. Bus. Strategy Series **11**(6), 343–362 (2010). Emerald Group Publishing Limited
25. Porter, M.E.: What is strategy? (1996). http://www.ipocongress.ru/download/guide/article/what_is_strategy.pdf. Accessed 16 Dec 2011
26. Brandenburger, A., Nalebuffm, B.: Co-opetition - a revolutionary mindset that combines competition and cooperation (1996)
27. Dagnino, G.B., Rocco, E.: Coopetition Strategy: Theory, Experiments and Cases. Routledge, London (2009)
28. Peltoniemi, M., Vuori, E.: Business ecosystem as the new approach to complex adaptive business environments. In: Frontier of E-Business Research (2004)
29. Wycisk, C., McKelvey, B., et al.: Smart parts supply networks as complex adaptive system: analysis and implications. Int. J. Phys. Distrib. Logist. Manage. **38**(2), 108–125 (2008)

Context-Aware Hand Pose Classifying Algorithm Based on Combination of Viola-Jones Method, Wavelet Transform, PCA and Neural Networks

Ngoc Hoang Phan[✉] and Thi Thu Trang Bui

Faculty of Information Technology, Ba Ria-Vung Tau University,
Truong Van Bang Street 01,
Vung Tau City, Ba Ria-Vung Tau Province, Vietnam
hoangpn285@gmail.com, trangbt.084@gmail.com
{hoangpn, trangbtt}@bvu.edu.vn

Abstract. In this paper we propose a novel context-aware algorithm for hand poses classifying. The proposed algorithm based on Viola-Jones method, wavelet transforms, PCA and neural networks. At first, the Viola-Jones method is used to find the location of hand pose in images. Then the features of hand pose are extracted using combination of wavelet transform and PCA. Finally, these extracted features are classified by multi-layer feedforward neural networks. In this proposed algorithm, for each training hand pose we create one neural network, which will determine whether an input hand pose is training hand pose or not. In order to test the proposed algorithm, we use known Cambridge Gesture database and divide it into 5 parts with difference light contrast conditions. The experimental results show that the proposed algorithm effectively classifies the hand pose in difference light contrast conditions and competes with state-of-the-art algorithms.

Keywords: Hand poses classifying · Method Viola-Jones · Wavelet transform · PCA · Neural networks

1 Introduction

Hand gesture recognition is one of the most difficult and required task in the field of image processing and computer vision. The hand gesture recognition systems are used to classify specific human hand gesture. The main aim of these systems is to transfer information or to manage difference devices, such as computers, televisions, etc. In this paper, the hand pose classifying task, which is one main subtask of hand gesture recognition, is considered.

In order to classify the hand pose in images, we can do these following steps:

1. Detecting and finding the location of hand pose in images;
2. Extracting the features of detected hand pose;
3. Classifying hand pose using extracted features.

© ICST Institute for Computer Sciences, Social Informatics and Telecommunications Engineering 2017
P. Cong Vinh et al. (Eds.): ICCASA 2016, LNICST 193, pp. 42–51, 2017.
DOI: 10.1007/978-3-319-56357-2_5

To detect and find the location of hand pose in images we use method Viola-Jones. Because of high processing speed and effectiveness, method Viola-Jones becomes one of the most used object detection methods. This method based on three ingredients to enable fast and accurate object detection: the integral image for feature detection, Adaboost for feature selection and an attentional cascade for efficient computational resource allocation. These ingredients allow method can perform the object detection in real time [1–4].

After location of hand pose is detected, the next step is its features extraction. In order to extract image features, wavelet transform is one of the most effective methods. Wavelet transform enables to obtain the necessary information about the image and it is also can be quickly calculated. The experimental results of image classification algorithms [5–10] showed that images, features of which extracted by using wavelet transform, were classified with 76–99.7% accuracy rate.

In the algorithms [4, 11–20] wavelet transform is effectively used to solve the task of pattern recognition on noisy images. In this case, the objects were recognized with 90–98.5% accuracy rate. Besides the experimental results of algorithms [4, 16–20] showed that using combination of wavelet transform, PCA and neural networks gave more effective performance of object recognition. In these algorithms, neural networks were used to recognize objects based on their features, which extracted by using the combination of wavelet transform and PCA.

Thus, using the combination of Viola-Jones method, wavelet transform, PCA and neural networks is perspective solution for development of novel context-aware hand pose classifying algorithm. In this paper we propose a novel context-aware algorithm for hand pose classifying based on combination of Viola-Jones method, wavelet transform, PCA and neural networks. In this case, the context is any information about an image such as: image light condition, contour, noise and so on.

2 Proposed Algorithm

The proposed hand pose classifying algorithm consists of following main steps:

1. Finding the hand pose location in image based on Viola-Jones method (Fig. 1);
2. Retrieving the features of hand pose using wavelet transform (Fig. 1);
3. Reducing dimension of extracted features vector based on PCA (Fig. 1);
4. Training neural networks using obtained feature vectors (Fig. 2);
5. Classifying hand pose based on obtained feature vectors and trained neural networks (Fig. 3).

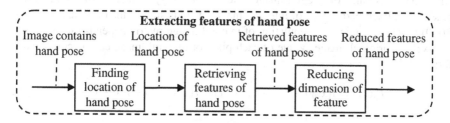

Fig. 1. Process of extracting features of hand poses.

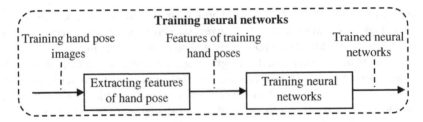

Fig. 2. Process of training neural networks.

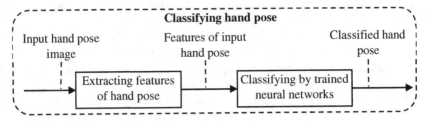

Fig. 3. Process of classifying hand poses.

2.1 Finding Hand Pose Location Using Viola-Jones Method

This method was developed and proposed in 2001 by Paul Viola and Michael Jones, and it is still effective to detect object in digital images and videos in real-time [1, 2]. Using simple cascade classifier, which is the feature detector instead of one complex classifier, is the main idea of this method. Based on this idea, it enables to construct a detector, which can work in real time.

Integral Image

In Viola-Jones method, integral image is used to rapidly compute rectangle features. The integral image is widely used in other methods, such as wavelet transforms, SURF, Haar filtering and etc. [21]. Pixel value of the integral image at location (x, y) contains the sum of pixels above and to the left of (x, y) and is computed by formula (1).

$$I(x,y) = \sum_{x' \le x, y' \le y} i(x', y'), \tag{1}$$

where $I(x, y)$ is value of integral image pixel (x, y); $i(x, y)$ – intensity of original image pixel (x, y). Each pixel value of integral image $I(x, y)$ is sum of the original pixels from $i(0, 0)$ to $i(x, y)$. Time of computation of integral image matrix depends on the number of pixels of original image. Value of each pixel of integral image can be computed by formula (2):

$$I(x,y) = i(x,y) - I(x-1, y-1) + I(x, y-1) + I(x-1, y). \tag{2}$$

Haar-like Features

Haar-like features are image features, which are used in the object recognition task. Viola and Jones adapted the idea of using an alternate feature set based on Haar wavelets instead of the usual image intensities of Papageorgiou et al. [22]. And they developed the new features called Haar-like features. A Haar-like feature considers adjacent rectangular regions at a specific location in a detection window, sums up the pixel intensities in each region and calculates the difference between these sums.

In the detection phase of the Viola–Jones object detection framework, a window of the target size is moved over the input image, and for each subsection of the image the Haar-like feature is calculated. This difference is then compared to a learned threshold that separates non-objects from objects. Because such a Haar-like feature is only a weak learner or classifier (its detection quality is slightly better than random guessing) a large number of Haar-like features are necessary to describe an object with sufficient accuracy. Examples of Haar-like features are presented in Fig. 4.

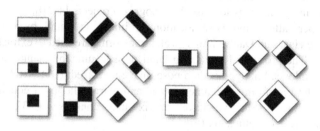

Fig. 4. Examples of Haar-like features.

Learning Classification Using Adaboost

Boosting is a machine learning meta-algorithm for performing supervised learning. Boosting is based on the question posed by Kearns [23]: can a set of weak learners create a single strong learner? A weak learner is defined to be a classifier which is only slightly correlated with the true classification (it can label examples better than random guessing). In contrast, a strong learner is a classifier that is arbitrarily well-correlated with the true classification.

Schapire's affirmative answer to Kearns' question has had significant ramifications in machine learning and statistics, most notably leading to the development of boosting [24].

For each feature, the weak learner determines the optimal threshold classification function, such that the minimum number of examples is misclassified. A weak classifier $h_j(x)$ thus consist of a feature f_j, a threshold j and a parity p_j indicating the direction of the inequality sign (formula 3):

$$h_j(z) = \begin{cases} 1, & \text{if } p_j f_j(z) < p_j \theta_j \\ 0, & \text{otherwise} \end{cases}, \tag{3}$$

where z is a 24×24 pixel sub-window of an image.

Development of this approach was development more perfect family algorithms of a boosting – AdaBoost, short for Adaptive Boosting, is a machine learning algorithm, formulated by Yoav Freund and Robert Schapire. It is a meta-algorithm, and can be used in conjunction with many other learning algorithms to improve their performance. AdaBoost is adaptive in the sense that subsequent classifiers built are tweaked in favor of those instances misclassified by previous classifiers.

For combining increasingly more complex classifier in a "cascade" which allows background regions of the image to be quickly discarded while spending more computation on promising object-like regions.

2.2   Extracting Hand Pose Features Using Wavelet Transforms

By using wavelet transform to extract image features, we will obtain the necessary information about the image. Besides we can also quickly calculate the wavelet transform. So wavelet transform becomes one of the most effective methods, which are used to extract image features to classify (recognize) objects [4–20].

In this paper, after hand pose location in image is found by using method Viola-Jones, the Haar and Daubechies wavelet transforms are used to extract hand pose image features. The process of extracting hand pose features by using wavelet transform works as follows. Firstly, the hand pose image is resized to 64 × 64 pixels. Then we apply wavelet transform to obtained image and extract the low-frequency wavelet coefficients. In the result, we have matrix that consists of $32 \times 32 = 1024$ low-frequency wavelet coefficients (Fig. 5).

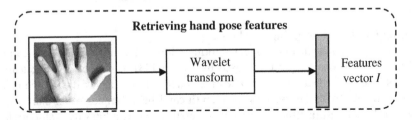

Fig. 5. Retrieving hand pose features using wavelet transform.

2.3   Dimension Reduction Using PCA

Before classifying by neural networks, dimension of hand pose feature vector is reduced. In this paper, PCA is used to solve this task. At first, eigenspace for hand poses (eigenhandpose) will be created using M images of hand poses. The process of creating hand pose eigenspace is carried out as follows.

In first step, the process of extracting features is applied to each of M images. After that we obtain a set of $\vec{I}_1, \ldots, \vec{I}_M$ feature vectors. Then we form the mean vector, the value of each element of which is calculated by the formula (4):

$$\vec{I}_{avg} = \frac{1}{M} \sum_{n=1}^{M} \vec{I}_n. \tag{4}$$

In second step, each vector of the M feature vectors is subtracted by mean vector using formula (5):

$$\vec{\Phi}_n = \vec{I}_n - \vec{I}_{cp}, \ n = 1, \dots, M. \tag{5}$$

In third step, an eigenspace, which consists of K eigenvectors of the covariance matrix C (6), is created. It is the best way to describe the distribution of these M feature vectors ($K < M$).

$$C = \frac{1}{M} \sum_{n=1}^{M} \vec{\Phi}_n \vec{\Phi}_n^T = AA^T, \quad A = \{\vec{\Phi}_1, \dots, \vec{\Phi}_M\}. \tag{6}$$

where k-th vector $\vec{u}_k$ satisfies maximization of the following formula (7):

$$\lambda_k = \frac{1}{M} \sum_{n=1}^{M} (\vec{u}_k^T \vec{\Phi}_n)^2 \tag{7}$$

and an orthogonality condition (8):

$$\vec{u}_l^T \vec{u}_k = \begin{cases} 1, & l = k \\ 0, & \text{otherwise} \end{cases}. \tag{8}$$

Vectors $\vec{u}_k$ and values λ_k are eigenvectors and eigenvalues of covariance matrix C. In order to create this eigenspace, firstly, we calculate M eigenvectors $\vec{u}_l$ of covariance matrix C by using eigenvectors of other matrix $L = A^T A$. Each vector $\vec{u}_l$ is calculated by the formula (9):

$$\vec{u}_l = \frac{1}{M} \sum_{k=1}^{M} v_{lk} \Phi_k, \ l = 1, \dots, M. \tag{9}$$

After that we select K eigenvectors, which have the largest eigenvalues from M obtained eigenvectors. The eigenspace is the set of K selected eigenvectors (Fig. 6).

When the hand pose eigenspace is created, the process of reducing dimension of hand pose feature vector $\vec{I}_{in}$ is carried out as follows.

Firstly, we decompose the hand pose feature vector on K eigenvectors $\vec{u}_i$ and calculate corresponding decomposition coefficients by the formula (10):

$$w_i = \vec{u}_i^T (\vec{I}_{in} - \vec{I}_{avg}), \ i = 1, \dots, K. \tag{10}$$

Then we form a novel hand pose feature vector using formula (11):

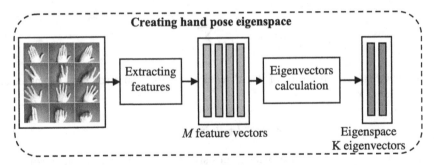

Fig. 6. Creation of hand pose eigenspace.

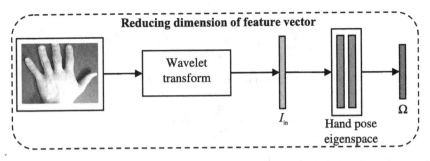

Fig. 7. Reducing dimension of hand pose feature vector.

$$\vec{\Omega}^T = \{w_1, \ldots, w_K\}. \tag{11}$$

This vector describes the distribution of each eigenvectors in presentation of hand pose feature vector. The novel hand pose feature vector is $\vec{\Omega}$, which consists of K elements. In this case, K is much less than 1024 (Fig. 7).

2.4 Hand Pose Classifying Using Neural Networks

In this proposed algorithm paper, we use back-propagation feed-forward neural networks to classify hand poses based on obtained feature vectors. For each hand pose of training set, we create one multilayered feed-forward neural network, which is trained by back propagation method. The input of these neural networks is the hand pose feature vector $\vec{\Omega}$ (11), which consists of K elements. These neural networks will return a value from 0 to 1, which determine whether an input hand pose is training hand pose or not.

The neural networks classify the input hand pose as follows. Firstly, feature vector of the input hand pose is extracted. After that the dimension of this vector is reduced. Finally, obtained hand pose feature vector is submitted to the inputs of all trained neural networks. Input hand pose is classified as a hand pose of training set, neural network of which returns the largest value (Fig. 8).

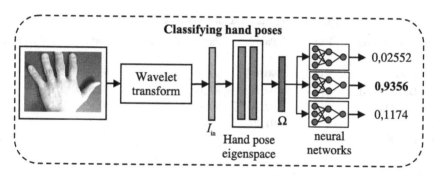

Fig. 8. Classifying hand poses.

3 Experimental Results

The proposed algorithm was tested using a part of the Cambridge Gesture database [25]. All experiments were performed on a laptop with the processor Intel Core Duo P7350 2.0 GHz and 2.0 GB of RAM. This hand pose database consists of 5 difference parts, which contain images in various light contrast conditions (Fig. 9).

Fig. 9. Examples of hand pose images of 5 difference parts

In the part 1 (Fig. 9a), the light is straight ahead the hand pose. The light comes from bottom right corner of the hand pose for part 2, top right corner – part 3 (Fig. 9c), top left corner – part 4 (Fig. 9d) and bottom left corner – part 5 (Fig. 9e).

Fig. 10. Examples of images of 12 classes of hand pose of dataset part 1.

In these experiments hand poses are divided into 12 classes presented on Fig. 10. For each part, we created one testing dataset, which contains 2400 hand pose images (20 images of each class). And for each part we also created one training dataset, which contains 1200 hand pose images (10 images of each class).

The experimental results are presented in Table 1. It is shown that the proposed hand pose classifying algorithm, which based on a combination of wavelet transform, PCA and neural networks, gave more accurate classifying results than algorithm [20].

Table 1. Accuracy rate of hand pose classifying.

Wavelet transform type	Part 1, %	Part 2, %	Part 3, %	Part 4, %	Part 5, %	All parts, %
[20] (Haar)	94,63	90,96	89,46	92,33	90,17	93,30
[20] (Daubechies)	93,67	90,17	87,58	90,79	87,63	92,57
Proposed (Haar)	96,75	92,34	90,58	94,15	91,53	94,96
Proposed (Daubechies)	95,49	91,40	88,69	92,32	88,75	93,88

The highest hand pose classifying accuracy was obtained for the dataset part 1, in which the light is straight ahead the hand pose. For other parts, the classifying accuracy is competed with each other. Besides, it is shown that in this case, using wavelet Haar gave more effective classifying results than using wavelet Daubechies.

4   Conclusion

In this paper we developed a novel algorithm for hand pose classifying based on method Viola-Jones, wavelet transform, PCA and neural networks. Developed algorithm enables effectively classifying hand pose with difference light contrast conditions.

The proposed algorithm gave the highest hand pose classifying accuracy 96,75%, which was obtained for the dataset part 1. In this part the light is strait ahead hand pose. The experimental results also showed that using wavelet Haar gave more accuracy rate of hand pose classifying than using wavelet Daubechies.

References

1. Viola, P., Jones, M.J.: Rapid object detection using a boosted cascade of simple features. In: IEEE Conference on Computer Vision and Pattern Recognition, Kauai, Hawaii, USA, vol. 1. pp. 511–518 (2001)
2. Viola, P., Jones, M.J.: Robust real-time face detection. Int. J. Comput. Vision **57**(2), 137–154 (2004)
3. Wang, Y.-Q.: An analysis of the Viola-Jones face detection algorithm. Image Process. On Line **4**, 128–148 (2014)
4. Phan, N.H., Bui, T.T.T., SpitsynVladimir, G.: Real-time hand gesture recognition base on Viola-Jones method, algorithm CAMShift, wavelet transform and principal component analysis. Tomsk State Univ. J. Control Comput. Sci. **2**(23), 102–111 (2013)
5. Mehdi, L., Solimani, A., Dargazany, A.: Combining wavelet transforms and neural networks for image classification. In: 41st Southeasten Symposium on System Theory, Tullahoma, TN, USA, pp. 44–48 (2009)
6. Weibao, Z., Li, Y.: Image classification using wavelet coefficients in low-pass bands. In: Proceedings of International Joint Conference on Neural Networks, Orlando, Florida, USA, pp. 114–118 (2007)

7. Chang, T., Jay, K.: Texture analysis and classification with tree-structured wavelet transform. IEEE Trans. Image Process. **2**(4), 429–440 (1993)
8. Daniel, M.R.S., Shanmugam, A.: ANN and SVM based war scene classification using wavelet features: a comparative study. J. Comput. Inf. Syst. **7**, 1402–1411 (2011)
9. Park, S.B., Lee, J.W., Kim, S.K.: Content-based image classification using a neural network. Pattern Recogn. Lett. **25**, 287–300 (2004)
10. Gonzalez, A.C., Sossa, J.H., Riveron, E.M.F., Pogrebnyak, O.: Histograms, wavelets and neural networks applied to image retrieval. In: Gelbukh, A., Reyes-Garcia, C.A. (eds.) MICAI 2006. LNCS (LNAI), vol. 4293, pp. 820–827. Springer, Heidelberg (2006). doi:10. 1007/11925231_78
11. Lai, J.H., Yuen, P.C., Feng, G.C.: Face recognition using holistic Fourier invariant features. Pattern Recogn. **34**, 95–109 (2001)
12. Kakarwal, S., Dsehmuhk, R.: Wavelet transform based feature extraction for face recognition. Informatica **15**(2), 243–250 (2004)
13. Zhang, B.-L., Zhang, H.: Face recognition by applying wavelet subband representation and kernel associative memory. IEEE Trans. Image Process. **4**(11), 1549–1560 (1995)
14. Gumus, E., Kilic, N., Sertbas, A., Ucan, O.N.: Evaluation of face recognition techniques using PCA, wavelets and SVM. Expert Syst. Appl. **37**, 6404–6408 (2010)
15. Wadkar, P.D., Wankhade, M.: Face recognition using discrete wavelet transform. Int. J. Adv. Eng. Technol. **3**(1), 239–242 (2012)
16. Mazloom, M., Kasaei, K.: Face recognition using PCA, wavelets and neural networks. In: Proceeding of the First International Conference on Modeling, Simulation and Applied Optimization, Sharjah, UAE, 1–3 February, pp. 1–6 (2005)
17. Phan, N.H., Bui, T.T.T., Spitsyn, V.G., Bolotova, Y.A.: Using a Haar wavelet transform, principal component analysis and neural networks for OCR in the presence of impulse noise. J. Comput. Opt. **40**(2), 249–257 (2016)
18. Phan, N.H., Bui, T.T.T.: Context-aware handwritten and optical character recognition using a combination of wavelet transform, PCA and neural networks. In: Vinh, P.C., Alagar, V. (eds.) ICCASA 2015. LNICSSITE, vol. 165, pp. 254–263. Springer, Cham (2016). doi:10. 1007/978-3-319-29236-6_25
19. Phan, N.H., Bui, T.T.T., Spitsyn, V.G., Bolotova Yu, A., Savitsky Yu, V.: Development of algorithms for face and character recognition based on wavelet transforms, PCA and neural networks. In: Proceedings of 2015 International Siberian Conference on Control and Communications (SIBCON). IEEE (2015)
20. Phan, N.H., Bui, T.T.T., Spitsyn, V.G.: Face and hand gesture recognition based on wavelet transforms and principal component analysis. In: 7th International Forum on Strategic Technology IFOST: Proceedings of IFOST 2012. IEEE (2012)
21. Gonzalez, R.C., Woods, R.E.: Digital Image Processing. Addison-Wesley, Reading (2001)
22. Papageorgiou, C., Oren, M., Poggio, T.: A general framework for object detection. In: International Conference on Computer Vision (1998)
23. Kearns, M.: Thoughts on hypothesis boosting. Unpublished manuscript in Machine Learning Class Project (1988)
24. Freund, Y., Schapire, R.E.: A short introduction to boosting. J. Japan. Soc. Artif. Intell. **14**(5), 771–780 (1999)
25. Kim, T.K., Wong, S.F., Cipolla, R.: Cambridge Hand Gesture Data set. http://www.iis.ee.ic. ac.uk/~tkkim/ges_db.htm

A Load Balancing Game Approach for VM Provision Cloud Computing Based on Ant Colony Optimization

Khiet Thanh Bui[1(✉)], Tran Vu Pham[1], and Hung Cong Tran[2]

[1] Faculty of Computer Science and Engineering, Ho Chi Minh City University of Technology, Ho Chi Minh City, Vietnam
khietbt@tdmu.edu.vn
[2] Training and Science Technology Department,
Posts and Telecoms Institute of Technology, Ho Chi Minh City, Vietnam

Abstract. The resource management on cloud computing is a major challenge. Resource management in cloud computing environment can be divided into two phases: resource provisioning and resource scheduling. In this paper, we propose VM provision solution ensure to balance the goals of the party stakeholders including service providers and customers based on game theory. The optimal or near optimal solution is approximated by meta-heuristic algorithm – Ant Colony Optimization (ACO) based on Nash equilibrium. In the experiments, the Ant System, Max-Min Ant System, Ant Colony System algorithm are applied to solve the game. The simulation results show how to use the coefficients to achieve load balancing in VM provision. These coefficients depend on objectives of cloud computing service providers.

Keywords: Load balancing · VM provision · Non-cooperative game · Ant Colony Optimization

1 Introduction

Infrastructure as a Service - IaaS cloud computing gives users such as network infrastructure, servers, CPU, memory, storage space as a virtual machine (VM) using server virtualization technology. Server virtualization technology allows to create multiple virtual machines on a physical machine (PM) and each VM is allocated in hardware resources as real machine with RAM, CPU, network card, hard drive, operating system and the individual applications. The resource management on cloud computing is a major challenge. Resource management in cloud computing environment can be divided into two phases: resource provisioning and resource scheduling. Resource provisioning phase determine resource requirements as well as quality of service for the customer which will be allocated somewhere in the system. Resource scheduling phase manage the life cycle of resource after it is allocated successfully. Customers and service providers often have different requirements and may conflict with each other. Service providers want to maximize profits by maximizing use of resources. However, maximum exploitation of resources may not satisfy customers

© ICST Institute for Computer Sciences, Social Informatics and Telecommunications Engineering 2017
P. Cong Vinh et al. (Eds.): ICCASA 2016, LNICST 193, pp. 52–63, 2017.
DOI: 10.1007/978-3-319-56357-2_6

with performance and quality of service provided. To ensure quality of services, providers must extend the same or refuse new service requirements. Optimal resource provision is essential in the use of cloud computing resources especially IaaS. Optimization problems of this type are usually NP-Hard class or NP-Complete [1]. Solution to this problems are usually based on specific characteristics which apply algorithms such as exhaustive algorithm, deterministic algorithm [2] or algorithm meta-heuristic [3–5]. In experiments, almost deterministic algorithms are than better algorithms exhaustive. However, deterministic algorithms are ineffective in distributed data environment, thereby leading to inappropriate scheduling issues in large-scale environment [6]. Meanwhile, cloud computing environment data is distributed, requiring scalability, ability to meet high customer requirements to access VM provision problems by meta-heuristic is feasible. Although meta-heuristic algorithms can give near optimal results in acceptable time, in this study, we propose provision solution ensure to balance the goals of the party stakeholders including service providers and customers based on game theory. Then, the algorithm used in particular meta-heuristic is Ant Colony Optimization (ACO) to find solutions which is an optimal or near optimal VM provision based on Nash equilibrium. The remainder of this paper is organized as follows. Section 2 describes state or art of the model game to solve resource provision. A game load balancing VM provision model is described in Sect. 3. The main purpose of Sect. 4 describes the ACO algorithms for the VM provision in cloud computing. Performance evaluation of the proposed and simulation results is described in Sect. 5. Finally, Sect. 6 presents the conclusions.

2 Related Work

According Grosu et al., there are 3 types of models for load balancing in single issues distributed to job class system: global, cooperative, non-cooperative [7]. The article suggested using Nash Bargaining Solution to provide a Pareto optimal allocation that fair allocation for all the jobs. The Fairness index is always one using the NBS which means allocation is fair to all jobs. Besides, load balancing in heterogeneous distributed system towards user-modeled optimal is proposed non-cooperative game by Grosu et al. proposed in [8]. But this proposal is only applied in static load balancing model, nor the dynamic load balancing model. For the proposed non-cooperative load balancing game, Aote et al. consider the structure of the Nash equilibrium [9]. They define the load balancing problem and the scheme to overcome it by using new area called game theory. Based on this structure they derive a new distributed load balancing algorithm. Minarolli et al. proposed CPU allocation for VMs in the IaaS cloud based on QoS aspects and operating cost [10]. Resource management model includes 2 levels: local controller undertake CPU allocation for VM to achieve optimal at the PM locally and global controller manages the VMs and live migration to other physical machines for achieving maximum global utility system. But this article is only interested in CPU resources that have not mentioned memory, disk and network. Using migration technique, Yang et al., guarantee for the full balance of the global system [11]. Ye et al. proposed non-cooperative games Strategic model for both the load balancing server problem and virtual machine placement problem [12]. The load balancing server problem is mapping a set of VMs which is described as a multi-dimensional vector to PM to achieve maximum load on a PM on any minimized dimension. VM placement problem is a set of VMs is assigned to the minimal number of PMs in which the load on each PM is in limited capacity. The VM and the PM are not identical in terms of capacity and configuration,... The VMs mapping PMs ensures using PMs resource efficiently. Efficiency issues are considered as the overload of the physical machine as using fewer machines for energy-saving materials [13]. This article suggests demand of forecasting algorithm based on resource using exponentially weighted moving average EWMA. Optimal changes in the use of resources on a physical machine to achieve the optimal across the system. This method can only achieve local optimal, not global optimization. This article only addresses allocation issues when required. When a request arrives, the service providers must decide whether to accept or not to meet the requirements of the system requirements of vendors that can handle this request in the external system - an affiliate vendor. To solve that problem, Tchernykh et al. modeled the problem towards energy-Efficient [14]. Algorithms scheduling algorithms are evaluated on the income provider and power consumption. To achieve the fairness between systems and customers in distributed systems, Siar et al. modeled the problem in non-cooperative game [15]. Using genetic algorithms and hybrid popularity algorithm is to find the optimal solution or the near optimal based on Nash equilibrium. In [16] Considering the demands of end users and service providers achieves multi-QoS indexes by calculating the load of each peer through quantitative analysis of costs, system and network. These are peer ratings, thanks to the weights determining whether peer matching the requirements of users while ensuring optimal goal of using resources to save money. Sui et al. proposed strategy and recoding Spectrum sharing on non-navigation-driven selection and Nash equilibrium cooperative game [17]. But in general cases, it is difficult to achieve all solutions. The best solution in the Nash game cannot describe the dynamic change of strategy players. Therefore, the Evolutionary game theory for network selection is proposed. [18] VM scheduling problem is solved by combining ant colony optimization algorithm and dynamic VM forecast scheduling (VM_DFS). Through the analysis of the historical using memory in each servers predicts the possibility of using the memory of the VM on the server in the future which is important as a basis for finding the optimal solution for scheduling based on ant colony optimization algorithm.

3   A Game Load Balancing VM Provision Model

3.1   VM Provision

In IaaS cloud, PMs can deploy VMs on itself based on virtualization technique. A VM requirements r (cpu, ram, disk) correspond to cpu, ram, the virtual machine's disk. Ensuring the efficient use of resources as well as the use of infrastructure services IaaS stability, allocates resources strategically in IaaS virtual machine reasonable. Maybe modeling scheduling problems on the cloud as a directed graph DAG (Directed acyclic Graph)) [19–21] G (V, E) where V is a set vertex represent tasks, E is the set of directed

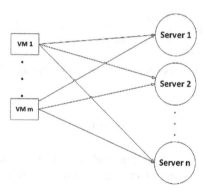

Fig. 1. VMs provision ability graph

edges represent dependency relationships between the vertices. In Fig. 1. Presents the ability of VM j is allocated on PM i.

3.2 A Game Load Balancing Model

To model this problem by game theory, we consider customers as the players in the VM provision game. To ensure the system is always efficient, well, how the system should maximize the use of PM resources evenly. To measure the efficiency of resource using a PM, using the following formula:

$$h_i = \frac{U_i}{T_i} \tag{1}$$

In which U_i is the resources that were used in the PM i is calculated using the formula:

$$U_i = \sqrt{c_i^{u^2} + r_i^{u^2} + d_i^{u^2}} \tag{2}$$

T_i is resources ith physical machine, is calculated as follows

$$T_i = \sqrt{c_i^2 + r_i^2 + d_i^2} \tag{3}$$

The load balancing system is measured by the following formula:

$$L = \frac{\sum_{i=1}^{n} (h_i - \bar{h})^2}{n} \tag{4}$$

The service providers avoid wasting the resources of the physical machine. When VM j is allocated on the host j, the waste of resources is calculated as follows:

$$W = \begin{cases} \sum_{i=1}^{k} A_i, & k \in n \, hosts \setminus host \, j \\ 0, & if \, vm \, j \, is \, not \, allocated \end{cases} \quad (5)$$

In which, A_i is ready to serve the resource requirements of the VM of PM i, it is calculated as follows:

$$A_i = \sqrt{c_i^{a^2} + r_i^{a^2} + d_i^{a^2}} \quad (6)$$

For parameter μ, $\lambda \in [0.1]$ to perform trade-offs between load balancing and profit maximization. The payoff gives players the j required to serve VMs represented by a linear combination of L_j, W_j

$$F_j = \mu L_j + \lambda W_j \quad (7)$$

3.3   Problem Solving

Nash equilibrium is a strategy game in which no player can increase profits while other players have a fixed strategy. Meanwhile, if the strategy of the first player i's optimal strategy is denoted p_i^*, the optimal strategy of the other players is denoted by p_{-i}^*, the Nash equilibrium strategy p_i^* will comply with the conditions [22], as follows:

$$F_i\left(p_{-i}^*, p_i^*\right) \geq F_i\left(p_{-i}^*, p_i\right) \quad (8)$$

In multi-agent system environment, equilibrium can be unstable [23]. Also, it's hard to find Pareto-efficiency of Nash equilibrium. To solve this problem, most of the algorithm is based on the algorithm meta-heuristic. The plan assigns VMs to feasible PMs to find the optimal based on ant colonies algorithms. From feasible plan that is based on Nash equilibrium conditions will select the best plan. When no player can reach further payoff past estimated near optimal, it means that all players have selected their approximated Pareto optimal strategies [15]. If F_j^{itr} presents player's payoff j in iterator itr of the ant colony optimization algorithms, $F_j^{itr} - F_j^{itr-1}$ presents the improment of player j's payoff. Termination condition is the sum of square deviation of all players' payoff less than a small number ε, i.e.:

$$\sum_{i=1}^{n} \left(F_j^{itr} - F_j^{itr-1}\right)^2 < \varepsilon \quad (9)$$

4   Ant Colony System Algorithm for Allocation VM

Ant colony optimization algorithm is proposed based on experiments on ants. Due to the nature and chemical characteristics, every ant on the move always leaves a chemical trail called pheromone trail along the way and they often take the path with dense smell. The pheromone trail is these chemicals evaporated over time. Enhancing the learning process has the effects of raising the efficiency of the algorithm in the process of the ants for finding the solutions. One of the first important thing in the application of the ACO algorithm is pheromone information. Here pheromone is likely a selected PM to allocate VM on demand, this ability depends on the current configuration and server heuristic information. Information heuristic will be recalculated after each allocation by the configuration information of the PM changes after each successfully allocated VM. The recalculation will enable more accurate heuristic information for next time allocation.

Algorithm : Ant Colony Optimization Meta-heuristic

```
While termination-condition not met do
  Initialization pheromone for host
  Initialization heuristic for host
  For each gamer
    For each request VM
      Calculate the probability of the valid Hosts
      Allocate VM Based on the probability of Hosts
      Update pheromone
    End For
  End For
End While
```

4.1 Ant System Algorithm

The Ant System algorithm (AS) has two major phases: building local solutions and updating pheromone trail. A heuristic argument is said to be good when the index starts the initial pheromone value slightly higher than the number of pheromone can create in each turn building local solutions [24]. After each iteration of the algorithm, pheromone value are updated by the smell of all the ants that had built solution on its loop. Value τ_{ji} on edge (j,i) is calculated as follows:

$$\tau_{ji} \leftarrow (1 - \rho).\tau_{ji} + \sum_{k=1}^{m} \Delta\tau_{ji}^{k} \qquad (10)$$

In which, $0 < \rho < = 1$ is the rate of evaporation of the pheromone trail. Parameters evaporation avoids excessive accumulation streak pheromone and eliminates the inefficient PMs were selected earlier. $\Delta\tau_{i}^{k}$ presents quality smell of ants on the edges (j,i) on the graph are calculated as follows:

$$\Delta \tau_i^k = \begin{cases} \frac{Q}{L_k} \text{ if the ant } k \text{ choose } (j,i) \\ \quad 0 \qquad otherwise \end{cases} \tag{11}$$

In which, Q is constant, L_k is the cost of the ant k through the edge (j, i).

For each VM requirement, the program will calculate to retrieve a valid PMs (which is eligible to allocate a VM) and the calculated probability of being selected for each PM. The probability of each valid PM selected to allocate VM is calculated using the formula:

$$p_{ji}^k = \begin{cases} \dfrac{([\tau_{ji}]^\alpha \cdot [\eta_{ji}]^\beta)}{\sum_{c_{jl} \in N(s^p)} ([\tau_{jl}]^\alpha \cdot [\eta_{jl}]^\beta)} if \ c_{ji} \in N(s^p) \\ \qquad\qquad 0 \quad otherwise \end{cases} \tag{12}$$

In which $N(s^p)$ is a valid set of PMs can meet the required VM k. Edge (j,l) that has not been visited by ant k. The parameter α, β used to determine the effects of pheromone and information value η_i heuristic, heuristic information are calculated using the formula $\eta_i = h_i$

4.2 Max-Min Ant System Algorithm

MAX - MIN Ant System [25] called MMAS is an improved version of AS with four modifications: First, the only ant finds the best solution is updated pheromone, but this can lead to delay when looking for new and better solutions for the following ants tend to move in the directions of high pheromone concentrations (usually in the direction of the ants before). To avoid this, a change is proposed to create limited access markings odor 2: max and min. Pheromone value is updated as follows:

$$\tau_{ji} = \left[(1 - \rho).\tau_{ji} + \Delta \tau_{ji}^{best} \right]_{\tau_{min}}^{\tau_{max}} \tag{13}$$

In which, the value τ_{max} and τ_{min} marginal value of pheromone, with operator

$$[x]_b^a = \begin{cases} a \ if \ x > a, \\ b \ if \ x < b, \\ x \ otherwise \end{cases} \tag{14}$$

$$\Delta \tau_{ji}^{best} = \begin{cases} \frac{1}{L_{best}} if \ (j,i) is \ used \\ \quad 0 \quad otherwise \end{cases} \tag{15}$$

In which, L_{best} is the heuristic of hosts which the best ants choose.

The pheromone concentrations are initialized by the value of the upper, which will help to enhance the search for better solutions when searching. If the case could not find a better solution after several attempts, the pheromone concentration trail will be reset.

4.3   Ant Colony System Algorithm

Ant Colony System Algorithm (ACS) [26] is proposed by Dorigo and Gambardella. First, the ability to search the gradual increase is expected to be better than the algorithm AS using the action selection rules. Second, the process of evaporation and distributed pheromone occur only when the ant is choosing the best solution. Finally, every time is selected to be one good solution and distribution, it also reduces the pheromone trail of surrounding solution's pheromone concentration.

Probability selected PM to allocate VM requirements calculated under the pseudorandom proportional: the probability that an ant selects an edge (j,i) depends on the random variable normal distribution $q \in [0, 1]$,

$$p = \begin{cases} argmax_{c_{il} \in N(s^p)} \left\{ \tau_{il} \eta_{il}^{\beta} \right\}, & if\ q \leq q_0 \\ p_{ji}^k, & if\ q > q_0 \end{cases} \tag{16}$$

Parameters q_0 will help choose the best PM in the iteration k by using heuristic information and pheromone concentration of PM. Using variable q_0, algorithm allows selection between PM – the best current configuration and looking for a different approach – a PM with more appropriate configuration.

In this algorithm, only the PM is determined to be the best in the iteration shall be updated pheromone. This can greatly affect the algorithm performance, the complexity of the algorithm in the function updates pheromone trail will be reduced from O (n^2) to O (n) (because of the need to update PM pheromone in each level found only 1). Pheromone value is updated as follows:

$$\tau_{ji} \leftarrow \begin{cases} (1 - \rho)\tau_{ji} + \rho \Delta \tau_{ji}\ n\hat{e}'u\ (j,i)\ is\ the\ best \\ \tau_{ji}\ \ \ otherwise \end{cases} \tag{17}$$

Like MMAS algorithm, L_{best} is the heuristic of hosts which the best ants choose.

5   Simulation Results

In this paper, we are concerned with the problems of the load balancing and resource extraction. With optimal ants algorithm classes, the results depend on the parameters $\varepsilon, \alpha, \beta$. Thus, in the experiments below, we find the appropriate parameters for the algorithms as well as the allocation of resources for customer VMs through load balancing levels of the system in the formula (4) and the level of resource wasting system resources by the formula (5).

In the Fig. 2 changing ε from 0.03 to 0.1, we can see ACS algorithm with a few numbers of iteration is stable. When increasing epsilon, MMAS and AS algorithms have reduced the number of iteration and are nearly equal to the number of iterations of the ACS. The iterations of MMAS is higher than AS and ACS. This shows that the algorithm MMAS has richer solutions.

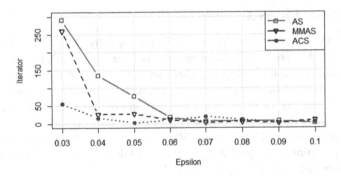

Fig. 2. Iteration of the algorithm with ε

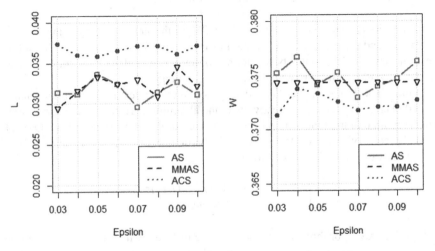

Fig. 3. Load balancing level and waste resource level with ε

In Fig. 3 when ε increases, the level load balancing and waste resource tends to increase. Therefore, within the limits of the paper we choose epsilon = 0.05 level for the next experiment. Choose other parameters $\varepsilon = 0.05$; $\mu = \lambda = 0.5$; $\rho = 0.2$; $p_0 = 0.9$. Let the number of clients from 10 to 70. Change α, β, then the load balancing level and waste resource level presents following (Figs. 4 and 5):

In general view, the load balancing level of all of algorithms has increased the propensity. We consider the load balancing level of all the algorithms. The ACS algorithm is more stable than AS and MMAS but its value is higher than AS and MMAS. The fluctuation band of MMAS is higher. When the α is larger than the β, all of algorithm has the same propensity.

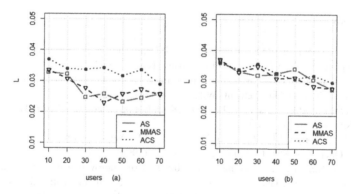

Fig. 4. (a) $\alpha = 0.1$; $\beta = 0.9$; (b). $\alpha = 0.9$, $\beta = 0.1$.

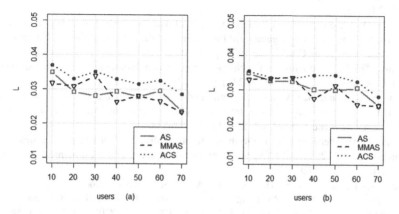

Fig. 5. (a) $\alpha = 0.3$; $\beta = 0.7$; (b) $\alpha = 0.7$; $\beta = 0.3$

6 Conclusions

In this paper, we use the non-cooperative game for the gamers in the VM provision to achieve load balancing. The game's payoff calculated by combining the two parameters load balancing and the waste resources. The load balancing parameter helps to distribute VMs to PMs based on current state of PMs. The waste resource helps service providers to achieve optimal profits. We propose the load balancing model take care both of customer and service provider are by using combination two parameters. The optimal solution is approximated by ant colony optimization based on Nash equilibrium. The experiments show how to use the coefficients to achieve load balancing in VM provision. These coefficients depend on objectives of the cloud computing service provider. In the next time, we study another optimization algorithms for this problem as well as study how to use the coefficients to achieve optimal or near optimal solution.

Acknowledgement. This work is supported by the Thu Dau Mot University's research program in 2016.

References

1. Gary, M.R., Johnson, D.S.: Computers and Intractability: A Guide to the Theory of NP-completeness. WH Freeman and Company, New York (1979)
2. Morton, T., Pentico, D.W.: Heuristic Scheduling Systems: With Applications to Production Systems and Project Management. Wiley, New York (1993)
3. Van Laarhoven, P.J., Aarts, E.H., Lenstra, J.K.: Job shop scheduling by simulated annealing. Oper. Res. **40**, 113–125 (1992)
4. Colorni, A., Dorigo, M., Maniezzo, V., Trubian, M.: Ant system for job-shop scheduling. Belg. J. Oper. Res. Stat. Comput. Sci. **34**, 39–53 (1994)
5. Ghumman, N.S., Kaur, R.: Dynamic combination of improved max-min and ant colony algorithm for load balancing in cloud system. In: 2015 6th International Conference on Computing, Communication and Networking Technologies (ICCCNT), pp. 1–5. IEEE (2015)
6. Tsai, C.-W., Rodrigues, J.J.: Metaheuristic scheduling for cloud: a survey. IEEE Syst. J. **8**, 279–291 (2014)
7. Grosu, D., Chronopoulos, A.T., Leung, M.-Y.: Load balancing in distributed systems: an approach using cooperative games. In: Proceedings of the IEEE-IEE Vehicle Navigation and Information Systems Conference 1993, p. 10. IEEE (1993)
8. Grosu, D., Chronopoulos, A.T.: Noncooperative load balancing in distributed systems. J. Parallel Distrib. Comput. **65**, 1022–1034 (2005)
9. Aote, S.S., Kharat, M.: A game-theoretic model for dynamic load balancing in distributed systems. In: Proceedings of the International Conference on Advances in Computing, Communication and Control, pp. 235–238. ACM (2009)
10. Minarolli, D., Freisleben, B.: Utility-based resource allocation for virtual machines in cloud computing. In: 2011 IEEE Symposium on Computers and Communications (ISCC), pp. 410–417. IEEE (2011)
11. Yang, C.-T., Cheng, H.-Y., Huang, K.-L.: A dynamic resource allocation model for virtual machine management on cloud. In: Kim, T.-h., Adeli, H., Cho, H.-s., Gervasi, O., Yau, Stephen, S., Kang, B.-H., Villalba, J.G. (eds.) GDC 2011. CCIS, vol. 261, pp. 581–590. Springer, Heidelberg (2011). doi:10.1007/978-3-642-27180-9_70
12. Ye, D., Chen, J.: Non-cooperative games on multidimensional resource allocation. Future Gener. Comput. Syst. **29**, 1345–1352 (2013)
13. Xiao, Z., Song, W., Chen, Q.: Dynamic resource allocation using virtual machines for cloud computing environment. IEEE Trans. Parallel Distrib. Syst. **24**, 1107–1117 (2013)
14. Tchernykh, A., Lozano, L., Bouvry, P., Pecero, J.E., Schwiegelshohn, U., Nesmachnow, S.: Energy-aware online scheduling: ensuring quality of service for IaaS clouds. In: 2014 International Conference on High Performance Computing & Simulation (HPCS), pp. 911–918. IEEE (2014)
15. Siar, H., Kiani, K., Chronopoulos, A.T.: An effective game theoretic static load balancing applied to distributed computing. Cluster Comput. **18**, 1609–1623 (2015)
16. Liu, L., Mei, H., Xie, B.: Towards a multi-QoS human-centric cloud computing load balance resource allocation method. J. Supercomputing **72**, 2488–2501 (2015)
17. Sui, N., Zhang, D., Zhong, W., Wu, L., Zhang, Z.: Evolutionary game theory based network selection for constrained heterogeneous networks. In: 2015 2nd International Conference on Information Science and Control Engineering (ICISCE), pp. 738–742. IEEE (2015)
18. Seddigh, M., Taheri, H., Sharifian, S.: Dynamic prediction scheduling for virtual machine placement via ant colony optimization. In: 2015 Signal Processing and Intelligent Systems Conference (SPIS), pp. 104–108. IEEE (2015)

19. Li, J., Qiu, M., Ming, Z., Quan, G., Qin, X., Gu, Z.: Online optimization for scheduling preemptable tasks on IaaS cloud systems. J. Parallel Distrib. Comput. **72**, 666–677 (2012)
20. Rahman, M., Li, X., Palit, H.: Hybrid heuristic for scheduling data analytics workflow applications in hybrid cloud environment. In: 2011 IEEE International Symposium on Parallel and Distributed Processing Workshops and Phd Forum (IPDPSW), pp. 966–974. IEEE (2011)
21. Saovapakhiran, B., Michailidis, G., Devetsikiotis, M.: Aggregated-DAG scheduling for job flow maximization in heterogeneous cloud computing. In: 2011 IEEE Global Telecommunications Conference (GLOBECOM 2011), pp. 1–6. IEEE (2011)
22. Osborne, M.J., Rubinstein, A.: A Course in Game Theory. MIT Press, Cambridge (1994)
23. Pendharkar, P.C.: Game theoretical applications for multi-agent systems. Expert Syst. Appl. **39**, 273–279 (2012)
24. Dorigo, M., Maniezzo, V., Colorni, A.: Ant system: optimization by a colony of cooperating agents. IEEE Trans. Syst. Man Cybern. Part B (Cybernetics) **26**, 29–41 (1996)
25. Stützle, T., Hoos, H.H.: MAX–MIN ant system. Future Gener. Comput. Syst. **16**, 889–914 (2000)
26. Dorigo, M., Gambardella, L.M.: Ant colony system: a cooperative learning approach to the traveling salesman problem. IEEE Trans. Evol. Comput. **1**, 53–66 (1997)

Optimizing the Algorithm Localization Mobile Robot Using Triangulation Map

Dao Duy Nam[1,2] and Nguyen Quoc Huy[1,3(✉)]

[1] SaigonTech, SaigonTech Tower, Lot 14, Quang Trung Software City,
District 12, Ho Chi Minh City, Vietnam
{namdd,huy.nq}@saigontech.edu.vn
[2] High School for the Gifted, VNUHCM, 153 Nguyen Chi Thanh, District 5,
Ho Chi Minh City, Vietnam
[3] Saigon University, 273 An Duong Vuong, District 5,
Ho Chi Minh City, Vietnam

Abstract. The problem of minimum distance localization in environments that may contain self-similarities is addressed. A mobile robot is placed at an unknown location inside a $2D$ self-similar polygonal environment P. The robot has a map of P and can compute visibility data through sensing. However, the self-similarities in the environment mean that the same visibility data may correspond to several different locations. The goal, therefore, is to determine the robot's true initial location while minimizing the distance traveled by the robot. We consider approximation algorithm for the robot localization problem. The algorithm is based on triangulation of a simple polygon representing a map. Based on the basis of the implemented program, we conducted experimental studies of this algorithm. The numerical results and their interpretation are better than others.

Keywords: Computational geometry · Robotics · Robot localization · Overlay polygon · Algorithm complexity · Approximation algorithm · Polygon triangulation

1 Introduction

In order to solve the application of mobile robot localization problem (MRLP), which relates to the field of robotics using computational geometry methods and algorithms. Substantially, MRLP for the case in a plane is formulated as follows: The mobile robot can move in the external environment, which can be represented as a free space plane and limited by wall (barrier). We assume that the external environment can be described by a simple polygon, the interior corresponding to the free space, and the polygon boundary (without self-intersections) corresponding to the barrier. Assume that the robot is provided an environment map as a simple planar polygon P with n vertices without holes. Initially, the mobile robot is placed in an unknown location at some point p within the polygon P. The robot is equipped with a compass and a sensor device, in which it carries out all-round visibility and the distance to obstacles. Robot must determine its true location in the external environment which locates yourself on the map. For this robot, firstly, it can view their surroundings and realize the visible

© ICST Institute for Computer Sciences, Social Informatics and Telecommunications Engineering 2017
P. Cong Vinh et al. (Eds.): ICCASA 2016, LNICST 193, pp. 64–71, 2017.
DOI: 10.1007/978-3-319-56357-2_7

region (so-called visibility polygon) $V = V(p)$ in the map. If the map has only one piece, which coincides with the visibility polygon, then the problem is solved. If the map has several pieces, it is necessary to determine which piece corresponds to the initial robot location. For this purpose, based on the analysis of polygons P and V, robot must generate a set of hypotheses H of its location $p_i \in P$ so that the visibility polygon $V(p_i)$ at the point p_i is congruent to V. Robot moves and surveys surroundings, then it can eliminate all false hypotheses of its location, and determine its true initial location. This requires that the total length of robot movement must be minimal.

2 Related Works

It proves that the optimization problem of mobile robot localization is an NP-hard problem [1]. The approximation (for polynomial computational complexity) algorithms for mobile robot localization are considered [2–4]. Here, as a rule, it focuses on the characteristics in which describe the deviation value of the optimal solution (the total length of the robot movements). Characteristics of the computational complexity of such algorithms are evaluated asymptotically, and the data of the real time operation algorithms typically are not provided due to the high computational complexity algorithms. For example, $O(n^5 log\ n)$ [2] or $\Omega(n^{12})$ [4]. In [5, 6], they proposed approximation algorithms with MRLP solutions based on the pre-triangulation of a simple polygon representing the map. Now we will discuss the improvements of these algorithms to gain more efficiency in computation time.

3 Solution

The well-known mobile robot localization algorithms [2–4] comprise two phases: hypothesis generation [7] and hypothesis elimination. The hypotheses generation phase computes the set of hypothetical locations $p_1, p_2, \ldots, p_k \in P$ that match the observations sensed by the robot at its initial location. The hypothesis elimination phase rules out incorrect hypotheses thereby determining the true initial location of the robot.

The hypothesis generation phase generates a set $H = \{h_1, h_2, \ldots, h_k\}$, $(\forall i \in 1..k| h_i : p=p_i)$ of hypothetical locations in P at which the robot might be located initially. Without loss of generality, we select an arbitrary hypothetical location p_i from H to serve as a reference point or origin. Next, for each hypothetical location p_j, $1 \leq j \leq k$, a translation vector $t_j = p_i - p_j$ is defined that translates location p_j to p_i $(p_i = p_j + t_j)$. As a result, we compute a set of copies $P_1, P_2, .., P_k$ of the environment polygon P, corresponding to the set of hypothetical H, such that P_j is congruent to P translated by vector t_j. Copy P_i is translated by the zero vector.

Computing the intersection of polygons is required in algorithms [3, 4], as well as in two further considered algorithms [5, 6]. Note that (1) when computing the shortest path in a simple polygon from a point to another, algorithm [8] uses the provisional triangulation of a polygon followed using "funnel", this is more effective than other approaches. Constructing the graph visibility [9] is an example; (2) through the using triangulation polygon can be more efficient to compute polygons visibility and its skeletons.

We give a description of the proposed improvement in the mobile robot localization algorithm using triangulation map presented before [6]. Our description has a different specification and a more detailed representation in some steps of the algorithm as well as evaluations of their complexity. In the future, their program will be better if using more systematic triangulation map.

As already mentioned, it is expedient to triangulate the polygon map localization algorithms using an auxiliary effect in case of computing the shortest path from a point in a simple polygon to another. In using the original polygon triangulation preprocessing, firstly, it is possible to effectively implement other action, such as the visibility polygon, and secondly, it is possible to partition the map into many triangles to select the robot movements on the hypotheses elimination phase. For example, a survey of the robot path can occur in the centers of the triangles or middle points of the triangulation edges. It can be considered as an alternative to triangulation on a polygon decomposition visibility cells used in [2, 7]. Number of cell triangulation (triangles) is $O(n)$, which gives a hope for the acceleration of the localization algorithm in using.

Robot localization algorithm using triangulation map [6] can be described by considering the previously given definitions. Let an input polygon map be P and the robot be placed in an unknown initial location in P. The algorithm consists of the following steps:

1. Compute the relative coordinates in the visibility polygon $V(p)$ and its skeleton $V^*(p)$ of the robot according to current sensors in the initial robot location p that the conformance has been not known on the map. Let m be the number of vertices of $V^*(p)$.
2. Make a triangulation of polygon map.
3. Generate set H of k hypotheses on the map P, corresponding to the obtained visibility polygon V. For this polygon skeleton visibility V^* specified in relative coordinates, it is mapped to polygon sequence of vertices based on marking edges skeleton. In places matches based on the use of map which is calculated triangulation skeleton of a polygon of visibility concerning, the alleged location of the robot and the two skeletons are compared. If both skeletons and visibility polygons are the same, then a new hypothesis is fixed.
4. [From P.4 to P.9 in further operations are performed for all active (not yet eliminated) h_j hypotheses $(j = 1, 2,..., k')$, initially $k' = k$.]. Choose an arbitrary hypothesis h_i from a variety of active hypotheses H and the corresponding point of the hypothetical location as a starting point for the construction of intersections. Transferring the vertices gotten from triangulated "displaced" polygon corresponding to other hypotheses (actually in triangulation, the numbers of given vertices do not change, and the "shift" only is occurred in the coordinates of the vertices).
5. For the active hypotheses, the connected component $F = InterS(P_1, P_2, \ldots, P_{k'})$ is calculated at a starting point. Calculate triangulation F.
6. Find the point r in a set of points at the midpoints of edges of the triangulation and at the center of triangles within the polygon F, the point r is the nearest to the

current location of the points of the robot which may eliminate some hypotheses. For this search, the problem is implemented in width by triangulation graph. The visibility polygon skeleton $V^*(q)$ is determined in each surveyed of the corresponding point q. This skeleton is associated with the skeletons which appear in the corresponding point q_j in copies map of active hypotheses, and is determined by the possibility elimination of hypotheses when the planned moves of robot are implemented to this point. For all of these points, the shortest path is calculated from the current location of the robot to the selected point r. Here we need to calculate the shortest path possible at the stage of the search to get the width of a set of triangles from the current location of the robot to the point r, and then immediately to build a funnel to calculate the shortest path. With this modification, it is important that the width of the search tree is not completely bypassed, as cut off subtrees, whose roots are found in terms of possible hypotheses elimination. This search limits in width search, maybe the total movement of the robot is longer, but it reduces the time of the algorithm.

7. Carry out the movement robot to a point r.
8. Eliminate hypothesis by comparing the current visibility polygon data of the robot at the point r, the data of visibility calculated equivalent in all points corresponding to the active hypotheses. Thus, if a hypothesis is confirmed, it eliminates one or more others, i.e. eventually it eliminates at least one of the hypotheses.
9. Let E be a set of hypotheses that have been corrected in the previous step. Replace k' to $k' - |E|$. Repeat steps 4–9 until the set of active hypotheses H does not remain only a hypothesis ($k' = 1$), which will correspond to the true initial location of the robot.

The computational complexity of this algorithm in stages and summary are shown in Table 1. Note that when the pre-triangulation calculation of the shortest path from

Table 1. The computational complexity of algorithm in stages and summary

Step	Actions	Complexity of integrated action
1–2	Triangulation polygon map	$O(n \log^* n)$
3,4	Generating hypotheses	$O(mn) + O(kn)$
5	Construction of intersection with respect to the selected hypothesis and triangulation of F (k'-the number of active hypotheses)	$(k' - 1)O(n) + O(n \log^* n)$
6,7	Examine 4 k'(n-2) points on the edges of the triangles and the centers to eliminate hypotheses. Calculation of the shortest paths to the points that eliminate hypotheses to determine the nearest of them	$4k'(n - 2)O(n) = k'O(n^2)$
8	Comparison of data on visibility polygons for active hypotheses and current robot location	$k'O(n)$
The full complexity	$O(mn) + O(kn) + O(n \log^* n) + \sum_{k'=1}^{k-1} [k'O(n^2) + k'O(n)] = O(n^4)$	

the current robot location is analyzed in terms of the worst case scenario for the time $O(n)$ [8], but this operation is required to apply repeatedly in step 6 each iteration of the algorithm that determines the total localization algorithm complexity.

Triangulation simple polygon has a theoretical complexity $O(n)$ [10], and can be implemented. For example, a known efficient and practical algorithm [11] for time $O(n\ log^*\ n)$ (Let $log^{(i)}\ n$ denote the ith iterated logarithm, i.e. $log^{(0)}n = n$ and for $i > 0$ we have $log^{(i)}n = log(log^{(i-1)}n)$. For $n > 0$ let $log^* n$ denote the largest integer l so that $log^{(l)}n \geq 1$) practically gives $O(n)$ in MRLP. The output of this algorithm is a set of triangles, the numbers of their given vertices. For further using the algorithm localization, the set of triangles is converted during the $O(n)$ in a special data structure [12]. This view, in fact, is one of the options adapted to the triangulation costal list used to represent a planar subdivision plane [9]. Each triangle in the structure is represented by its three vertices and three-pointers on the adjacent triangles to its adjacent through edges.

Structure triangulation is obtained in two stages. First, a set of given triangles forming a triangulation, and each vertex of the triangulation create a list of triangles in which include the vertex. Then, a proper structure of triangulation with the information about the adjacent triangles is obtained from each pair of the vertices of the triangle by analyzing lists obtained at the first stage. The structure is complemented by inputs array of vertices and edges of the triangulation.

The triangulation structure is used to effectively implement some basic operations of the localization algorithm. For example, it can be systematically used by the operation of construction of the polygon, and the visibility of its skeleton is implemented on the basis of the breadth-first search on the graph by using a dual triangulation. Thus, it is possible, as a rule, to avoid viewing maps all vertices of a polygon, to analyze the triangles adjacent to the current.

4 Implementation

To analyze the effectiveness of the proposed algorithms was carried out an experimental study based on their program implementation (Visual C++ 2010), as well as implementations of algorithms [2–4] and compare their properties as the value of the total travel path of the robot and the running time localization. It has previously been established [13] that the algorithm [3] using the randomization in hypothesis elimination is more efficient than the algorithm [2] using the decomposition map to cell visibilities and having an asymptotic complexity $O(n^5 log\ n)$, and also more effective than algorithm [4] based on the solution semigroup Steiner problem and having a computational complexity $\Omega(n^{12})$. Therefore, the comparison is further provided with an algorithm [3]. On algorithms participating in the experiment will be cited, indexed them for brevity Roman numerals: I - mobile robot localization algorithm (MRLA) using triangulation map; II - MRLA randomization using hypothesis elimination [3] (the number of points placed randomly in the test area, $X = 100$); III - the same MRLA [3], but the number of points placed randomly in the study area, $X = 500$; IV - MRLA using windows in the polygon map [5].

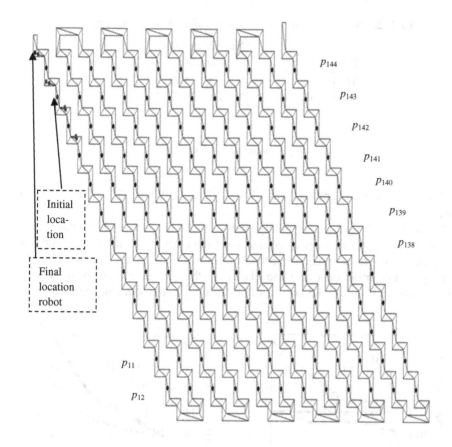

Fig. 1. Generation map $n = 672$ and $k = 144$

Generate maps of various model types used during the experiment. Generation was carried out in several patterns. The combination of the parameters defines the size of the template of the overall size map n, and a generation of its numerical value can be adjusted as a rule approximately. Figure 1 shows an example of generation size map $n = 672$ and $k = 144$ number of hypotheses location p_i ($i = 1..144$). Note that such map structure provides a relatively large ratio of k/n, here $k/n = 0.21$.

Preliminary analysis showed that the resulting characteristics of the algorithms (path length d, traversed by the robot to the final location, and time work t localization algorithm) essentially depend on the initial location of the robot (by hypothesis number). For this reason, it is reasonable to calculate the average of hypotheses, not the characteristics obtained for different algorithms and their relationship. The average will be characterized by the relative efficiency of the algorithms. Choose characteristics of triangulation algorithm (algorithm number I) as the "standard" for comparison. Those algorithms (with a number) will be calculated (here, i - number of hypotheses).

Table 2. The values of the ratios for the configuration shown in Fig. 1.

Feature (x)	Number algorithm			
	I	II	III	IV
The length of the path	1	1.57	1.01	1.63
Time localization	1	17.1	26.7	26.9

$$s_i^{(a)} = \frac{x_i^{(a)}}{x_i^{(l)}}, \text{ where } x = d \text{ or } x = t. \tag{1}$$

Averaging over k hypothesis was $\bar{s}^{(a)} = \frac{1}{k}\sum_{i=1}^{k} s_i^{(a)}$. Where $\bar{s}_i^{(l)} = 1$ and $\bar{s}^{(l)} = 1$ (Table 2).

The algorithm I based on triangulation shows that the time is much better than that of the others, but it gives a somewhat greater path length than randomization algorithm in variant III. Similar relations are obtained and other map configurations. Figures 2 and 3 show a plot of the mean values of these relations on the size map polygon n. Many types of line graphs in Figs. 2 and 3 are algorithms with their corresponding numbers.

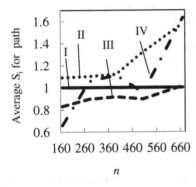

Fig. 2. Average S_i for path

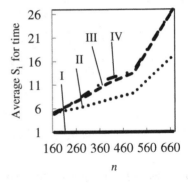

Fig. 3. Average S_i for time

5   Conclusions

The data in these figures show that the range of values the size maps n in the algorithm I above indicates that the operating time is the least, and the second one is the algorithm II.

The experiments with other model configurations maps showed the same results, and our improvement of approximate MRLA algorithms provides comparable accuracy, but the operating time of two modified MRLA algorithms using triangulation map and using windows in the polygon map is smaller than that of others. Here the best algorithm by time results is algorithm I, systematically using triangulation map. This result differs from the previously obtained for the original (unmodified) version of the algorithm [5, 6], using triangulation, where the best results showed the algorithm II at that time.

References

1. Dudek, G., Jenkin, M.: Computational Principles of Mobile Robotics, 2nd edn., 406 p. Cambridge University Press (2010)
2. Dudek, G., Romanik, K., Whitesides, S.: Localizing a robot with minimum travel. SIAM J. Comput. **27**, 583–604 (1998)
3. Rao, M., Dudek, G., Whitesides, S.: Randomized algorithms for minimum distance localization. Internat J. Robotics Research **26**, 917–934 (2007)
4. Koenig, S., Mitchell, J.S.B., Mudgal, A., Tovey, C.: A near-tight approximation algorithm for the robot localization problem. SIAM J. Comput. **39**, 461–490 (2009)
5. Дао Зуй Нам, Ивановский С.А. Приближенный алгоритм локализации мобильного робота с использованием окон в многоугольнике карты. Известия СПБЭТУ «ЛЭТИ» . № 3, С. pp. 38–43 (2014)
6. Дао Зуй Нам, Ивановский С.А. Приближённые алгоритмы локализации мобильного робота. Научный вестик НГТУ. № 2, С, pp. 109–121 (2014)
7. Guibas, L.J., Motwani, R., Raghavan, P.: The robot localization problem. SIAM J. Comput. **26**, 1120–1138 (1997)
8. Hershberger, J., Snoeyink, J.: Computing minimum length paths of a given homotopy class. Comput. Geom. Theory Appl. **4**, 63–98 (1994)
9. De Berg, M., Cheong, O., Van Kreveld, M., Overmars, M.: Computational Geometry: Algorithms and Applications, 3rd edn., 386 p. Springer, Heidelberg (2008)
10. Chazelle, B.: Triangulating a simple polygon in linear time. Discrete Comput. Geom. **6**(1), 485–524 (1991). Springer-Verlag
11. Seidel, R.: A simple and fast incremental randomized algorithm for computing trapezoidal decompositions and for triangulating polygons. Comput. Geom. Theory Appl. **1**(1), 51–54 (1991)
12. Скворцов А.В. Триангуляция Делоне и её применение. – Томск: Изд-во Том. ун-та, 2002. – 128 с
13. Дао Зуй Нам, Ивановский С.А. Экспериментальный анализ алгоритмов локализации мобильного робота. Известия СПБЭТУ «ЛЭТИ» . № 1. С, pp. 19–24 (2014)

Enhanced Human Activity Recognition on Smartphone by Using Linear Discrimination Analysis Recursive Feature Elimination Algorithm

Loc Tan Nguyen[✉]

Thu Dau Mot University, Binh Duong, Vietnam
locnt@tdmu.edu.vn

Abstract. Human Activity Recognition (HAR) is a challenging research topic in tracking a person's state of motion and interaction with the surroundings. HAR plays an important role in developing many applications helping improve quality of life. Applications based on HAR could be used in checking the state of health, identifying a mobile phone's context, keeping track of user's physical activities, etc. In this research, we applied Recursive Feature Elimination based on Linear Discrimination Analysis (RFELDA) to (http://topepo.github.io/caret/rfe.html#rfe) reduce the dimensionality of dataset before applying classification algorithms to assign subject's activities. The experiment results on dataset showed that RFELDA improved performance and reduced processor time better than original dataset did.

Keywords: Feature Selection · Smartphones · Human Activity Recognition

1 Introduction

In recent years, Human Activity Recognition (HAR) is a special branch of research in tracking the state of motion. It attracted many researchers' as well as technology companies' special interest. This shows that research in HAR is of great importance. Firstly, the intelligent application systems are based on the identification of human activities and the surroundings. Secondly, HAR somewhat helps identify human being's psychological complexity. Thirdly, in the era of Internet of Things, the applications based on HAR are developed to focus primarily on supporting human beings. Therefore, human activity recognition needs to be studied to develop the system of applications related to human activity.

Applications based on human activity recognition could be used in: checking the state of health [1], detecting the fall status of patients [2], recognizing outdoor contexts, keeping track of individual's daily activities [3–5], recognizing terrorists or crimes in the crowd, etc.

HAR would be based on various devices including camera, mobile devices (smartphones, smartwatches, glasses, etc.) and home sensors. However, human activity recognition is primarily based on smartphone. Firstly, a smartphone is normally equipped with many sensors such as acceleration, gyroscope, GPS, image, audio, light,

© ICST Institute for Computer Sciences, Social Informatics and Telecommunications Engineering 2017
P. Cong Vinh et al. (Eds.): ICCASA 2016, LNICST 193, pp. 72–81, 2017.
DOI: 10.1007/978-3-319-56357-2_8

temperature, etc. Secondly, the smartphone is one of the intelligent devices which are used most in our society because of their small size, wearability and modern functions like computing power. Thirdly, in recent years, research in human activity recognition based on sensor-embedded smartphones has been conducted by organizations and companies, and has stimulated the great interest among researchers [4].

For these reasons, in our research, we deployed the Human Activity Recognition System (HARS) on Androi-based cell phones which are equipped with two popular sensors: three-dimensional acceleration sensor-xyz, and gyroscope-xyz. Data collection and application development are conducted on Android because its operating system is free, open-source, easy to program. The system we developed helps identify and classify a user's daily activities including: walking, going upstairs, going downstairs, sitting, standing, and lying.

We apply RFELDA to select features and reduce dimensionality of dataset. Machine learning algorithms (Naïve Bayes, k-nearest – neighbor (KNN), Random Forest) are used to identify user's activities. The results of our experimental research are very positive and promising. The accuracy of Random Forest method is 91.89%, k-nearest neighbor is 85.81%, and Naïve Bayes is 69.69%.

This paper is structured in the following way: Related work is depicted in Sect. 2; The Human Activity Recognition System is presented in Sect. 3; The Evaluation Method is described in Sect. 4; the experiment results are showed in Sect. 5; The Conclusion is described in Sect. 6.

2 Related Work

Human activity recognition is a fundamental step in building the intelligent application systems. In general, stages of processing information in the intelligent systems include: data collection, data analysis, decisive orientation and response to the surrounding context. Human activity recognition is conducted in two first stages. The goal is to classify the simple-to-complex activities. In order to reach this goal, researchers used different instruments to monitor a user's activity level. However, two most common instruments are cameras (image sensors) and wearable devices. Through these instruments, human activities can be divided into five main groups (see Table 1).

Table 1. Activities and applications based on human activity recognition

Application	Example
Daily activity	Watching television, ironing, eating, bathing, cleaning, and watering
Locomotion	Cycling, driving, drop, falling, standing, and sitting
Community	Calling, chatting, and talking
Security	Detecting terrorism and crime
Sports/Fitness	Jumping, weightlifting, swimming, and skiing

Yet, using cameras to monitor a user's activity level is most likely limited and has some disadvantages. For example, cameras equipped in rooms where the user stays must be high-resolution. Additionally, using cameras is able to cause the user's feelings of be uncomfortable. Thus, the use of wearable devices may be more effective because they are equipped with various sensors and easy to carry. For this reason, many research projects have been conducted on mobile devices, like cell phone, in order to build applications which are used in the elderly's healthcare [6, 7] and the falling state detection [8, 9]. Activities recognized from sensors associated with the surroundings are also analyzed in order to avoid the situation in which the user's cell phone is falling onto the floor. Additionally, applications based on HAR to keep track of a person's daily exercise and measure the level of energy consumption [10, 11] have also been developed to give users the necessary advice for fitness.

In another research project, N. Ravi [12] used acceleration sensors to identify human activities. He left them on the participant's pelvic to identify seven actions including: standing, walking, jogging, climbing stairs, going downstairs, vacuuming, and sitting upright. He used decision trees, k-Nearest Neighbors, SVM, Naïve Bayes to evaluate the accuracy.

In 2013, Guiry et al. [13] used algorithms including C4.5, CART, SVM, Multi-Layer Perceptrons, Naïve Bayes to collect data from sensor-based cell phones. A total of 24 volunteers participated in the experimental research. The sensors were placed inside the participants' chest. And, the results showed that the accuracy of recognizing activities including lying, sitting, standing, walking, jogging and cycling was 98%. Additionally, in 2015, Capela et al. [14] proposed a method to increase the capability for classifying human activities including sitting, standing and lying. The experimental research was conducted on Blackberry Z10 smartphone with two sensors: acceleration and gyroscopes with a view to collecting 16 daily activities. The total of 30 people of different ages participated in the study. The Blackberry Z10 smartphone was placed on the participants' right-front hip. The researchers focused on recognizing the transitioning-into and transitioning-out state of a sitting to evaluate accurately the sitting activity. Sang et al. [15] also used smartphone devices with two common sensors (accelerometer and gyroscope) to collect data on human activities including: going downstairs, going upstairs, sitting with the phone in a pocket, driving and putting the phone on the table. They used two algorithms including k-Nearest Neighbors (kNN) and Artificial Neural Network (ANN) to classify user's activities. The result showed that the accuracy of recognizing five activities was 74% for kNN and 75.3% for ANN.

Differing from other researchers, several groups of researchers primarily focus on the preprocessing stages: feature extraction and selection to reduce the dimensionality of data, selection of the optimal feature subsets. For example, Tuan Dinh and Chung Van [16] applied Correlation-based Feature Selection method and the Instance-Based Learning Algorithms Family (IB3) to remove redundant instances and irrelevant features.

Therefore, for the classification to be better, we applied RFELDA method to our research. This method helps reduce the redundant features and the processor time better than using the original dataset.

3   The Human Activity Recognition System

The human activity recognition system consists of four components: data collection, feature extraction, dimensionality reduction and classification labels (Fig. 1).

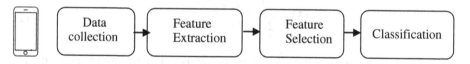

Fig. 1.   The process of activity recognition

3.1   Data Collection

Dataset was collected from the smartphone with accelerometer and gyroscope sensors. The smartphones were placed on the left of the participants' waist. The acceleration and gyroscope signals have proved to be effective for human activity recognition. Because accelerometer sensor is used to determine acceleration though a three-axis accelerometer identifying the changes of the cell phone's direction, whereas gyroscope plays as a rotation sensor to determine the rotation of the phone.

3.2   Feature Extraction

The collected signals with noise will be pre-processed to eliminate some unwanted features. The unwanted features will be eliminated by applying noise filters and then divided into small sliding windows of 2.56 s and 50% overlap (128 readings/window). Feature extraction will be carried out with the time domain and frequency domain. For each row in the dataset, it is 561 feature vectors with time domain and frequency domain, user's activity labels and the subject in the experiment.

3.3   Feature Selection

We included a correlation matrix to remove redundant features with threshold 0.95 before using the backward recursive feature elimination selection. This is a method which starts with all features, and then removes redundant features based on ranking criteria until satisfied with a stop condition. For Linear Discrimination Analysis, it is an application of RFE using LDA criteria for ranking. The goal is to project a dataset onto a lower-dimensional space with good subset of features. The LDA algorithm and cross validation method are used repeatedly to evaluate the model. It is configured to explore good subset of the features. The RFELDA would give a good rank variables and the error prediction would be lowered.

Linear Discrimination Analysis was performed on the basis of the minimum total error of classification model. The observation is assigned to the class label with the highest probability. It is also called Bayes rule. According to Bayes' rule, if there are n classes, observation x will be assigned to class i:

$$P(i \mid x) > P(j \mid x), \forall j \neq i$$

Formula in Bayes theory describes the relationship between two conditional probabilities $P(i|x)$, $P(x|i)$:

$$P(i \mid x) = \frac{P(x \mid i) * P(i)}{\sum_{\forall j} P(x \mid j) * (P(j))} \tag{1}$$

To make it convenient for the calculation, statisticians have found equivalent conversion formula called discrimination Analysis.

$$f_i = \mu_i C^{-1} x_k^T - 1/2 \, \mu_i C^{-1} \mu_i^T + \ln(p_i) \tag{2}$$

To assign an observation to the ith class label if the probability f_i is the highest. In the formula (2), the component $\mu_i C^{-1} \mu_i^T$ is Mahalanobis distance to measure the distance discrimination among groups.

LDARFE Algorithm following steps:

Inputs:

Step 1: Initalize

Training examples $F = \{f_1, f_2, \dots f_k, \dots f_n\}$

Set p=n // p: number of features, p=152 features

Class labels : y = [walking, walking up,walking down, sitting,standing, lying]

Feature ranked list r = { }

Step 2: Train data the classifier LDA

Step 3: Calculate discriminant coefficients of eigen vector from LDA classifier to evaluate the relevancy of each feature for activity classification by using k-cross validation

Step 4: Find the feature f_i with the smallest F-value ranking which is removed

Step 5: Update feature ranked list

$r = \{r \cup [F(fi), r]\}$

F={F-fi} and set p=p-1
Go to step 2 unitl p=1 or F={ }

Output: Feature ranked list r.

3.4 Classification Algorithms

The Machine Learning algorithms are applied to classify user's activities after reducing original dataset. In this system, we were recommended to use Random Forest, Naïve

Bayes, KNN because they help us obtain good performances better than other classifications do. To evaluate classifications, we used k-cross validation to estimate the performance models.

4 Evaluation Method

To evaluate the performance system, we use confusion matrixes, precision (P), recall (R), F-measure (F) and the accuracy metrics.

The accuracy was calculated by the following formula:

$$Accuracy = \frac{TP + TN}{TP + TN + FP + FN}$$

Where,

TP (True Positives): The number of positive observations was assigned to positive class label.

TN (True Negatives): The number of negative observations was assigned to negative class label.

FP (False Positives): The number of negative observations was assigned to positive class label.

FN (False Negatives): The number of positive observations was assigned to negative class label.

Precision (P) is positive predictive value:

$$Precision = \frac{TP}{TP + FP}$$

Recall (R) is true positive rate:

$$Recall = \frac{TP}{TP + FN}$$

F-measure (F) is a value to be derived from recall and precision

$$F\text{-}measure = \frac{2 * P * R}{P + R}$$

5 Experiment Results

5.1 Experiment Design

Dataset was collected from 30 participants of the age between 19 and 49. Each participant wore Samsung Galaxy II cell phone on the waist and then performed six physical activities including: walking, going upstairs, going downstairs, sitting, standing, and lying down. The Samsung Galaxy smartphone was equipped with two sensors: accelerometer and gyroscope. The former is to determine 3-axial linear acceleration and the latter is to determine 3-axial angular velocity at a constant rate of 50 Hz.

Dataset was divided into two sets, 70% for training the classifier and 30% for testing. Noise signals in datasets will be eliminated by applying noise filters and then divided into small sliding windows of 2.56 s and 50% overlap (128 readings/window) for feature extraction from the time domain and frequency domain. Each row in dataset has 561 feature time and frequency domain. We used parallel computing using R tool and caret package. The Human Activity Recognition Dataset (UCIHAR) was downloaded from UCI's website.

We included a correlation matrix to remove redundant features with threshold 0.95 and obtained 277 features before applying RFELDA algorithms to reduce dimensionality of dataset from 277 features to only 152 features. Finally, we used algorithms to classify users' activities.

5.2 Feature Selection Result

LDA recursive feature elimination algorithm selected important features from the 277 features in the dataset. We plot the result of RFELDA algorithm and choose features which have greater value than threshold 0.9. We obtained 152 features compared to 561 features of original dataset (Fig. 2).

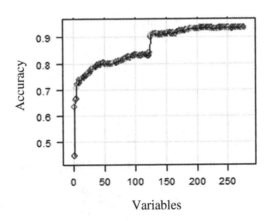

Fig. 2. The variable importance chart

5.3 Result of Classification

Confusion Matrix. The results are presented in Tables 2, 3 and 4. We observed the Precision, the Recall and The F-Measure of classifications. We found that the results of random forest are better than others. Particularly in the case of lying state, using random forest algorithm obtained the highest precision (100%).

Table 2. Confusion matrix of kNN results on testing data

	Walking	Upstairs	Downstairs	Sitting	Standing	Lying	Recall %
Walking	473	67	105	0	0	0	0.733
Upstairs	14	401	65	2	0	0	0.832
Downstairs	9	3	250	0	0	0	0.954
Sitting	0	0	0	336	41	0	0.891
Standing	0	0	0	153	491	20	0.739
Lying	0	0	0	0	0	517	1
Precision %	0.954	0.851	0.595	0.684	0.923	0.963	
F-measure %	0.829	0.842	0.733	0.744	0.821	0.981	

Table 3. Confusion matrix of Naïve Bayes results on testing data

	Walking	Upstairs	Downstairs	Sitting	Standing	Lying	Recall %
Walking	365	45	76	0	0	0	0.751
Upstairs	58	401	61	5	12	7	0.747
Downstairs	73	25	283	0	0	0	0.743
Sitting	0	0	0	356	267	0	0.571
Standing	0	0	0	25	120	1	0.822
Lying	0	0	0	105	133	529	0.69
Precision %	0.736	0.851	0.674	0.725	0.226	0.985	
F-measure %	0.743	0.796	0.707	0.639	0.354	0.811	

Table 4. Confusion matrix of random forest results on testing data

	Walking	Upstairs	Downstairs	Sitting	Standing	Lying	Recall %
Walking	462	28	25	0	0	0	0.897
Upstairs	26	437	50	1	0	0	0.85
Downstairs	8	6	345	0	0	0	0.961
Sitting	0	0	0	408	13	0	0.969
Standing	0	0	0	77	519	0	0.871
Lying	0	0	0	5	0	537	0.991
Precision %	0.931	0.928	0.821	0.831	0.976	1	
F-measure %	0.914	0.887	0.886	0.895	0.92	0.995	

Activities in the same group could be missing classification against different group. Static activity compared to dynamic activity. For example, sitting, standing and lying in the same group is difficult and missing classification. However, activities in different group could be clearly classified.

Accuracy. With regard to the accuracy of classifications by using kNN, Naïve Bayes, and Random forest classifiers, Table 5 shows that the accuracy of Random forest model was 91.89% higher than Naïve Bayes (69.69%) and KNN model (85.8%). This indicates that Random forest model is the best approach and should be chosen. The calculation of the error of Random forest model is $1.00 -$ accuracy (0.0811).

Table 5. The accuracy of testing classifications

Method	Accuracy %
KNN	85.81
Naïve Bayes	69.69
Random forest	91.89

Sensitivity (Recall), Specificity. We plot the sensitivity and specificity rate of our results in Fig. 3. We found that Random forest is better in both aspects.

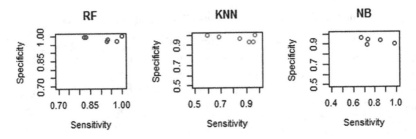

Fig. 3. The sensitivity (recall) and specificity models

6 Conclusion

In this paper, we proposed a new method for reducing irrelevant features. Our experimental results show that the system improved processor time and enhanced the accuracy of recognizing the user's activities better than original UCI dataset did. However, this approach could be further improved in several aspects. In the future, we are investigating feature subsets with higher classification and obtaining a small size with other classifications such as Support Vector Machine (SVMRFE), Principle Component Analysis (PCA). It is able to further improve the model performance by tuning the model parameters and collecting more users' activities.

References

1. Avci, A., Bosch, S., Marin-Perianu, M., Marin-Perianu, R., Havinga, P.: Activity recognition using inertial sensing for healthcare, wellbeing and sports applications: a survey. In: 23rd International Conference on Architecture of Computing Systems, pp. 167–176 (2010)
2. Chen, J., Karric, K., Chang, D., Luk, J., Bajcsy, R.: Wearable sensors for reliable fall detection. In: 27th Annual International Conference of the Engineering in Medicine and Biology Society 2005, pp. 3551–3554. IEEE-EMBS (2005)
3. Anjum, A., Ilyas, M.U.: Activity recognition using smartphone sensors. In: Consumer Communications and Networking Conference (CCNC) 2013, pp. 914–919. IEEE (2013)

4. Kwapisz, J.R., Weiss, G.M., Moore, S.A.: Activity recognition using cell phone accelerometers. SIGKDD Explor. Newsl. **12**, 74–82 (2011)
5. Kose, M., Incel, O.D., Ersoy, C.: Online human activity recognition on smart phones. In: ACM 2nd International Workshop on Mobile Sensing, Beijing, China (2012)
6. Anguita, D., Ghio, A., Oneto, L., Parra, X., Reyes-Ortiz, Jorge, L.: Human activity recognition on smartphones using a multiclass hardware-friendly support vector machine. In: Bravo, J., Hervás, R., Rodríguez, M. (eds.) IWAAL 2012. LNCS, vol. 7657, pp. 216–223. Springer, Heidelberg (2012). doi:10.1007/978-3-642-35395-6_30
7. Chetty, G., White, M., Akther, F.: Smart phone based data mining for human activity recognition. Procedia Comput. Sci. **46**, 1181–1187 (2015)
8. Marschollek, M., Wolf, K.-H., Gietzelt, M., Nemitz, G., Meyer zu Schwabedissen, H., Haux, R.: Assessing elderly persons' fall risk using spectral analysis on accelerometric data - a clinical evaluation study. In: 30th Annual International Conference of the IEEE Engineering in Medicine and Biology Society 2008, EMBS 2008, pp. 3682–3685 (2008)
9. Yabo, C., Yujiu, Y., Wenhuang, L.: e-FallD: a fall detection system using android-based smartphone. In: 2012 9th International Conference on Fuzzy Systems and Knowledge Discovery (FSKD), pp. 1509–1513 (2012)
10. Khan, A.M.: Human activity recognition using a single tri-axial accelerometer. Thesis for the Degree of Doctor of Philosophy (2011)
11. Sazonov, E.S., Fulk, G., Hill, J., Schutz, Y., Browning, R.: Monitoring of posture allocations and activities by a shoe-based wearable sensor. IEEE Trans. Biomed. Eng. **58**, 983–990 (2011)
12. Ravi, N., Dandekar, N., Mysore, P., Littman, M.L.: Activity recognition from accelerometer data. In: Proceeding of the National Conference on Artificial Intelligence 2005, pp. 1541–1546 (2005)
13. Guiry, J.J., van de Ven, P., Nelson, J., Warmerdam, L., Riper, H.: Activity recognition with smartphone support. Med. Eng. Phys. **36**, 670–675 (2014)
14. Capela, N.A., Lemaire, E.D., Baddour, N.: Improving classification of sit, stand, and lie in a smartphone human activity recognition system. In: IEEE International Symposium on Medical Measurements and Applications (MeMeA), pp. 473–478 (2015)
15. Sang, V.N.T., Thang, N.D., Toi, V., Hoang, N.D., Khoa, T.Q.D.: Human activity recognition and monitoring using smartphones. In: Toi, V.V., Lien Phuong, T.H. (eds.) 5th International Conference on Biomedical Engineering in Vietnam. IFMBE, vol. 46, pp. 481–485. Springer, Heidelberg (2015). doi:10.1007/978-3-319-11776-8_119
16. Tuan Dinh, L., Chung Van, N.: Human activity recognition by smartphone. In: 2015 2nd National Foundation for Science and Technology Development Conference on Information and Computer Science (NICS), pp. 219–224 (2015)

LCD-Based on Probability in Content Centric Networking

Dang Tran Phuong[1], Tuan-Anh Le[2(✉)], Le Phong Du[3], Tuyet Anh Thi Nguyen[2], and Phuong Luu Vo[4]

[1] VNPT-NET, Ho Chi Minh City, Vietnam
tranphuong@vnpt.vn
[2] Faculty of Information Technology, Thu Dau Mot University, Thu Dau Mot, Binh Duong Province, Vietnam
{letuanh,tuyetnta}@tdmu.edu.vn
[3] Lac Hong University, Bien Hoa, Dong Nai Province, Vietnam
lpdu@tvu.edu.vn
[4] School of Computer Science and Engineering, International University - VNUHCM, Ho Chi Minh City, Vietnam
vtlphuong@hcmiu.edu.vn

Abstract. Nowadays, Content Centric Networking (CCN) could be the future Internet architecture for its advance feature: In-network caching due to cheaper to cache than to transmit contents nowadays. Besides, the popularity of content in CCN gives much challenge to researchers, but there are a few solutions for that, such as LCD (Leave Copy Down). LCD policy is known as simple and effective caching mechanism so far. This work presents a new way of cooperation between CCN nodes in caching mechanism. Our caching mechanism is an optimization of LCD that some CCN nodes can help the others for their work on caching decision policy. This cooperation method doesn't require both additional signaling packet and much computation resource to work. Experiments show that this optimization in terms of cache hit can achieve better than convention LCD does. In additional, our solution is simple and very low overhead.

Keywords: CCN · Optimization · Caching · Cooperation · Probability · LCD

1 Introduction

CCN has been nominated as a hopeful alternative to Internet connection-oriented model which use TCP/IP protocol. The principle "connection" is not be used in CCN anymore; the "content" will be central, other aspects as request and respond data, cache, store, routing or security is based on content which are given name to identify. The name of content is distinct in global scope, the named content with different sizes is split into chunks with equal size as a transmission units. The idea of CCN is to try to reuse content for many consumers' need by caching it at every CCN node. All network nodes are routers which equipped with memories for purpose of caching chunk. So that in-network caching is respected as CCN's key feature.

In CCN, the consumer shows his need to network by sending a stream of request packets for chunks of every needed content. After sending request packets, the consumer will waiting for incoming data packets that the network responds or he will resend his need again since time-out. All the request packets will propagate through node to node in network to find its suitable chunk until it hit cache at CCN node. For every request packet, the CCN node responds with a data packet - in case of hitting cache - to the requester or forward that request packet to its neighbors as it is a requester by using its forwarding policy - in case of missing cache. The CCN node use its caching policy (i.e. decision policy, replacement policy) to treat with every received data packet, these policies help it knows whatever chunk to cache to memory or to discard from the memory because of space for new one. By this way, CCN can push needed content closer to consumer than before so that can reduce network's bandwidth consumption and the content retrieval times is shorter than in TCP/IP protocol.

However, the CCN's policy (i.e. forwarding policy, decision policy and replacement policy) have been exposing many challenges for researchers. Like the importance of routing in host-to-host network paradigm which was researched well in recent decades, caching is the most important factor to CCN performance base on named content that has much attention but few studies so far. There are many studies of network caching for World Wide Web which pointed out in [2] but are not completely suitable for CCN, except one of them, LCD [2, 10] is simple and more effective than original LCE (Leave Copy Everywhere) not only in World Wide Web caching but also in CCN which [3] pointed out.

With the advances of LCD for CCN, our work in this paper proposes a novel method of caching which use LCD mechanism combines with dynamic probability. Not the same as convention LCD that always cache chunks with probability equal 1, in our work, the CCN nodes will cooperate with each other's to calculate the probability to cache chunk. Our simulations result has proved to achieve more gain to network performance than convention LCD does.

The remaining paper is structured as follows. Section 2 is a brief express of some related works. The details of this scheme and algorithm are described in Sect. 3. The simulation results are analyzed in Sect. 4 and a brief conclusion is in Sect. 5.

2   Related Work

Caching is reliable not a new topic, with many work relating with Web caching replacement policies and decision policies [1]. Relating with caching policies, as indicate in [2], much attention has been paid for cache replacement problems (more than 38 strategies were overviewed in [1]), however, the other aspect, cache decision policies, there are few studies relating with [3].

With the policy for replacement an object in cache memory, the most popular is Least Recently Used (LRU) which has been used in the CCN context [4–6] and of the more general ICN context [7–9]. Some others related with Most Recently Used (MRU) and Most Frequently Used (MFU) in ICN context [8].

For decision policies, generally the assumption is made that any new content gets always cached, these use Leave Copy Down (LCE) mechanism. As in [3], few exceptions to this rule come from the Web caching [2, 10, 12, 13] or CCN [11] contexts. In those solutions, the approach in [12] is too complexity to apply in CCN, while DEMOTE [13] is known to poorly perform on network of caches. Beside, another simple policy is considered in [11], where caching decisions are taken uniformly at random with a fixed probability FIX(P). FIX(P) can make a quite good result in caching performance of Web caching with a small probability (P approximate 0.2) in some cases. FIX(P) with small probability (0.2) may avoid many replacement errors (replacement error occurs when a higher popularity content was replaced with lower popularity in caching memory [2]) but the results of applying FIX(P) to web caching are so different depend on network topology and the amount of content or cache size. However, FIX(P) has not been applied or evaluated in CCN so far. Another decision policy that [2] introduces is MCD (Move Copy Down), with its mechanism, MCD can have a good result in web caching than LCE because of well treat to popularity contents and fewer replacement errors.

With this respect, only the Leave Copy Down (LCD) policy [2, 10] is simple enough to be worth implementing in CCN. LCD has been applied in CCN and it shown that LCD achieves much better than LCE in caching performance, especially for contents with classified popularities.

On the other hand, only a few explicit cache coordination policies (e.g., see [14] for Web, and [15] for ad hoc domain) but [3] points out that they would likely violate CCN line of speed constraint.

In direct approaches, [3, 16] study arbitrary networks of CCN caches with special attention to different caching replacement (e.g., LRU, MRU, etc.) and decision policies (e.g., LCD [1], etc.). In these works, the CCN network is considered with homogeneous cache sizes, e.g., content store of CCN nodes have the equal size.

In this work, we still focus on decision policy of CCN which use LCD in a novel way base on the idea of probability and CCN node can cooperate with each other in making a decision to cache contents.

3   Scheme Design and Algorithm

In this section introduce LCD-based on probability, called LCD-Prob. The idea of LCD-Prob is to improve cache-hit ratio of some CCN nodes with lowest performance, so that the cache-hit ratio of whole network, in average, will be better. In this scheme, with every content requested by consumer, the first node, that the request packet for each content come to, called edge node, and the others, on the path of this request packet forwarded to the repository, called core node, as shown in Fig. 1.

In imitation, when all CCN nodes are implemented with the same memory size (Content Store), we found that the core nodes usually have lower cache-hit ratios than the edge nodes in using LCD as decision policy. Since the traffic throughput at core nodes are more than at edges that lead the replacement of chunk, in limited memory, occur more frequently.

To improve the effectiveness of caching at these core nodes, they must try to retain the most popular contents in their memory. The least the memory replacement occur in core nodes, the more chance the popular contents would be retained. LCD-Prob will try to keep contents at core nodes not be changed so regularly in CCN network, so that the

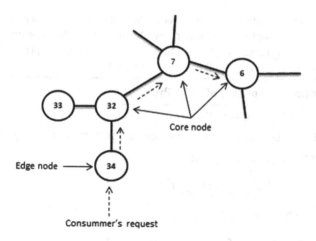

Fig. 1. Topology

decision to cache a content of LCD now is based on probability. The probability to cache is a dynamic parameter which can be calculated based on the correlation cache-hit ratio between core node and edge node. The probability denotes as: the smaller the cache-hit ratio of node is, the smaller the probability to cache a new chunk will be.

The current cache-hit ratio of edge node will be sent to next node (also core node) in every request packet that it forwards to and it will be retained in data packet on the backward path, the information is used to calculate the probability at the node which is chosen to cache the chunk by LCD's decision.

The calculation of probability is defined as follow:

n_{hit} is the number of request packet at a CCN node that hit cache;
n_{miss} is the number of request packet at a CCN node that miss cache;
C_{edge} is current cache-hit ratio of the edge node which receives request packet from consumer;
P is probability to cache a chunk in the memory of considering node;
C_{core} is current cache-hit ratio of the node which calculating probability (P) for caching a chunk;
C_x (x = core or edge) is computed by

$$C_x = \frac{n_{hit}}{n_{hit} + n_{miss}}$$

P is calculated as

$$P = MIN(1, \frac{C_{core}}{C_{edge}^k}) \tag{1}$$

where k is a constant which $k \geq 1$.

The algorithm for data packet processing at each CCN node where LCD policy decides to cache the chunk to node's memory, this node uses the information contained in data message (C_{edge}) and its information (C_{core}) to calculate the probability P. Then the CCN node will cache the chunk with probability P.

Algorithm 1: Algorithm of LCD-Prob.

```
1: Receive a data packet
2: IF (LCD policy decide to cache the chunk) DO
3:    IF(C_edge > C_core) DO
```

$$P = C_{core} / (C_{edge})^k$$

```
5:    ELSE P = 1.0
6:    Generate a random number R ∈ [0,1]
7:       IF (R ≤ P) DO
8:           Cache the chunk
9:       END IF
10:   END IF
11: END IF
12: Forward data message to next node
```

When a CCN node receives a data packet, the LCD-Prob policy is used to decide to cache down this chunk or not. The same as convention LCD, for every request packet that got cache hit event at a CCN node, only the next node on the backward way (toward consumer) have chance to cache down this chunk. To cache this chunk, the CCN node must use C_{edge} (i.e., it is piggybacked in data packet) and its cache hit ratio (C_{core}) to retrieve probability P in case $C_{edge} > C_{core}$ or P will be 1, that is $P \in [0,1]$. To use P, the core node will generate a random R which $R \in [0,1]$ then compare R to P as: If $R \leq P$, the caching is successful. Oppositely, $R > P$ will cause the caching fail. The parameter k is used to adjust the change of P according to the change of C_{core}.

Finally, the data packet will be forwarded to next node toward consumer without caching down at any others.

LCD-Prob doesn't require any message packet or bandwidth to operate, it only requires a little CPU resource to calculate (1), generate a random R and compare them.

4   Evaluation

To evaluate LCD-Prob, we simulate it on CCN network by using Watts-Strogatz (WS) model [18], which can capture characteristics of Internet topology structure. Our simulation tool is implemented by C++ programming language. Consumer's requests follow Zipf distribution with the parameter $0.7 \leq \alpha \leq 1.5$. The key performance indicators are focus on average cache-hit ratio and average hop-count (i.e., total hops on the path of a request until hitting the chunk). The parameters are set in our simulation as described in Table 1.

Table 1. Parameter setting

Parameter	Value	Parameter	Value
Number of CCN node	44	Forwarding	Shortest path routing
Number of repository	12	Decision	Convention LCD
Number of consumer	24		LCD-Prob
Replacement policy	LRU	Content store	200
k	5	Number of content	5000

As shown in Figs. 2 and 3, LCD-Prob achieves better results in cache-hit ratio and hop count than convention LCD with the content following the Zipf distribution and the parameter $0.7 \leq \alpha \leq 1.5$: the network average cache-hit ratio is higher up to 16% and the network average hop count are lower 11% (Fig. 4).

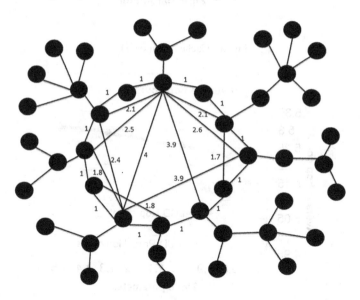

Fig. 2. Simulation topology

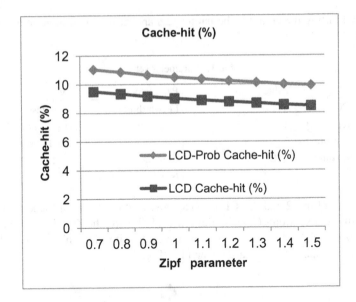

Fig. 3. Cache hit ratio (%)

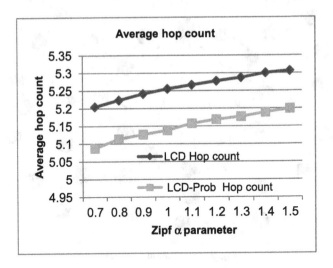

Fig. 4. Average hop count

The cache-hit ratio higher means caching performance is better and the hop count lower means LCD-Prob pushes needed content closer to consumer than LCD.

With a limit cache-hit ratio at every edge node, most of the requests will be forwarded to nearest core node to find provision server. This causes the throughput through core nodes are much higher than in edge nodes. The incoming requests are much higher but network cache size is homogeneous for all nodes will cause cache hit ratio at core nodes are smaller than at edge nodes. Moreover, LCD mechanism treats popularity content well at edge nodes but badly at core nodes, especially at the nodes next to provision server, LCD does the same as LCE.

Our mechanism can avoid that problem of LCD by caching with probability at every node especially at core nodes. The core nodes always have smaller cache-hit ratio can have smaller probability to cache a new chunk. Like the result of FIX(P) [2] has shown to us, with small probability to cache a new chunk, node CCN can reduce a lot of replacement errors would happen through caching replacement. When a node reduce this error through caching, that means it retain higher popularity contents in its memory instead of replacing them with lower popularity ones. In this case, the node' caching performance is better. With many core nodes have better performance, the network average cache hit ratio increases as we achieve in experiments.

5   Conclusions

In this paper, we propose a lightweight way to cooperate with each other on caching using statistic cache-hit ratio and without sending any additional message. Cache-hit ratio is sent to next node within request message and will be retained in data packet on backward path; CCN nodes use this info to calculate the probability to cache the chunk in combination with LCD algorithm. The proposal improves the caching performance in some nodes in network so that they have higher caching performance of network. In additional, our solution is simple and very low overhead. However, the parameter k is effected in network topology that need to be optimized to find the suitable value to achieve proposal's best result, our next work will find out this question.

Acknowledgment. This research is funded by Vietnam National Foundation for Science and Technology Development (NAFOSTED) under grant number 102.02-2015.36.

References

1. Podlipnig, S., Osz, L.B.: A survey of web cache replacement strategies. ACM Comput. Surv. **35**(4), 374–398 (2003)
2. Laoutaris, N., Che, H., Stavrakakis, I.: The LCD interconnection of LRU caches and its analysis. Perform. Eval. **63**(7), 609–634 (2006)
3. Rossini, G., Rossi, D.: Caching performance of content centric networks under multi-path routing (and more). Technical report, Telecom Paris- Tech (2011)
4. Psaras, I., Clegg, R.G., Landa, R., Chai, W.K., Pavlou, G.: Modelling and evaluation of CCN-caching trees. In: IFIP Networking (2011)
5. Carofiglio, G., Gallo, M., Muscariello, L., Perino, D.: Modeling data transfer in content-centric networking. In: ITC (2011)
6. Carofiglio, G., Gallo, M., Muscariello, L.: Bandwidth and storage sharing performance in information centric networking. In: ACM SIGCOMM, ICN Worskhop, pp. 1–6 (2011)
7. Choi, J., Han, J., Cho, E., Kwon, T.T., Choi, Y.: A survey on content-oriented networking for efficient content delivery. IEEE Commu. Mag. **49**(3), 121–127 (2011)
8. Katsaros, K., Xylomenos, G., Polyzos, G.C.: MultiCache: an overlay architecture for information-centric networking. Comput. Netw. 1–11 (2011)

9. Rosensweig, E.J., Kurose, J.: Breadcrumbs: efficient, best-effort content location in cache networks. In: IEEE INFOCOM (2009)
10. Laoutaris, N., Syntila, S., Stavrakakis, I.: Meta algorithms for hierarchical web caches. In: IEEE ICPCC (2004)
11. Arianfar, S., Nikander, P.: Packet-level caching for informationcentric networking. In: ACM SIGCOMM, ReArch Workshop (2010)
12. Che, H., Tung, Y., Wang, Z.: Hierarchical web caching systems: modeling, design and experimental results. IEEE J. Sel. Areas Commun. **20**(7), 1305–1314 (2002)
13. Wong, T., Ganger, G., Wilkes, J.: My cache or yours? making storage more exclusive. In: USENIX Annual Technical Conference (2002)
14. Wolman, A., Voelker, G.M., Sharma, N., Cardwell, N., Karlin, A., Levy, H.M.: On the scale and performance of cooperative web proxy caching. In: ACM SOSP, pp. 16–31 (1999)
15. Fiore, M., Mininni, F., Casetti, C., Chiasserini, C.-F.: To cache or not to cache. In: IEEE INFOCOM, pp. 235–243 (2009)
16. Rossi, D., Rossini, G.: A dive into the caching performance of content centric networking. Technical report, Telecom ParisTech (2011)
17. Jacobson, V., Smetters, D., Briggs, N., Thornton, J., Plass, M., Braynard, R.: Networking named content. In: ACM CoNEXT (2009)
18. Watts, J., Strogatz, H.: Collective dynamics of 'small-world' networks. Nature **393**, 440–442 (1998)

Multivariate Cube for Representing Multivariable Data in Visual Analytics

Hong Thi Nguyen[1], Anh Van Thi Tran[2], Tuyet Anh Thi Nguyen[4],
Luc Tan Vo[3], and Phuoc Vinh Tran[4(✉)]

[1] University of Information Technology (UIT),
Vietnam National University - HCMC, Hochiminh City, Vietnam
hongnguyen1611@gmail.com
[2] Hochiminh City Economics College, Ho Chi Minh City, Vietnam
ttvanh26@gmail.com
[3] Eastern International University, Binhduong, Vietnam
luc.vo@eiu.edu.vn
[4] Thudaumot University (TDMU), Binhduong, Vietnam
{tuyetnta,Phuoctv}@tdmu.edu.vn, Phuoc.gis@gmail.com

Abstract. The data visualization enables users to contribute their knowledge and experience to the analysis of data stored in storages or resulted from collecting systems in real time. Visual techniques displaying data table as 2D or 3D charts, pies, lines, and so on, do not completely enable to explore multivariable data. Multivariate cube is modified from parallel coordinates by rotating the reference axis to the direction perpendicular to parallel coordinates plane. Multivariate cube represents multivariable data to enable users to answer elementary tasks in visual analytics by associating a point with its references on axes of 3-dimensional coordinates. Multivariate cube represents visually multivariable data to enable users to answer synoptic tasks in visual analytics by viewing the variation of data along the reference axis for each variable, or viewing the correlation between variables on the plane being perpendicular to and moving along the reference axis. Multivariate cube is illustrated in this paper with two case studies for visual analytics, the evaluation of learning outcomes of a program of higher education and the happenings of a disease.

Keywords: Visual analytics · Multivariate cube · Multivariable data · Data visualization

1 Introduction

Techniques of visualization display data tables as charts, pies, lines, and so on, on two-dimensional screen. Many visual softwares supply with 2D and 3D charts to display data tables as columns arranged in a cube but not enable more tools of flexible interaction to explore information or analyze data. Parallel coordinates [1–4] represent data variables on parallel axes on a plane but not share reference variables to enable to answer tasks in visual analytics. Meanwhile, visual analytics demands to show multivariable data with shared reference variables to answer analytical tasks, specially

© ICST Institute for Computer Sciences, Social Informatics and Telecommunications Engineering 2017
P. Cong Vinh et al. (Eds.): ICCASA 2016, LNICST 193, pp. 91–100, 2017.
DOI: 10.1007/978-3-319-56357-2_10

synoptic questions. It also needs tools of complete and flexible interaction to discover new knowledge from data and estimate the correlation between data variables.

The main idea of this study is to apply multivariate cube which is modified from parallel coordinates for representing data sets of multi-attributes. In that, each of attribute is considered as a data variable, the key reference variable is chosen to represent on the reference axis perpendicular to the plane of parallel coordinates. The attribute axis is an axis on parallel coordinates plane and perpendicular to axes of parallel coordinates. The axes of parallel coordinates are arranged along the attribute axis, where each axis indicates the values of an attribute, termed characteristic axis. The reference axis, the attribute axis, and characteristic axes constitute a cube to represent characteristics referring to a reference variable, termed multivariate cube. The multivariate cube displaying visually characteristics as data variables enables user to answer analytical tasks including elementary and synoptic questions [5].

This paper is structured as follows. The next section presents the constitution of multivariate cube from parallel coordinates by rotating the reference axis to the direction perpendicular to parallel coordinates plane. The third section is the first case study that applies multivariate cube for representing the statistical evaluation by recruiters, alumni, last-year students, and lecturers on learning outcomes of information system program by TDMU to enable users to analyze the educational state of the program at TDMU. The fourth section is the second case study that applies multivariate cube for representing and analyzing visually the data concerning hand, foot, and mouth disease in Binhduong province during 2012–2014. The last section summarizes main contents of the paper.

2 Multivariate Cube for Representing Multivariable Data

2.1 Related Works

A data table is structured as a 2-dimensional matrix of columns and rows. Each column represents an attribute as a set of values of a variable and each row is a data tuple representing a relation between variables. Data variables shown in table may be divided into reference variables and characteristics [5]. Data visualization is studied as a conversion of a data variable of table into a visual variable as an axis or an colored axis (Fig. 1).

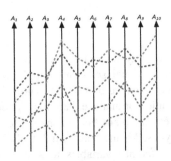

Fig. 1. The parallel coordinates.

Parallel coordinates composed of parallel axes on a plane are utilized to represent a data table, where each axis shows data of a column considered as a data variable, polylines connect the values on axes, which associate with each other on the same row of data table [1–3]. The parallel coordinates does not limit the number of variables as well as the number of rows of data table. However, parallel coordinates do not define reference axes as well as not enable completely to answer questions relating the variation of a variable corresponding to an interval of reference variable or questions concerning the correlation between variables.

Space-time cube is a cube of 3-dimensional orthogonal coordinates, where 2 axes indicate ground locations and another axis indicates time [6]. Space-time cube enables to represent and analyze visually space-time and moving objects [7–10]. However, it does not enable to represent objects of multivariable data. Therefore, some authors have tried to expand space-time cube to represent movement data including space-time location and attributes [11, 12].

2.2 Multivariate Cube Constituted from Parallel Coordinates

Multivariate cube is constituted from parallel coordinates as follows. Parallel coordinates are composed of parallel axes on a plane, each of which is utilized to represent a data variable. The axis representing the key reference variable, termed reference axis, is rotated to the direction perpendicular to the plane of parallel axes. Other parallel axes, termed characteristic axes, are arranged on the characteristic plane and along the attribute axis perpendicular to them. The orthogonal axes of reference, characteristic, and attribute form multivariate cube. In the cube, a characteristic value which associates with a point on the characteristic axis and a point on the reference axis is displayed as a bar or a point. The plane formed by the reference axis and a characteristic axis displays visually the variation of the characteristic with respect to the reference variable within displayed reference interval. The planes perpendicular to the reference axis at various reference values show the relation and correlation between characteristics at the reference values (Fig. 2).

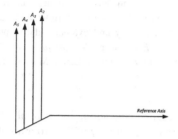

Fig. 2. Multivariate cube constituted from parallel coordinates.

3 Case Study 1: The Evaluation of Higher Education Program of Information System at Thu Dau Mot University

Thu Dau Mot University (TDMU) is a provincial university located in Thu Dau Mot city belonging Binhduong province, Vietnam, which borders on Hochiminh City in the north. The TDMU provides with diverse programs for undergraduate and graduate students. Expected as a big center providing with human resources for the provinces in the southeast of Vietnam, the TDMU not only provides students with academic knowledge but also skill and attitude (Fig. 3). The TDMU always enhances educational qualification by evaluating repeatedly student's competence with respect to the demand of society. The information system is one of programs made evaluation in academic year 2015–2016.

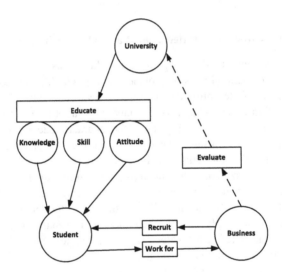

Fig. 3. The triad of higher education "University – Student – Business". The triad represents the relation between university, student, and business, where university educates students on knowledge, skill, and attitude to meet the need of recruiter and business, meanwhile business recruits students graduated from university and evaluates the response rate of university with respect to its demand (Source: *"Evaluating the competence of students graduated from information technology programs in Hochiminh City."* Master dissertation by Anh Van Thi Tran).

Based on the triad of higher education, the school of information technology belonging to the TDMU carried out a survey of the program of information system with interviewees who are business and recruiters considered as receivers the results of the program, alumni and last-year students as results of the program, and lecturers as executers of the program. Each learning outcome on knowledge, skill, and attitude is evaluated on five levels. The evaluation results are summarized in three tables, the

Table 1. The statistics on the cognition of importance of learning outcomes (Source: Survey by Tuyet Anh Thi Nguyen in a study funded by TDMU in 2016)

Learning outcome, symbol of learning outcome	Business & recruiters	Alumni	Last-year students	Lecturers
Knowledge of basic science, KBS	3	2.61	2.96	3.61
Knowledge of basic engineering, KBE	3.47	3.4	3.67	3.88
Knowledge of advanced engineering, KAE	3.4	3.46	3.91	3.95
Knowledge of supplement, KOS	3.41	3.22	3.42	3.32
Capacity of reasoning, analyzing, and solving problems, RAS	3.88	3.42	3.66	3.08
Researching and exploring knowledge, REK	3.69	3.53	3.02	3.66
Thought of systematic level, TSL	3.88	2.97	3.09	3.55
Team work, TWK	3.88	4	3.37	3.76
Communication, COM	3.68	3.49	3.56	3.08
English-based communication, EBC	4.11	3.69	4.2	2.97
Society and environment, SAE	3.23	3.1	2.4	2.74
Job context and business, JCB	3.04	3.63	3.53	2.75
Constituting idea and managing technical system, MTS	3.04	3.63	3.53	2.75
Designing system of information technology, SIT	3.4	3.3	3.5	2.54
Implementation, IMP	3.48	3.02	2.71	2.71
Operating and maintaining system of information technology, OAM	3.21	2.85	3.46	2.59
Attitude, idea, and education, AIE	4.22	3.92	3.56	4.09
Morality and justice, MAJ	3.93	3.71	3.39	3.88

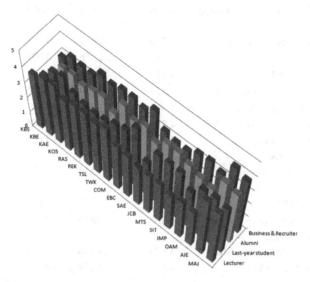

Fig. 4. The multivariate cube representing visually data of the Table 1 on the interviewees' cognition of importance of learning outcomes.

cognition of the importance of learning outcomes, the expectation of the achievement of learning outcomes from students, and the possibility of students' response of learning outcomes. The first two tables are utilized in this paper to illustrate the application of multivariate cube for visual analytics in evaluating higher education.

The surveyed data on information system program of TDMU in the academic year 2014–2015 are represented on the multivariate cubes at Figs. 4 and 5. Various tools of data visualization softwares such as show/hide, rotation, slide bar, zoom, selection, and so on, enable users to analyze the results evaluating learning outcomes by different groups of interviewees. The multivariate cubes show generally that the elementary questions relating interviewee and learning outcome can be answered easily by referring to corresponding axes. The cubes also shows on learning outcome axis the difference in evaluating different learning outcomes by an interviewee. The cubes provide users with the correlation of cognitions of the importance (Fig. 4) as well as the correlation of expectations of the achievement from students (Fig. 5) between recruiters, last-year students, alumni, and lecturers for each learning outcome.

Table 2. The statistics on the expectation of achievement of learning outcomes from students (Source: Survey by Tuyet Anh Thi Nguyen in a study funded by TDMU in 2016).

Learning outcome, symbol of learning outcome	Business & recruiter	Alumni	Last-year students	Lecturers
Knowledge of basic science, KBS	4.141	3.694	3.866	4.305
Knowledge of basic engineering, KBE	4.141	3.694	3.866	4.305
Knowledge of advanced engineering, KAE	4.313	4.019	4.081	4.583
Knowledge of supplement, KOS	4.177	3.944	3.657	4.068
Capacity of reasoning, analyzing, and solving problems, RAS	4.281	4.083	3.614	4.234
Researching and exploring knowledge, REK	4.406	3.972	3.651	4.344
Thought of systematic level, TSL	4.219	3.917	4.219	4.094
Team work, TWK	4.55	4.356	3.956	4.288
Communication, COM	4.112	3.689	4.201	2.969
English-based communication, EBC	3.875	4.333	4.485	3.412
Society and environment, SAE	4	3.714	4.04	3.17
Job context and business, JCB	4.25	3.762	4.025	3.223
Constituting idea and managing technical system, MTS	4.25	3.762	4.025	3.223
Designing system of information technology, SIT	4.063	3.444	4.091	3.177
Implementation, IMP	4.05	3.622	4.065	2.75
Operating and maintaining system of information technology, OAM	4.208	3.833	4.081	2.927
Attitude, idea, and education, AIE	4.625	4.238	3.756	4.429
Morality and justice, MAJ	4.6	4.378	3.847	4.463

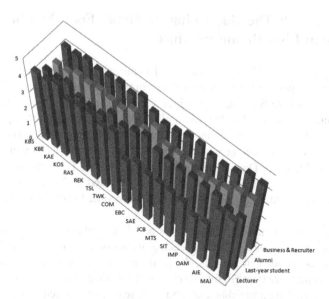

Fig. 5. The multivariate cube representing visually the data Table 2 showing the statistics on the interviewees' expectation of achievement of learning outcome from students.

The multivariate cube of Fig. 4 represents visually the data of the Table 1. The cube shows the very low correlation between the evaluations by recruiter and evaluations by lecturer on the importance of several learning outcomes as Capacity of reasoning, analyzing, and solving problems (RAS), Communication (COM), English-based communication (EBC), Society and Environment (SAE), Job context and business (JCB), Constituting idea and managing technical system (MTS), Designing system of information technology (SIT), Implementation (IMP), Operating and maintaining system of information technology (OAM), and so on.

Similarly, the multivariate cube of Fig. 5 represents the data of the Table 2. The cube displays the very low correlation between the expectations of recruiters and the expectations of lecturers on achievement from students for several learning outcomes as Capacity of reasoning, analyzing, and solving problems (RAS), Team work (TWK), Communication (COM), English-based communication (EBC), Society and Environment (SAE), Job context and business (JCB), Constituting idea and managing technical system (MTS), Designing system of information technology (SIT), Implementation (IMP), Operating and maintaining system of information technology (OAM), and so on.

The visual analysis on the Figs. 4 and 5 results in the necessity for making or adjusting the policy to improve the educational qualification of the university. Technically, an extended multivariate cube can be studied to represent and analyze the development as well as the improvement of the evaluation on information system program when the survey is carried out in several academic years.

4   Case Study 2: The Happenings of Hand, Foot, Mouth Disease in Binh Duong Province

Binhduong province borders on northern Hochiminh City, Vietnam. It is about 2,700 km² large with over 1.7 million habitants. In the study of the disease of hand, foot, and mouth in the whole Binhduong province, the related attributes are composed of the total of patients, the total rainfall, the average humidity, and the average temperature. The attributes change over time and are recorded every week during 2012–2014. In that, the total of patients is recorded in the whole Binhduong province and its administrative units as Thudaumot, Thuanan, Dian, Bencat, Dautieng, Phugiao, Tanuyen according to the administrative map in 2013; the total rainfall is recorded at 7 stations in the whole province; the average humidity and temperature are recorded at one station in the whole province.

The visual representation of data enables people to make visual analysis to understand the happenings as well as the outbreaking of the disease. The data variables related to the disease as the total of patients, the total rainfall, the average humidity, and the average temperature are converted to visual variables, where time variable is converted to the time axis, each data variable related to the disease is converted to an axis used as a planar variable associating with a color variable. Each disease data variable changing over time is represented on a 2D-coordinate system, where an axis represents time and another associating with a color represents the variable concerning the disease. The 2D-coordinate systems representing the variables related to the disease may be arranged on parallel planes so that they share the time axis. The combination of 2D-coordinate systems constitutes a multivariate cube representing the data variables related to the disease (Fig. 6). In the study, the intensity of color is used to show the value weight of variable over time to perceive more easily the correlation between disease data variables.

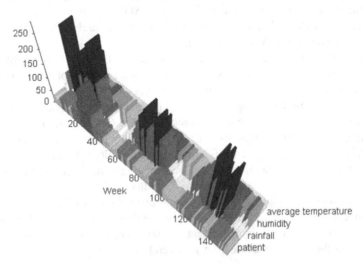

Fig. 6. The multivariate cube representing visually the data of disease of hand, foot, and mouth in Binhduong province during 2012–2014. (Data provided by Binhduong Medical Center for Providing Against Possible Contingencies)

The interactive tools of software as time selection, attribute selection, rotation, zoom, and so on provide user with different viewings to extract information for analytical tasks. Viewing along the time axis of the Fig. 6, user can cognize the developments of the disease. Viewing on the plane perpendicular to the time axis at a time point, user may percept the relation between the total of patients and rainfall, humidity, temperature. In that, the correlation between the total of patients and rainfall or humidity is high, meanwhile the correlation between the total of patients and temperature is very low. The correlation shows that hand, foot, and mouth disease happens when the rainfall and humidity increase and temperature does not affect the development of the disease. This result enable epidemiologists to build scenarios of warning the disease.

5 Conclusion

The multivariate cube is modified from parallel coordinates, where one of axes is rotated to the direction perpendicular to the plane of other axes. The multivariate cube is suitable for representing data sets of several attributes for visual analytics. This paper presents two case studies applying multivariate cube for analyzing the data of evaluating educational result of information system program at Thu Dau Mot University, and the data of hand, foot, and mouth disease provided by Binhduong Medical Center for Providing Against Possible Contingencies. Viewing data displayed on the multivariate cube for educational evaluation of information system program, TDMU's University Board can cognize that the thought of lecturers does not meet the demand of business and recruiters with respect to several learning outcomes. Viewing data shown on the multivariate cube for hand, foot, and mouth disease, epidemiologist can detect the law developing the disease.

References

1. Inselberg, A.: The plane with parallel coordinates. Visual Comput. **1**, 69–91 (1985)
2. Inselberg, A., Dimsdale, B.: Parallel coordinates: a tool for visualizing multi-dimensional geometry. In: IEEE, pp. 361–378 (1990)
3. Andrienko, G., Andrienko, A.: Parallel coordinates for exploring properties of subsets. Presented at the International Conference on Coordinated & Multiple Views in Exploratory Visualization (CMV 2004), pp. 93–104 (2004)
4. Inselberg, A.: Parallel Coordinates: Visual Multidimensional Geometry and Its Applications. Springer, New York (2008)
5. Andrienko, N., Andrienko, G.: Exploratory Analysis of Spatial and Temporal Data - A Systematic Approach. Springer, Heidelberg (2006)
6. Hagerstrand, T.: What about people in regional science? Presented at the Ninth European Congress of Regional Science Association (1970)
7. Tran, P.V., Nguyen, H.T.: Visualization cube for tracking moving object. Presented at the Computer Science and Information Technology, Information and Electronics Engineering (2011)

8. Nguyen, H.T., Duong, C.K.T., Bui, T.T., Tran, P.V.: Visualization of spatio-temporal data of bus trips. Presented at the IEEE 2012 International Conference on Control, Automation and Information Science, ICCAIS 2012, Hochiminh City, Vietnam (2012)
9. Tran, P.V., Tran, T.V., Nguyen, H.T.: Visualization-based tracking system using mobile device. In: Sobecki, J., Boonjing, V., Chittayasothorn, S. (eds.) Advanced Approaches to Intelligent Information and Database Systems. SCI, vol. 551, pp. 345–354. Springer, Cham (2014). doi:10.1007/978-3-319-05503-9_34
10. Bach, B., Dragicevic, P., Archambault, D., Hurter, C., Carpendale, S.: A review of temporal data visualizations based on space-time cube operations. In: Eurographics Conference on Visualization (EuroVis), pp. 1–19 (2014)
11. Tran, P.V., Nguyen, H.T., Tran, T.V.: Approaching multi-dimensional cube for visualization-based epidemic warning system - dengue fever. Presented at the 8th International Conference on Ubiquitous Information Management and Communication, ACM IMCOM 2014, Siem Reap, Cambodia (2014)
12. Nguyen, H.T., Tran, T.V., Tran, P.V., Dang, H.: Multivariate cube for visualization of weather data. Presented at the IEEE 2013 International Conference on Control, Automation and Information Science, ICCAIS 2013, Nha Trang, Vietnam (2013)

An Approach to Analyzing Execution Preservation in Java Program Refactoring

Thi-Huong Dao[1], Hong Anh Le[2(✉)], and Ninh Thuan Truong[1]

[1] VNU, University of Engineering and Technology, Hanoi, Vietnam
{huongdt.di12,thuantn}@vnu.edu.vn
[2] Hanoi University of Mining and Geology, Hanoi, Vietnam
lehonganh@humg.edu.vn

Abstract. Code refactoring is a technique that improves the existing code in order to make software easier to understand and more extensible without changing the external behavior. Software design patterns, programming language independent reusable solutions to comment problems, are well-known in Java communities. On one hand, the refactoring using design patterns brings many benefits such as cost saving, flexibilities, and maintainability. On the other hand, it potentially causes bugs or changes execution behavior of Java programs. This paper proposes a new approach to checking behavior preservation properties of Java programs after applying design patterns. We present new definitions to compute pre/post conditions of program behavior. In the next step, the paper makes use of Java Modeling Language (JML) to represent and check if the refactored program neglects to preserve the external behavior. A motivating example of Adaptive Road Traffic Control (ARTC) is given to illustrate the approach in detail.

Keywords: Refactoring · Design patterns · Consistency · ARTC

1 Introduction

Software development is an elaborated and time-considerable process involving many steps in which maintenance phase plays an important role. This phase takes a high cost if the designs or codes are poor that makes software difficult to understand. As a consequence, developers find hard to maintain, modify, or create new features.

Software refactoring, originally introduced by Opdyke in his dissertation [10], is techniques, which are widely adopted for improving existing designs or codes without altering the external behavior. It includes a series of small transformations restructuring the software system. The software is expected to execute correctly as same as it does before refactoring.

During refactoring process, if developers realize smell codes, they will find solutions to improve these with a new structure. Design patterns [6] are general repeatable reusable solution to a commonly occurring problem within a given

© ICST Institute for Computer Sciences, Social Informatics and Telecommunications Engineering 2017
P. Cong Vinh et al. (Eds.): ICCASA 2016, LNICST 193, pp. 101–110, 2017.
DOI: 10.1007/978-3-319-56357-2_11

context in software design. It is a description or template for how to solve a problem that can be used in many different situations.

Refactoring to Patterns is the process of improving the design of existing code with patterns, the classic solutions to recurring design problems. Refactoring to Patterns suggests that using patterns to improve an existing design is better than using patterns early in a new design. We should improve designs with patterns by applying sequences of low-level design transformations, known as refactorings. Patterns are language independent, they have been broadly used in many programming languages including Java.

However, a big problem with design patterns in refactoring process is that we can not assure the execution behavior of the original program and its refactored one is consistent. It means that some execution may not be preserved in new one. Several approaches have been proposed to checking the consistency between programs using graph transformation techniques [2,12], and XML metadata interchange [5]. In this paper, we propose an approach to checking the consistency of execution behavior of Java programs before/after refactoring. The main contributions of the paper are (1) defines how to compute pre/post conditions of software execution behavior (i.e. program scenario), (2) utilize JML notations and tools to describe the constraint in refactored program to check the consistency property, and (3) illustrate the proposed approach with a case study of ARTC program.

The rest of the paper is organized as follows. In the following section, we review related work. Section 3 gives an overview of Strategy pattern and JML. A motivation example of Adaptive Road Traffic Control system is displayed in Sect. 4. Section 5 presents the approach to checking consistency software refactored programs. Section 6 concludes and gives some directions for future works.

2   Related Work

As mentioned earlier, William Opdyke [10], whose first introduced the *refactoring* term for object-oriented software, opened a new research direction in the field of software engineering. His research interested in describing the prerequisites and automatic program restructurings required to guarantee preservation of behavior. Moreover, he also developed a refactoring tool for Smalltalk.

According to analyzing of different criteria (e.g. the activities of refactoring, the specific techniques and formalisms), Tom Mens et el. [9] provided an extensive overview of existing research area. Particularly, they also discussed about various formal techniques which are used in refactoring process, such as invariants, pre/postcondition, graph transformation, program slicing, software metric, etc. Their research was very valuable with others people whose study in refactoring.

In [4], JML was used to specify the behaviors of a Java program. With the support tools [3] the program will be static and dynamic testing. Static testing will return syntax error and the invalided type of variables, dynamic testing (run-time assertion checking) will notify all kinds of run-time assertion violations.

Nevertheless, these studies were only done purely on a software program and have no related to refactoring process.

Some studies represent the behaviors of the software system via the assertions (invariants, pre/postconditions) [10,11], one problem is that the static checking of some preconditions may require very expensive analysis, or may even be impossible.

In comparison to prior works, our approach focuses on analyzing execution preservation between original program and evolution itself in refactoring process. Based on the JML specification to represent pre/post-conditions of a scenario, we use OpenJML tool to automated checking these constraints on both programs and answer the question whether the refactored program is satisfied initial behaviors specification or not? The advantages of our work is feasibility in experiment and semi- automated in checking behavior consistency.

3   Background

We interested in design pattern term as well as Java Modeling Language (JML) as a theory foundation to execute our method in the next section.

3.1   Strategy Pattern

Design pattern, is a general reusable solution to a commonly occurring problem within a given context in software design, has become popular since 1994 by GOF [6], in which they have categorized the design patterns into three groups, namely creational, structural, and behavioral patterns.

In this section, we clarify one behavioral pattern, namely **Strategy pattern**. It *encapsulates, defines a family of algorithms and makes them interchangeable independently from clients.* The strategy object changes the *executing algorithm* in the particular context object.

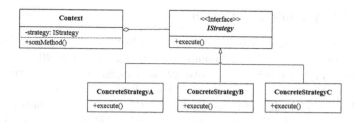

Fig. 1. Strategy pattern

The **Strategy pattern** has three participants as shown in Fig. 1:

– **IStrategy:** The interface that is shared among the concrete strategy classes in the family. Class *Context* uses this interface to call the algorithm defined by a concrete strategy.

– **ConcreteStrategy:** Where the real implementation of strategy takes place.
– **Context:** The class maintains a reference of type *IStrategy*. In some cases, *Context* may implement operations so that *ConcreteStrategy* can access its data.

The advantage of using strategy pattern is that encapsulating algorithms in individual classes will render reusing code much more convenient and hence, the behavior of the **Context** can be altered at run-time dynamically.

3.2 Java Modeling Language

Java Modeling Language (JML) [7] is a *behavioral interface specification language* (BISL) that can be used to specify Java classes and interfaces. JML specifications or assertions can be added directly to source code as a special kind of comments called annotation comments, or they can live in separate specification files. These assertions are usually written in a form that can be compiled, so that their violations can be detected at run-time.

The two main advantages in using JML are [7]:

– the precise, unambiguous description of the behavior of Java program modules (i.e., classes and interfaces), and documentation of Java code,
– the possibility of tool support [3].

JML's syntax is very close to the Java programming language, so it easily used by programmers who have familiar with Java. In this section, we only present a brief overview about functions as well as features of JML. For more details, one can refer to [8].

4 A Motivating Example: Adaptive Road Traffic Control System

4.1 ARTC System's Description

Traffic congestion is an ever increasing problem in towns and cities all over the world. Local authorities must continually work to maximize the efficiency of their road networks and to minimize any disruptions caused by accidents and events.

From the object-oriented perspective, the initial ARTC system is described by a simplistic model with four classes, namely *Detector, TrafficController, Road* and *Optimizer*. The UML class diagram of initial ARTC system is shown in Fig. 2.

The UML sequence diagram have accomplished the task of showing how the objects interact with each other in scenario. We will portray our approach with the two significant methods: *gettrafficFlow()* and *optimizeTraffic()*. The sequence diagram for Scenario of functional processes is depicted in Fig. 3.

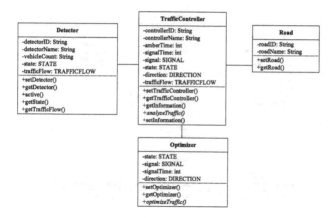

Fig. 2. The initial class diagram of ARTC system

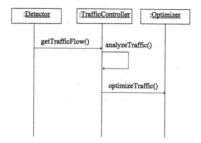

Fig. 3. Sequence diagram for calculating optimal control

4.2   Selected Patterns

In Fig. 2, the method *optimizeTraffic()* belong to class *Optimizer*, which is employed to optimize light signals of the ARTC system. However, the system design may have following problems with the *optimizeTraffic()* of the class *Optimizer*:

– Algorithms are so **complex** to implement in one, therefore make the source code as large and arduous to maintain.
– It takes **time** as well as **effort** to add new algorithms to the existing ones.
– The code of the existing algorithms are **difficult to reuse**, especially when one want to create a hierarchy from *Optimizer* class.

In order to overcome these limitations and improve the system, we are going to optimize it by using **Strategy pattern**. As illustrated in Fig. 4, we detach three optimization strategies (*SignalOptimizeStrategy, TimeLimitOptimizeStrategy, AdjacentOptimizeStrategy*) from the class *Optimizer* then formed a hierarchy of algorithm classes that share the interface *OptimizerStrategy*. After applying Strategy pattern, the sequence diagram of the scenario calculating optimal control is re-drawn in Fig. 5.

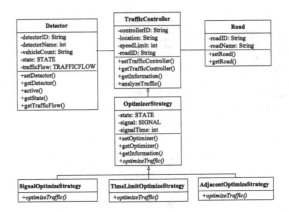

Fig. 4. Class diagram of ARTC system after applying Strategy pattern

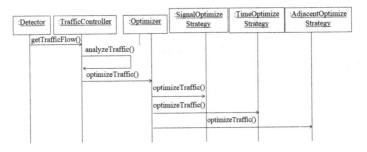

Fig. 5. Sequence diagram for calculating optimal control after applying Strategy pattern

4.3 Behaviour Preservation

ARTC system has a real time characteristic because of immediate responses to variant of traffic flow conditions, some identified constraints need to be preserved are[1]:

- If the **state** is *heavyTraffic* and the **signal** is *red*, it will be ensured that the **signal** is turned to *green*.
- If the **state** is *lowTraffic* and **signal** is *red*, it will be ensured that the **signal-Time** is increased.
- If the **state** is *highTraffic* and **direction** is *noChoose*, it will be ensured that the **direction** is turned to *choose*.

If we implement these constraints as a purely Java code, it may be not enough to guarantee the correct behavioral execution. As a consequence, we employ the JML' code to annotate it in order to two purposes, firstly, ensuring the performance of the source code is correctly, secondly, automated validation of software programs.

---

[1] Due to space considerations, we do not display completed constraints here.

5   Approach to Checking Consistency

5.1   Formal Representation of a Software Program

In order to automated checking the consistency between two programs after applying design patterns in refactoring, we introduce a formal representation of a software program as follows:

Definition 1 (Program). *A program P is formally represented by a 2-tuple $\langle C_P, S_P \rangle$, where C_P is a set of classes and S_P is a sequence of method invocation statements in the main body of a program.*

Definition 2 (Class). *A class $C_{i_P} \in C_P$ is represented by a 3-tuple $C_{i_P} = \left\langle M_{C_{i_P}}, A_{C_{i_P}}, I_{C_{i_P}} \right\rangle$, where $M_{C_{i_P}}$ is a set of public methods, $A_{C_{i_P}}$ is a set of public attributes, and $I_{C_{i_P}}$ states a set of class invariants.*

Definition 3 (Method precondition). *The precondition $PRE_{m_{i_P}}$ of the method $m_{e_i} \in M_{C_{i_P}}$ in the class C_{i_P}, is a condition that it has to satisfy when it begins to execute.*

Definition 4 (Method postcondition). *The postcondition $POST_{m_{i_P}}$ of the method $m_{e_i} \in M_{C_{i_P}}$ in the class C_{i_P}, is a condition that it has to satisfy after executing.*

In Definition 1, S_P is a set of sequence statements of invoking methods which begins with the entry point of the main function in program P. In this paper, we employ the "*scenario*" term to refer the S_P signal.

Definition 5 (Scenario). *A scenario S_P is represented by a 4-tuple $S_P = \langle C_{S_P}, PRE_{S_P}, M_{S_P}, POST_{S_P} \rangle$, where $C_{S_P} \subseteq C_P$ represents a set of classes involved in the scenario, PRE_{S_P} is the scenario precondition, M_{S_P} is a sequence of methods of involved classes, and $POST_{S_P}$ states the scenario postcondition.*

Definition 6 (Scenario method). *A method in the scenario is a 4-tuple $M_{k_{S_P}} = \left\langle PRE_{k_{S_P}}, M_{k_{S_P}}, POST_{k_{S_P}}, k \right\rangle$, where $PRE_{k_{S_P}}$ states the method precondition, $M_{k_{S_P}}$ is the public method of the involved in the scenario, $POST_{k_{S_P}}$ is the method postcondition, and k is the execution order of method in the scenario.*

In this paper, we consider the case that pre/postcondition of a method is the conjunction of predicates on the attributes of classes involved in the scenario, i.e., $PRE_{k_{S_P}} = \bigwedge P(A_{CijP})$, where $A_{CijP} \in A_{CiP}$ is a attribute, $CiP \subseteq C_{SiP}$ and P is predicate. A scenario consists of a sequence of methods, hence its pre/postcondition are formed by their pre/postcondition. A scenario pre/postcondition is defined on pre/postconditions of all methods involved in the scenario as follows.

Definition 7 (Scenario precondition). *The scenario precondition PRE_{S_P} is defined by the precondition of the first happened method in the scenario.*

The precondition of the first method in the scenario specifies constraints of all scenario-related public attributes.

Definition 8 (Scenario postcondition). *The scenario postcondition $POST_{S_P}$ is defined by the conjunction of the constraint on public attribute A_{C_P} in the method postcondition $POST_{k_{S_P}}$ of the last happened method in M_{S_P}.*

Let a scenario $S = (m_1, m_2, ..m_n)$, where m_i, $i = \overline{1..n}$, is the i-th method happened in the scenario. From Definition 6, we have $m_i = (pre_{mi}, m_{mi}, post_{mi}, i)$ and $post_{(}mi) = \bigwedge P_k(A_kC)$, where P_k are the predicate on A_kC, which is the attribute of class C involved in the scenario. Assume that the scenario has one public attribute A_C that appears in both postconditions of two methods m_i and m_j such that $1 \leq i < j \leq n$. Then we have $post_{mi} = P_i(A_C)$ and $post_{mj} = P_j(A_C)$. Since m_i happens before m_j, $P_j(A_C)$ must be hold after executing the j-th method.

Definition 9 (Refactor). *A refactor R using design patterns is denoted $R : P \xmapsto{D} P'$, where P and P' are the original program and its evolution, respectively, D is the applied pattern name.*

5.2 Consistency Rules of Program Refactoring

In Subsect. 5.1, we address that the pre/postcondition of a scenario can be computed from pre/postcondition of involved operations. In practice, the execution of a scenario must be preserved its pre/postcondition.

Proposition 1 (Execution preservation of original program). A program P is said to be execution preservation if with each scenario, its preconditions and its postconditions are preserved before and after execution, respectively.

Formally, $PRE_{S_P}[S_P]POST_{S_P}$.

Proposition 2 (Execution preservation of refactored program). A refactored program P' is said to be execution preservation with the original one P if with the same scenario execution, its preconditions are preserved before and its postconditions are hold after execution.

Formally, $PRE_{S_P}[S_{P'}]POST_{S_P}$.

In this proposition, the scenario pre/postcondition of the refactored program are figured out through the scenario one of the original program according to Definitions 7 and 8.

5.3 Applying the Proposed Approach to Check the Execution Preservation of ARTC System

Back to the example in Sect. 4, all initial behaviors specification of the ARTC system have been validated checking on Eclipse software by plug-in OpenJML.

Now, after refactoring, we are going to consider whether evolution program is satisfied all behaviors specification of initial program or not?

In experiments, we have carried out the implementation the source code of the ARTC system after refactoring. Based on the set of rules which was built in these Section, we have shown the pre/postcondition of the evolution scenario as well as checked the constraints on it. The experimental results are illustrated in Fig. 6.

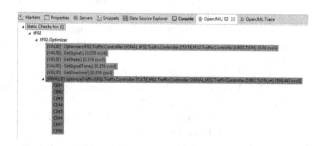

Fig. 6. The result of checking behavior preservation on refactored program

In other words, the refactored program not preserves all behaviors of initial program in execution, so it should consideration how to the corrected refactoring process.

6 Conclusion and Future Work

In this paper, we have proposed an approach to verify the execution preservation of refactored program which is performed by design patterns in software program. In addition, JML is used to describe constraints of class behaviors. We have proposed consistent rules to verify if the scenario execution of the original program and refactored one is preserved the same constraints in evolution process.

It has been many works to check the consistency of a program, however, these works focus on the consistency between different phases of life cycle development model (e.g., implementation and design phase) or different diagrams of a model (e.g., state diagrams and sequence diagrams), but our research pays attention in checking consistency between original program and its evolution in the implement phase.

To demonstrate the approach, we have implemented a program of an ARTC system in UML. In the case study, we have just illustrated only the consistency verification when applying Strategy pattern in the only a pair of scenario, respectively in the both programs, others scenarios may be done in a similar way for the more complex system.

As portrayed in the case study, we can see that the calculation of pre and post-condition of scenarios is time-consuming and error-prone if we do it manually. For the future works, we will adopt tools to calculate automatically constraints and verify the program evolution process.

References

1. Alexander, C., Ishikawa, S., Silverstein, M.: Pattern Languages. Center for Environmental Structure, vol. 2 (1977)
2. Bottoni, P., Parisi-Presicce, F., Taentzer, G.: Coordinated distributed diagram transformation for software evolution. Electron. Notes Theoret. Comput. Sci. **72**(4), 59–70 (2003)
3. Burdy, L., Cheon, Y., Cok, D.R., Ernst, M.D., Kiniry, J.R., Leavens, G.T., Rustan, K., Leino, M., Poll, E.: An overview of JML tools and applications. Int. J. Softw. Tools Technol. Transfer **7**(3), 212–232 (2005)
4. Cok, D.R.: OpenJML: software verification for Java 7 using JML, OpenJDK, and Eclipse. arXiv preprint arXiv:1404.6608 (2014)
5. Dong, J., Sheng, Y., Zhang, K.: A model transformation approach for design pattern evolutions. In: 2006 13th Annual IEEE International Symposium and Workshop on Engineering of Computer Based Systems, ECBS 2006, pp. 10–92 (2006)
6. Gamma, E., Helm, R., Johnson, R., Vlissides, J.: Design Patterns: Elements of Reusable Object-Oriented Software. Addison-Wesley Longman Publishing Co., Inc., Boston (1995)
7. Leavens, G.T., Baker, A.L., Ruby, C.: Preliminary design of JML: a behavioral interface specification language for Java. ACM SIGSOFT Softw. Eng. Notes **31**(3), 1–38 (2006)
8. Leavens, G.T., Poll, E., Clifton, C., Cheon, Y., Ruby, C., Cok, D., Müller, P., Kiniry, J., Chalin, P., Zimmerman, D.M., et al.: JML reference manual (2008)
9. Mens, T., Tourwe, T.: A survey of software refactoring. IEEE Trans. Software Eng. **30**(2), 126–139 (2004)
10. Opdyke, W.F.: Refactoring: a program restructuring aid in designing object-oriented application frameworks. Ph.D. thesis, University of Illinois at Urbana-Champaign (1992)
11. Roberts, D.B., Johnson, R.: Practical analysis for refactoring. University of Illinois at Urbana-Champaign (1999)
12. Zhao, C., Kong, J., Zhang, K.: Design pattern evolution and verification using graph transformation. In: 2007 40th Annual Hawaii International Conference on System Sciences, HICSS 2007, p. 290a, January 2007

A New Method to Analyze Graphical User Interfaces of Android Applications

Hong Anh Le[1][✉] and Ninh Thuan Truong[2]

[1] Hanoi University of Mining and Geology,
18 Pho Vien, Bac Tu Liem, Hanoi, Vietnam
lehonganh@humg.edu.vn
[2] VNU - University of Engineering and Technology,
144 Xuan Thuy, Cau Giay, Hanoi, Vietnam
thuantn@vnu.edu.vn

Abstract. In recent years, the number of Android smartphones increase dramatically and new applications are added numerously in Google store. Android developers usually have to deal with the difficulties such as limited capacity battery, screen design, and limited resources. Among them, specifying graphical user interfaces (GUI) of an application is one of the most important issues. This paper presents a new method to analyze GUI specifications of an Android application. We employ Event-B formal method and its refinement mechanism to formalize the specifications and to check if the constraints are satisfied. A running example of a Note application is given to illustrate the proposed method in detail.

Keywords: GUI specification · Event-B · Android applications

1 Introduction

With the rapid development of hardware technologies, smartphones become more powerful and much cheaper than ten years ago. Smartphones provide many advanced utilities to users and are in hands of a lot of people around the world. In the smartphone market, the devices using Android operating system contribute to around 65% in 2016. Currently, Google play store, the biggest market, contains more than 1.5 billions applications.

In software development process, specifying GUI is one of the most important step. Specifically, GUI of an mobile application becomes more critical because of various screen resolutions and limited resources. The developers who are based on the collection of GUI requirements design the screens and activities of their components before they actually write the code of the application. The GUI requirement documents often consist of UI objects and their semantic executions. One problem arises is that GUI specifications come with informal representation. Software developers, therefore, might misunderstand or can not realize the defects of GUI specifications. The earlier these faults are detected, the smaller cost of development is.

© ICST Institute for Computer Sciences, Social Informatics and Telecommunications Engineering 2017
P. Cong Vinh et al. (Eds.): ICCASA 2016, LNICST 193, pp. 111–120, 2017.
DOI: 10.1007/978-3-319-56357-2_12

Formal methods have been used for describing, validating, and verifying GUI specifications of software systems. Authors [10] proposed a formal language, Fruit (Functional Reactive User Interface Toolkit), to write concise specification of GUI programs. Some model-based approaches [4,12,13] using different kinds of existing methods, e.g. Petri Nets, Z, Spec#, to formally describe GUI requirements. Mobile developers design GUI with components provided in the rich Android GUI framework. These existing methods are not specified enough for analyzing Android GUI designs. Hence, formally checking the design to find defects is an emerging issue and is needed to be more investigated.

This paper present a new method which employs Event-B [2] and its refinement mechanism to model and verify Android GUI requirements. Event-B, which uses set theory as modeling notations and mathematical proofs, is suitable for system modeling. The Event-B refinement allows to develop the system from abstract level to more concrete and precise levels. Moreover, we can make use of many platforms supported for Event-B such as RODIN to specify and to prove desired properties either automatically or iteratively. After verification phase at design level, EventB2Java or EventB2C can be used to generate executable programs from Event-B models. The contributions of the paper are (1) presents a formalization of Android GUI requirements in Event-B notations, (2) proposes refinement-based approach of GUI modeling which is suitable for mobile software development, and (3) shows that desired properties can be verified in the RODIN and the resulted Event-B models can be translated into executable implementations.

The rest of the paper is organized as follows. Section 2 provides a brief introduction of GUI design, Event-B, and the RODIN platform. The main work of the paper is presented in Sect. 3. In the next section, we apply the proposed method to analyze a Note application. Section 5 outlines some related work. Finally, Sect. 6 concludes the paper and gives some research directions.

2   Background

In this section, we outline some principles of GUI design in software system as well as in Android smartphone. After that, Event-B and its support tool RODIN is sketched.

2.1   GUI Design

The user interface is one of the most important parts of a software system. It defines how users interact with the system, e.g. using hands, keyboards, and voice, and how the system delivers the results to users, e.g. via screens and voice. Designing GUI is a subset of Human-Computer interaction studies.

GUI of Android applications contains a collection of graphical elements, e.g., Layout, Text, Button, etc., provided by the framework. Android framework provides several ways to intercept events from users' interaction with View or Activity class. An Activity provides a window screen for users to interact with the application. An application usually contains multiple activities in which a main activity is defined for the first appeared screen when lunching the application. An activity has four essential states such as *running* (the activity is in the foreground), *paused* (it has lost focus but still visible), *stopped* (the activity retains all its data but is invisible), and *destroyed* (the activity is killed from the memory).

2.2   Event-B

Event-B is a kind of formal method which combines mathematical techniques from the set theory and the first order logic. It is an evolution of B-method. Event-B is suitable for modeling large and reactive systems. The basic structure of an Event B model consists of a MACHINE and a CONTEXT.

Contexts form the static part of the model while machines form the dynamic part. Contexts can extend (or be extended by) other context and are referred (seen) by machines. Being considered as the static part of the model, the context is used to store, for instance, the types and constants used during the development of the system. The machine contains the dynamic part of the model. It describes the system state, the operations to interact with the environment together with the properties, conditions and constraints on the model. A Machine is defined by a set of clauses which is able to refine another Machine. We briefly introduce main concepts of an machine as follows:

- Variables: represents the state variables of the model of the specification.
- Invariants: describes by first order logic expressions, the properties of the attributes defined in the variable clauses. Typing information, functional and safety properties are described in this clause. These properties are true in the whole model. Invariants need to be preserved by events clauses.
- Events: $E(v)$ present transitions between states. Each event has the form $evt =$ **any** x **where** $G(x, v)$ **then** $A(x, v, v')$ **end**, where x are local variables of the event, $G(x, v)$ is a guard condition and $A(x, v, v')$ is an action. An event is enabled when its guard condition is satisfied. The event action consists of one or more assignments. We have three kinds of assignments for expressing the actions associated with an event: (1) a deterministic multiple assignment $(v := E(t, v))$, (2) an empty assignment (skip), or (3) a non-deterministic multiple assignment $(v : |P(t, v, x'))$.

A Context consists of the following items:

- Sets: describes a set of abstract and enumerated types.
- Constants: represents the constants used by the model.
- Axioms: describes with first order logic expressions, the properties of the attributes defined in the CONSTANTS clause. Types and constraints are described in this clause.

To deal with complexity in modeling systems, Event-B provides a refinement mechanism that allows us to build the system gradually by adding more details to get a more precise model. A concrete Event-B machine can refine at most one abstract machine. A refined machine usually has more variables than its abstraction as we have new variables to represent more details of the model. In superposition refinement, the abstract variables are retained in the concrete machine, with possibly some additional variables. In data refinement, the abstract variables v are replaced by concrete ones w. Subsequently, the connections between them are represented by the relationship between v and w, i.e. gluing invariants $J(v, w)$.

2.3 RODIN

Rodin, an extension of the Eclipse platform, allows to create Event-B models with an editor. It also automatically generates the proof obligations of a model that can be discharged automatically or interactively. The architecture of the tool is illustrated in Fig. 1. Event-B UI provides users interfaces to edit Event-B models. Event-B Core has three components: static checker (checking the syntax of Event-B models), the proof obligation generator (producing simplified proof obligations that make them easier to discharge automatically), and the proof obligation manager (managing proof obligations and the associated proofs). The Rodin Core consists of two components: the Rodin repository (managing persistence of data elements) and the Rodin builder (scheduling jobs depending on changes made to files in the Rodin repository).

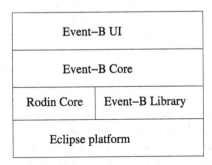

Fig. 1. Rodin tool architecture

3 Refinement-Based Approach to Analyzing Android GUI Designs

In this section, we first introduce the overall picture of our proposed method. After that, The formalization of Android GUI elements is given. Following this, we show how to model this formalization in Event-B notations and verify the desired properties with RODIN platform.

3.1   The Approach Overview

In the early phase of software development process, stakeholders often work together to initially define the GUI of the software. They then can add more precise and detail descriptions to GUI designs of the application. GUI design specifications of a general software system as well as Android applications describe the structure of each screen which is composed of UI elements and explain expected results or logic flows when users interact with these elements. The proposed approach consists of several steps depicted in Fig. 2.

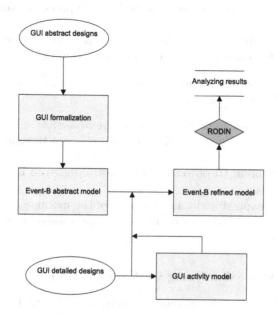

Fig. 2. The approach overview

The first steps in the proposed method is formalizing informal abstract GUI requirements and encoding them in Event-B notations. Along with development iterative phases, GUI designs are being more precise and detailed. These requirements, based on the refinement mechanism, are added to create a concrete Event-B one. The archived Event-B models in each steps can be verified via RODIN platform and its support plug-ins.

3.2   Formalization of Android GUI Elements

An Android application is different from an Android service as it has the GUI for users' interactions. Its GUI design describe each screen of the application which consists of UI elements, events, and corresponding actions. We define an application P as a 3-tuple $\langle W, S, C \rangle$, where

- W: a set of screens which are provided by *Activity* class in the framework.
- S: denotes the states of each screen including three essential ones of an Android activity.
- C: states the global constraints between screens.

Each screen composed of a collection of UI objects, events, and the corresponding actions. A screen $s \in S$ is formally defined as a 3-tuple $\langle Go, Ev, Ac \rangle$, where

- Go: denotes a set of graphical objects used in the screen. An object $o \in Go = \langle Pr, St \rangle$, where Pr and St represents its dynamic properties and state values respectively.
- Ev: states the intercept events when users interact with the screen.
- Ac: represents the consequences after the corresponding events happen.

Following the above definitions, we propose some rules to encode GUI requirements in Event-B notation as follows.

1. A screen s is mapped to an Event-B machine M.
2. Dynamic properties Pr of an UI object $o \in Go$ are translated to Event-B variables.
3. State values St of an UI object $o \in Go$ are translated to Event-B sets, constants, or axioms.
4. Events Ev are mapped naturally to events of the machine M.
5. Actions Ac associated with an event $e \in Ev$ are translated to assignments in THEN clauses of e.

3.3   Refinement for Analyzing GUI Specifications

In Sect. 3.2, we formalize the individual screen of an Android application with Event-B notations. One issue raised in verifying GUI specification is that analyzing multiple screens and verify the constraints between them. For simplicity, let assume that the application starts from the main activity, then goes into several branches. We continue to exploit Event-B refinement to formalize these (Fig. 3).

Following the rules presented in Sect. 3.2, we start by translating the main activity into the first abstract Event-B model. Then, we can visit other n screens from it. These, using the main activity's states, are modeled by refining the first abstract model. The remaining screens are modeled analogously.

4   A Running Example: Note Application

4.1   GUI Specifications

Note is a king of basic and popular Android applications providing users functionalities to create and view their personal memorial notes. It basically consists of four activities including *MainActivity*, *CreateActivity*, *EditActivity*, and

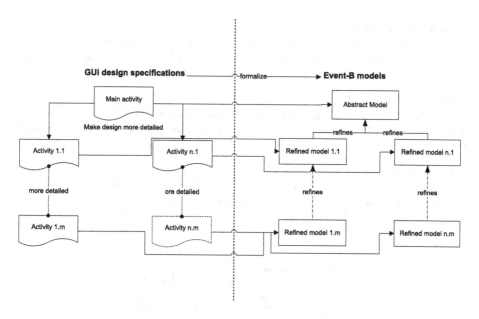

Fig. 3. Refinement for modeling UI designs

ViewActivity where *MainActivity* is the start-up screen. From the main screen, users can visit *CreateActivity*, *EditActivity*, or *ViewActivity* screens.

The *CreateActivity* screen has two events which are attached to two buttons such as *Save* and *Cancel*. The former allows users to save the note and go back to the previous screen. When users press the latter, they will ignore the current note and go back to the previous screen. The *EditActivity* screen acts in the similar way. The *ViewActivity* has only *Close* button to return the previous screen.

The application has to meet the requirement that only one of three screens *EditActivity*, *ViewActivity*, and *CreateActivity* activates at the same time. If *MainActivity* is active, then all other screens are destroyed.

4.2 Modeling and Verifying GUI Designs

We apply the proposed refinement-based approach to modeling the GUI specifications of *Note* application as follows.

Step 1. Initial model

The main activity is modeled as a context C_0 containing a set S representing four essential states of an Android activity and an abstract machine M_0 which *sees* C_0 and has four BOOL variables *main*, *createAtive*, *editActive*, and *viewActive* representing the active status of four activities.

Step 2. Refinement
CreateActivity is added into the design. This activity is modeled by a refined machine *M_CREATE* which refines machine *M_MAIN* and has a more variable *memo* and two events *Save* and *Cancel*.

Step 3. Refinement
Similarly, *EditActivity* is formalized by a refined machine *M_EDIT* which refines machine *M_MAIN* and has a more variable *memo* and two events *Save* and *Cancel*.

Step 4. Refinement
ViewActivity is modeled by a refined machine *M_VIEW* which refines machine *M_MAIN* and has a more variable *memo* and one event *Cancel*.

The paradigm of the translated model is depicted in Fig. 4.

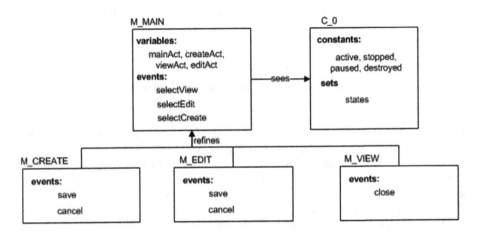

Fig. 4. Structure of the target model

The behavior constraints are formalized as two invariants:

$INV1$: ($editState = active \implies \neg(viewState = active \lor createsState = active) \land (viewState = active \implies \neg(editState = active \lor createsState = active) \land (createState = active \implies \neg(viewState = active \lor editState = active)$
and

$INV2$: $mainState = active \implies viewState = destroyed \land createState = destroyed \land editState = destroyed$

Verification results are depicted in Table 1. One discharged PO of *M_View* shows that in the screen *ViewActivity*, if users click *Save* button, it leads to the violation of the behavior constraint[1].

---

[1] The RODIN archive can be downloaded at http://125.212.233.56/NoteExample.zip.

Table 1. PO obligations statistics in RODIN

Machine	Total POs	Auto	Manual	Discharged
M_Main	19	19	0	0
M_Create	14	14	0	0
M_Edit	14	14	0	0
M_View	14	13	0	1

5   Related Work

GUI modeling is an emerging issue extracting many researchers. Many papers have been dedicated to formal modeling and checking UI specifications with different techniques. Bowen [5] provides formal notations of X11 programs' UI based on Z language. The author precisely specifies operations such as create, manipulate, and destroy windows to avoid ambiguity UI requirements. This method, however, does not provide a way to verify the desired properties. Clement, in [8], adopts VDM and its proof obligations to develop Window interfaces. The approach also makes use of VDM support tools to generate the implementation of the system in Prolog language. The difference between this paper and their paper is that we can generate the executable program in several languages (e.g., Java, C++) from the target Event-B model. Palanque *et al.* present a formalism called Interactive Cooperative Objects, which is based on high-level Petri nets. Their proposed approach is suitable for discrete interaction between users and application. It can check several properties of interface requirements such as absence of a deadlock, integrity constraints, etc. Judy Bowen *et al.*, in [4], integrate both user-centric design methods and Z formal method to propose a formal model of UI. The works presented in [3,9] also use Event-B proof obligations as the foundation to validate HCI requirements. These works need a hypothesis that the requirements are described in Concur Task Tree (CTT) models.

The common issue of these papers, in our opinions, is that they are unspecific enough to apply for Android applications in which dialogs inherit *Acivity* class. One of advantages of our method is that we can apply the tool, in [7], to generate Android codes from Event-B models.

6   Conclusions and Future Work

GUI requirement analysis plays an important role in mobile application development. Many work has been dedicated to GUI verification at early phase to reduce the cost. In this paper, we propose a new refinement-based method for modeling and verifying Android GUI designs. The defects of the design can be realized at any refinement step. Desired properties can be checked based on the generated proof obligations and almost be proved automatically. One limitation of this method is that Event-B primitives data type are not rich enough to describe all Android UI elements. This, however, can be overcome by incorporating with

Theory Plugin [6] to define more data structures. We also intend to expand this work with analyzing concurrency issues of Android application interfaces.

Acknowledgments. This work is partly supported by the project no. 102.03–2014.40 granted by Vietnam National Foundation for Science and Technology Development (Nafosted).

References

1. Event-B and the Rodin platform (2012). http://www.event-b.org
2. Abrial, J.-R.: Modeling in Event-B: System and Software Engineering, 1st edn. Cambridge University Press, New York (2010)
3. Ait-Ameur, Y., Baron, M.: Formal and experimental validation approaches in hci systems design based on a shared event b model. Int. J. Softw. Tools Technol. Transf. **8**(6), 547–563 (2006)
4. Bowen, J., Reeves, S.: Formal models for informal GUI designs. Electron. Notes Theor. Comput. Sci. **183**, 57–72 (2007)
5. Bowen, J.P.: X: why z? Comput. Graph. Forum **11**, 221–234 (1990)
6. Butler, M., Maamria, I.: Practical theory extension in event-b. In: Liu, Z., Woodcock, J., Zhu, H. (eds.) Theories of Programming and Formal Methods. LNCS, vol. 8051, pp. 67–81. Springer, Heidelberg (2013). doi:10.1007/978-3-642-39698-4_5
7. Cataño, N., Rivera, V.: EventB2Java: a code generator for event-b. In: Rayadurgam, S., Tkachuk, O. (eds.) NFM 2016. LNCS, vol. 9690, pp. 166–171. Springer, Cham (2016). doi:10.1007/978-3-319-40648-0_13
8. Clement, T.: The formal development of a windows interface. In: Proceedings of the 3rd BCS-FACS Conference on Northern Formal Methods (3FACS 1998), p. 6, Swinton, UK. British Computer Society (1998)
9. Cortier, A., d'Ausbourg, B., Aït-Ameur, Y.: Formal validation of java/swing user interfaces with the event b method. In: Jacko, J.A. (ed.) HCI 2007. LNCS, vol. 4550, pp. 1062–1071. Springer, Heidelberg (2007). doi:10.1007/978-3-540-73105-4_116
10. Courtney, A.A.: Modeling user interfaces in a functional language. Ph.D. thesis, New Haven, CT, USA. AAI3125177 (2004)
11. Le, H.A., Nakajima, S., Truong, N.T.: Formal analysis of imprecise system requirements with event-b. SpringerPlus **5**(1), 1000 (2016)
12. Palanque, P., Paternó, F. (eds.): Formal Methods in Human-Computer Interaction, 1st edn. Springer, New York (1998)
13. Palanque, P.A., Bastide, R.: Petri net based design of user-driven interfaces using the interactive cooperative objects formalism. In: Paternó, F. (ed.) Interactive Systems: Design, Specification, and Verification. Focus on Computer Graphics: Tutorials and Perspectives in Computer Graphics. Springer, Heidelberg (1995)

An Efficient Method for Time Series Join on Subsequence Correlation Using Longest Common Substring Algorithm

Vo Duc Vinh[1]([✉]), Nguyen Phuc Chau[1], and Duong Tuan Anh[2]

[1] Faculty of Information Technology, Ton Duc Thang University, Ho Chi Minh City, Vietnam
voducvinh@tdt.edu.vn, 51303240@student.tdt.edu.vn
[2] Faculty of Computer Science and Engineering, Ho Chi Minh City University of Technology,
Ho Chi Minh City, Vietnam
dtanh@cse.hcmut.edu.vn

Abstract. Joining two time series on subsequence correlation provides useful information about the synchronization of the time series. However, finding the exact subsequence which are most correlated is an expensive computational task. Although the current efficient exact method, JOCOR, requires $O(n^2 lgn)$, where n is the length of the time series, it is still very time-consuming even for time series datasets with medium length. In this paper, we propose an approximate method, LCS-JOCOR, in order to reduce the runtime of JOCOR. Our proposed method consists of three steps. First, two original time series are transformed into two corresponding strings by PAA transformation and SAX discretization. Second, we apply an algorithm to efficiently find the longest common substrings (LCS) of two strings. Finally, the resulting LCSs are mapped back to the original time series to find the most correlated subsequence by JOCOR method. In comparison to JOCOR, our proposed method performs much faster while high accuracy is guaranteed.

Keywords: Time series · Subsequence join · Longest common substring · Correlation coefficient

1 Introduction

Joining two time series on subsequence correlation is considered as a basic problem in time series data mining and appears in many practical applications such as entertainment, meteorology, economy, finance, medicine, and engineering [2]. Assume that we have two time series representing the runoffs at the two measurement stations in Mekong River, Vietnam as in Fig. 1. Meteorologists may concern about in what periods the runoffs of these two stations (in pink curve and dotted curve in Fig. 1) are similar. Subsequence join can bring out some useful information about the runoffs at different stations in the same river by finding subsequences which are most correlated based on some distance function (see the red (bold) subsequence in Fig. 1). Moreover, this approach can be extended easily to find *all* pairs of subsequences from the two time series that are considered similar. Thanks to these resultant subsequences, meteorologists can predict about the runoff of the river in future.

© ICST Institute for Computer Sciences, Social Informatics and Telecommunications Engineering 2017
P. Cong Vinh et al. (Eds.): ICCASA 2016, LNICST 193, pp. 121–131, 2017.
DOI: 10.1007/978-3-319-56357-2_13

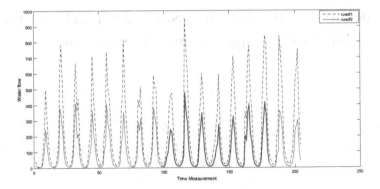

Fig. 1. Two time series of the runoff at the two stations in Mekong River, Vietnam. (Color figure online)

The subsequence join over time series can be viewed in different aspects. The first view is joining two time series based on their timestamps [8]. This approach does not carry out any similarity comparison because it just concerns about the high availability of timestamps and ignores the content of time series data. The second view of subsequence join is based on a nested-loop algorithm and some distance functions like Euclidian distance or Dynamic Time Warping [6, 7]. This joining approach returns all pairs of subsequences drawn from two time series that satisfy a given similarity threshold. This approach has some disadvantages such as time consumption because distance function is called many times over a lot of iterations. Moreover, the threshold for determining the resulting sets needs to be given by user. To reduce the runtime for nested-loop algorithm, some works tend to approximately estimate the similarity between two time series by dividing time series into segments. In this approach, Y. Lin et al. [6] introduced solutions for joining two time series based on a non-uniform segmentation and a similarity function over a feature-set. Their method is not only difficult to implement but also requires high computational complexity, especially for large time series data. To avoid these drawbacks, the work in [7] proposed joining based on important extreme points to segment time series. And then, the authors applied Dynamic Time Warping function to calculate the distance between two subsequences. The resulting sets are determined based on a threshold given from user. Although this method executes very fast, it may suffer some false dismissals because it ignores some data points when shifting the sliding window several data points at a time.

A recent work on subsequence join proposed by Mueen et al. in 2014 [2] can find the *exact* correlated subsequence. Mueen et al. introduced an exhaustive searching method, JOCOR, for discovering the most correlated subsequence based on maximizing Pearson's correlation coefficient in two given time series. Although the authors incorporated several speeding-up techniques to reduce the complexity from $O(n^4)$ to $O(n^2 lgn)$, where n is the length of two time series, the runtime of JOCOR is still unacceptable even for many time series datasets with moderate size. For example, running JOCOR on the input time series with length of 40000 data points will take more than 12 days to find the resulting subsequence. Furthermore, in [2], Mueen et al. also proposed an approximate method, α-approximate-JOCOR. This algorithm finds the nearly exact correlation subsequence by assigning the step size a value greater than one in each iteration depending on datasets. A natural question arises as to what reasonable value for step size. This is like a blind search.

To improve the time efficiency of JOCOR algorithm, in this work, our proposed method combines PAA dimensionality reduction, SAX discretization and an efficient Longest Common Substring algorithm to find the candidates of the most correlated subsequence before applying the JOCOR algorithm to post-process the candidates. The preprocessing helps to speed-up the process of finding the most correlated subsequence without causing any false dismissals. The experiment results demonstrate that our proposed method not only is more accurate than α-approximate-JOCOR but also achieves the high accuracy, even 100%, when being compared to *exact* JOCOR while the time efficiency is much better.

2 Background

2.1 Basic Concepts

Definition 1. A *time series* $T = t_1, t_2, ..., t_n$ is a sequence of n data points measured at equal periods, where n is the length of the time series. For most applications, each data point is usually represented by a real value.

Definition 2. Given a time series $T = t_1, t_2, ..., t_n$ of length n, a *subsequence $T[i: i + m -1] = t_i, t_{i+1}, ..., t_{i+m-1}$* is a continuous subsequence of T, starting at position i and length m ($m \leq n$).

This work aims to approximately join two time series T_1 and T_2 of length n_1 and n_2, respectively. The problem of time series join was defined by Mueen et al. [2] which is described as follows.

Problem 1. *(Max-Correlation Join)*: Given two time series T_1 and T_2 of length n_1 and n_2, respectively (assume $n_1 \geq n_2$), find the most correlated subsequences of T_1 and T_2 with *length $\geq$ minlength*.

The definition for Problem 1 can be extended to find *α-Approximate join*.

Problem 2. *(α-Approximate Join)*: Given two time series T_1 and T_2 of length n_1 and n_2, respectively, find the subsequences of T_1 and T_2 with *length $\geq$ minlength* such that the correlation between the subsequences is within α of the most correlated segments.

When joining two time series, we refer to finding the most correlated subsequence by calculating Pearson's correlation coefficient. The correlation coefficient is defined as follows.

$$C(x, y) = \frac{1}{n} \sum_{i=0}^{n-1} \left(\frac{x_i - \mu_x}{\sigma_x} \right) \left(\frac{y_i - \mu_y}{\sigma_y} \right) \tag{1}$$

where x and y are two given time series of equal length n, with average values μ_x and μ_y, and standard deviations σ_x and σ_y, respectively.

The value of Pearson's correlation coefficient ranges in $[-1, 1]$. Besides, the z-normalized Euclidean distance is also a commonly used measure in time series data mining. The distance between two time series $X = x_1, x_2,\ldots, x_n$ and $Y = y_1, y_2,\ldots, y_n$ with the same length n is calculated by:

$$d(x,y) = \sqrt{\sum_{i=1}^{n} (\hat{x}_i - \hat{y}_i)^2} \qquad (2)$$

where $\hat{x}_i = \dfrac{1}{\sigma_x}(x_i - \mu_x)$ and $\hat{y}_i = \dfrac{1}{\sigma_y}(y_i - \mu_y)$

Because we just pay attention to maximizing positive correlations and ignore the negatively correlated subsequences, we can take advantage of the relationship between Euclidian distance and positive correlation as follows.

$$C(x,y) = 1 - \frac{dist^2(x,y)}{2n} \qquad (3)$$

In this work, we will take advantage of statistics for computing correlation coefficient as follows.

$$C(x,y) = \frac{\sum xy - n\mu_x\mu_y}{n\sigma_x\sigma_y} \qquad (4)$$

$$d(x,y) = \sqrt{2n(1 - C(x,y))} \qquad (5)$$

This approach brings us two benefits. Firstly, the algorithm just takes one pass to compute all of these statistic variables. Secondly, it enables us to reuse computations and reduce the amortized time complexity to *constant* instead of *linear* [2]. In this paper, the above formulas will be used for computing correlation coefficient and z-normalized Euclidian distance between two subsequences.

2.2 Symbolic Aggregate Approximation (SAX)

A time series $T = t_1 \ldots t_n$ of length n can be represented in a reduced w-dimensional space as another time series $D = d_1 \ldots d_w$ by segmenting T into w equally-sized segments and then replacing each segment by its mean value d_i. This dimensionality reduction technique is called Piecewise Aggregate Approximation (PAA) [4]. After this step, the time series D is transformed into a symbolic sequence $A = a_1 \ldots a_w$ in which each real value d_i is mapped to a symbol a_i through a table look-up. The lookup table contains the *breakpoints* that divide a Gaussian distribution in an arbitrary number (from 3 to 10) of equi-probable regions. This discretization is called Symbolic Aggregate Approximation

(SAX) [5] which is based on the assumption that the reduced time series have a Gaussian distribution.

Given two time series Q and C of the same length n, we transform the original time series into PAA representations, Q' and C', we can define lower bounding approximation of the Euclidean distance between the original time series by:

$$DR(Q', C') = \sqrt{\frac{n}{w}} \sqrt{\sum_{i=1}^{w} (q_i' - c_i')^2} \tag{6}$$

When we transform further the data into SAX representations, i.e. two symbolic strings Q'' and C'', we can define a MINDIST function that returns the minimum distance between the original time series of two words:

$$MINDIST(Q'', C'') = \sqrt{\frac{n}{w}} \sqrt{\sum_{i=1}^{w} (dist(q_i'', c_i''))^2} \tag{7}$$

The $dist()$ function can be implemented using a table lookup as shown in Table 1. This table is for an alphabet $a = 4$. The distance between two symbols can be read off by examining the corresponding row and column. For example, $dist(a, b) = 0$ and $dist(a, c) = 0.67$.

Table 1. A look-up table used by the MINDIST function.

	a	b	c	d
a	0	0	0.67	1.34
b	0	0	0	0.67
c	0.67	0	0	0
d	1.34	0.67	0	0

3 The Proposed Method

In Fig. 2 we presents our proposed method for joining two time series based on the Pearson's correlation coefficients of their subsequences. The process of time series join consists of two main phases: (1) reducing the dimensionality of the two time series, discretizing the reduced time series and (2) joining the discretized time series based on a Longest Common Substring (LCS) algorithm. We will explain these two main phases.

3.1 Phase 1: Reducing the Dimensionality and Discretizing the Time Series

This phase consists of the following steps.

Step 1: Two original time series will be normalized by z-normalization. This normalization has two advantages. It helps our proposed method minimize the effect

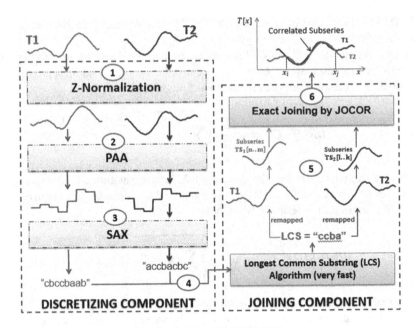

Fig. 2. Outline of LCS-JOCOR.

of noise and makes the whole dataset to fluctuate around x-axis while reserving the shape of time series.

Step 2: After being normalized, the time series will be dimensionally reduced by Piecewise Aggregate Approximation (PAA) transformation. PAA is chosen in this work since it is an effective and very simple dimensionality reduction technique for time series. In this work, the PAA compression rate will range from 1/20 to 1/5 depending on each type of datasets.

Step 3: The z-normalized PAA representations of the two time series are mapped into two strings of characters by applying Symbolic Aggregate Approximation (SAX) discretization. Thus, we have transformed our original problem of joining two long time series based on their most correlated subsequence into the problem of finding the Longest Common Substring (LCS) of two given strings.

In the next subsection, we will describe how to find the LCS of two strings efficiently.

3.2 Phase 2: Joining Two Time Series based on LCS Algorithm

This phase consists of the following steps.

Step 1: After discretizing two original time series, we get two strings, S_1 corresponding to time series T_1 and S_2 corresponding to time series T_2. We apply the algorithm of finding the Longest Common Substring (LCS) of the two strings S_1 and S_2. Our LCS algorithm is an iterative approach which is based on a *level-wise* *search*. The main idea of our LCS algorithm is that the k-character common substrings are used to explore $(k + 1)$-character common substrings. The algorithm is described as follows:

(i)   Find all unique single character strings in the first string S_1.
(ii) Find the positions of each of these single character strings in the second string S_2.
(iii) Then check if we can extend any of these single characters into two (or longer) character strings that are in common between the two strings. Find the positions of all these common strings in the second string S_2. Repeat (iii) until we can not find any longer common substrings in the two strings.

Note that in the above algorithm, we introduce two versions of finding LCS: exact matching and approximate matching. Exact matching simply considers the operator '=' between two characters. In contrast, approximate matching checks whether two compared characters equal or not depending on MINDIST(.) function introduced at Subsect. 2.2.

Step 2: After executing the LCS algorithm successfully, we will have two resulting substrings, one for exact matching and one for approximate matching. These longest common substrings will be mapped back to get the corresponding subsequences in the original time series. These subsequences are potentially the most correlated subsequences when compared to other ones in the whole time series.

Step 3: At the final step, we will apply JOCOR algorithm to calculate the Pearson's correlation coefficient and find the most correlated subsequence among the candidate subsequences found in Step 2. The main idea of JOCOR is to reuse the sufficient statistics for overlapping correlation computation and then prune unnecessary correlation computation admissibly. The JOCOR algorithm is described in details in [3].

4   Experimental Evaluation

We implemented all the methods in MATLAB and carried out the experiments on an Intel(R) Core(TM) i7-4790, 3.6 GHz, 8 GB RAM PC. We will conduct two experiments. First, we compare the performance of our proposed method to that of *exact* JOCOR on three measurements: the correlation coefficient of resulting subsequence, the runtime of algorithm and the length of the resulting subsequence. Second, we compare the performance of our proposed method to that of α-approximate-JOCOR also on the three above measurements.

4.1   Datasets

Our experiments were conducted over the datasets from the UCR Time Series Data Mining archive [1] and from [2]. There are 10 datasets used in these experiments. The names and lengths of 10 datasets are as following: Power (29,931 data points), Koski-ECG (144,002 data points), Chromosome (999,541 data points), Stock (2,119,415 data points), EEG (10,957,312 data points), Random Walks (RW2 - 1,600,002 data points), Ratbp (1,296,000 data points), LFS6 (180,214 data points), LightCurve (8,192,002 data points), and Temperature (2,324,134 data points). The datasets may be categorized into two types. The first type is that two long time series are from same source. In this case, we divide the time series into two equal halves. The first subseries will be T_1. The second one will be T_2. The second type is that two time series are from different sources. In this case, time series data downloaded from UCR will be T_1. Basing on T_1, we randomly generate the synthetic dataset T_2 by applying the following rule:

$$x_i = x_{i-1} \pm |x_{i-1} - \varepsilon| \quad \text{where } \varepsilon = \frac{\sum_{i=1}^{6} x_i}{6}$$

In the above formula, + or − is determined by a random process. Time series data T_2 is generated after the correspondent dataset has been normalized; therefore, there is no effect of noise in T_2.

4.2   LCS-JOCOR Versus *Exact* JOCOR

When operating some task on very long time series, the response time is one of the most challenging factors for researchers. In this experiment, we plan to compare the performance of our proposed method with that of *exact* JOCOR. The performance of each method is evaluated by three measurements: the maximum correlation coefficient of resulting subsequence, the runtime of the method, and the length of the resulting subsequence. Because the lengths of the resulting subsequences of the two methods are nearly similar, we exclude them from our comparison.

From Table 2, with datasets Stock, Koski-ECG and Chromosome, our LCS-JOCOR produced the same maximum correlation values as the exact JOCOR. In average of all experiments, our maximum correlation coefficients reach 95% of JOCOR's results. Regarding the runtime, our method outperforms JOCOR for eight out of ten datasets. Especially, with RW2 dataset, in the experiment with 15,000 data points, the runtime of our method was more than 15,000 times faster than that of JOCOR. The differences between the two runtimes of LCS-JOCOR and JOCOR are wider when the length of the datasets increases. Nevertheless, with Stock and LightCurve datasets, JOCOR runs slightly faster than our method. This is because the time series are undergone several transformations without being really preprocessed.

4.3   LCS-JOCOR Versus *α-approximate*-JOCOR

In this experiment, we compare the performances of LCS-JOCOR to that of α-approximate-JOCOR introduced in [2]. We recorded three measurements: the length of the resulting subsequence (Length), the runtime of algorithm (RT), and the maximum correlation coefficient (MC). Firstly, we examined the performances on 8,000 data points with the same setting as in [2]. For α-approximate-JOCOR, we conducted the

Table 2. Experimental results of LCS-JOCOR and JOCOR over 7 datasets (RT: runtime in secs; MC: maximum correlation).

Dataset	Length = 1000		Length = 4000		Length = 15000		Method
	RT	MC	RT	MC	RT	MC	
Stock	8.86	1.00	490.02	0.9986	187.06	0.9637	LCS-JOCOR
	8.26	1.00	478.02	0.9986	>12 hs	N/A	JOCOR
RW2	0.06	0.79	17.29	0.9295	21.25	0.9511	LCS-JOCOR
	1.19	0.97	409.46	0.979	10460.6	0.9853	JOCOR
RATBP	0.37	0.97	0.15	0.9755	0.67	0.9947	LCS-JOCOR
	12.47	0.98	426.46	0.996	10197.8	0.9992	JOCOR
Power	0.70	0.87	64.11	0.9403	98.44	0.9403	LCS-JOCOR
	24.17	0.87	1675.3	0.9403	23882.8	0.9403	JOCOR
LSF6	0.11	0.97	2.32	0.9847	4.88	0.9947	LCS-JOCOR
	13.05	1.00	339.42	0.9968	8075.71	0.9981	JOCOR
Koski-ECG	3.63	1.00	182.93	0.996	317.09	0.9973	LCS-JOCOR
	8.47	1.00	508.61	0.996	7579.06	0.9973	JOCOR
EEG	1.65	0.88	5.30	0.9042	31.63	0.8852	LCS-JOCOR
	31.92	0.90	1793.4	0.908	>8 hs	N/A	JOCOR
Chromosome	11.34	1.00	230.26	0.9993	7378.49	0.9994	LCS-JOCOR
	9.80	1.00	220.12	0.9993	7174.64	0.9994	JOCOR
Temperature	0.29	0.74	0.80	0.4218	10364.5	0.6854	LCS-JOCOR
	25.07	0.97	696.10	0.9717	20823.5	0.9818	JOCOR
LightCurve	1.97	1.00	10.25	0.9998	4.14	0.9997	LCS-JOCOR
	7.57	1.00	435.46	0.9999	10439.0	1.0000	JOCOR

experiments at different α values (2, 8, 16, 32, 64), and then we took average of each parameter. Table 3 presents experimental results for comparison.

With Power and Lightcurve datasets, LCS-JOCOR outperformed α-approximate-JOCOR in all three measures, especially the runtime of LCS-JOCOR is remarkably smaller. With datasets RW2, RATBP, and EEG, our method achieved the results approximately equivalent to α-approximate-JOCOR. Our method did not perform well on Chromosome and Stock datasets where we obtained the same MC but with greater runtime and shorter length; however, the differences are insignificant.

In general, the results show that the runtime of LCS-JOCOR is smaller than that of α-approximate-JOCOR for most datasets, the length of resulting subsequence and the

Table 3. Experimental results of LCS-JOCOR and α-approximate-JOCOR over 7 datasets.

Dataset	Length	Runtime (sec)	MC	Method
LightCurve	123	5	0.9999	LCS-JOCOR
	106	747	0.9999	α-JOCOR (avg)
RW2	112	87	0.9860	LCS-JOCOR
	116	821	0.9839	α-JOCOR (avg)
RATBP	100	0	0.9846	LCS-JOCOR
	101	1003	0.9991	α-JOCOR (avg)
Power	216	1058	0.9923	LCS-JOCOR
	204	1091	0.9919	α-JOCOR (avg)
EEG	105	41	0.8647	LCS-JOCOR
	104	1858	0.8807	α-JOCOR (avg)
Chromosome	6788	1462	0.9998	LCS-JOCOR
	6808	958	0.9998	α-JOCOR (avg)
Stock	4252	2578	0.9990	LCS-JOCOR
	4250	797	0.9990	α-JOCOR (avg)

value of Pearson's correlation coefficient is nearly equivalent. This is because LCS-JOCOR exploits dimensionality reduction and discretization to preprocess the two time series before applying the efficient LCS algorithm to find the candidates of the most correlated subsequence between the two time series while α-approximate-JOCOR jumps k data points in each iteration without considering the characteristic features of the two time series.

5   Conclusion and Future works

Subsequence join provides useful information about the synchronization of the time series. Solving method to the problem can be used as an analysis tool for several domains. In this paper, we proposed a new method, called LCS-JOCOR, to find approximate correlated subsequence of two time series with acceptable time efficiency. The experimental results show that our method runs faster than JOCOR and α-approximate-JOCOR while the accuracy of our approach is nearly the same as that of exact JOCOR, and higher than that of the α-approximate-JOCOR. We attribute the high performance of our method to the use of PAA to reduce the dimensionality of the two time series and the LCS algorithm to speed up the finding of the most correlated subsequence. As for future work, we intend to apply some more efficient LCS algorithm which is based on suffix tree [9] to our LCS-JOCOR in order to improve further its time efficiency.

Acknowledgement. We would like to thank Mr. John, a member of Matlab forum, for introducing some valuable ideas on the algorithm for finding LCS of two strings.

References

1. Keogh, E.: The UCR time series classification/clustering homepage (2015). http://www.cs.ucr.edu/~eamonn/time_series_data/
2. Mueen, A., Hamooni, H., Estrada, T.: Time series join on subsequence correlation. In: Proceedings of ICDM 2014, pp. 450–459 (2014)
3. Chen, Y., Chen, G., Ooi, B.-C.: Efficient processing of warping time series join of motion capture data. In: Proceedings of ICDE 2009, pp. 1048–1059 (2009)
4. Keogh, E., Chakrabarti, K., Mehrotra, S., Pazzani, M.: Dimensionality reduction for fast similarity search in large time series databases. Knowl. Inf. Syst. 3(3), 263–286 (2001)
5. Lin, J., Keogh, E., Lonardi, S., Chiu, B.: A symbolic representation of time series with implications for streaming algorithms. In: Proceedings of 8th ACM SIGMOD Workshop on Research Issues in Data Mining and Knowledge Discovery, pp. 2–11 (2003)
6. Lin, Y., McCool, Michael D.: Subseries join: a similarity-based time series match approach. In: Zaki, Mohammed J., Yu, J.X., Ravindran, B., Pudi, V. (eds.) PAKDD 2010. LNCS (LNAI), vol. 6118, pp. 238–245. Springer, Heidelberg (2010). doi:10.1007/978-3-642-13657-3_27
7. Vinh, V.D., Anh, D.T.: Efficient subsequence join over time series under dynamic time warping. In: Król, D., Madeyski, L., Nguyen, N.T. (eds.) Recent Developments in Intelligent Information and Database Systems. SCI, vol. 642, pp. 41–52. Springer, Cham (2016). doi:10.1007/978-3-319-31277-4_4
8. Xie, J., Yang, J.: A survey of join processing in data streams. In: Data Streams. Advances in Database Systems, vol. 31, pp. 209–236. Springer, US (2007)
9. Gusfield, D.: Algorithms on Strings, Trees and Sequences. Computer Science and Computational Biology. Cambridge University Press, New York (1997)

An ORM Based Context Model
for Context-Aware Computing

Annet Nishantha Anton Yogarajah, Shiluka Raveen Dharmasena,
Gobinath Loganathan$^{(\boxtimes)}$, Srinath Perera,
Vishnuvathsasarma Balachandrasarma, and Malaka Walpola

Department of Computer Science and Engineering,
University of Moratuwa, Moratuwa, Sri Lanka
slgobinath@gmail.com

Abstract. Context-aware applications are the future of modern smartphones. Now we have mobile devices with enough sensing and processing capabilities but combining them and developing a context-aware application for mobile devices is still a challenging task for developers. Context-aware middleware support is a solution to reduce the complexity in developing context-aware applications. Context modeling is one of the key requirement for a successful context-aware middleware for context representation and reasoning. This paper presents a new Object-Role Modeling (ORM) based context model which uses the advantage of modern graph databases and overcomes the problems associated with previous context models including their lack of context reasoning ability and poor spatial and temporal context modeling support.

Keywords: Context modeling · Context reasoning · Context awareness · Context-aware computing · Pervasive computing · Object-role modeling

1 Introduction

The most profound technologies are those that disappear [1]. In today's world, smartphones become an inevitable requirement for people to capture their surrounding, listen to music, watch videos, read email, access social media, chat with friends and even more. Here, a single device has access to various contextual information of its owner and others who share their information through the network which is connecting all the smartphones. The numerous sensors packed in modern smartphones let them track user's activities without interrupting the user. For example, my phone knows where I am and what I am doing right now to a certain extend without my concern. This seamless interaction of smartphones makes them the suitable candidate for context-aware computing. Context-awareness is the ability of a software to adapt according to the location of use, the collection of nearby people, hosts, and accessible devices, as well as

© ICST Institute for Computer Sciences, Social Informatics and Telecommunications Engineering 2017
P. Cong Vinh et al. (Eds.): ICCASA 2016, LNICST 193, pp. 132–141, 2017.
DOI: 10.1007/978-3-319-56357-2_14

to changes to such things over time [2]. Context is any information that can be used to characterize the situation of an entity. An entity is a person, place, or object that is considered relevant to the interaction between a user and an application, including the user and applications themselves [3].

However, still developing a context-aware application is a challenge for mobile application developers because implementing a context-aware system requires addressing many issues: (1) How does the system represent context internally? (2) How frequently does the system need to consult contextual information? What is the overhead of considering context? (3) What are the minimal services that an environment must provide to make context awareness feasible? (4) What are the relative merits of different location-sensing technologies? [4].

In this paper, we address the first issue and present an ORM context model using Neo4j graph database to support context modeling and reasoning as the solution. Our model represents the contextual information of people using nodes and links in a graph. The underlying database engine is used to store and process the contexts. This paper is organized as follows. Related work is discussed in Sect. 2. An introduction to Neo4j database and why we have selected it are described in Sect. 3. We discuss our context model in Sect. 4 and its context reasoning ability in Sect. 5. Section 6 describes the evaluation and results followed by the conclusion and future work in Sect. 7.

2   Related Work

There are remarkable researches conducted on context modeling and reasoning in middlewares. In this section, we analyze the major modeling techniques which were successfully adapted to general context modeling and the most successful implementation of each type.

Ontology-oriented modeling: This modeling is used by most of the existing middlewares because of its expressiveness and reasoning support. Dejene Ejigu et al. [5] developed a multi-domain ontology based reusable model. Comprehensive Structured Context Profiles (CSCP) was developed based on Resource Description Framework (RDF) as an improved representation technique [6]. SOCAM middleware uses the ontology to represent generic contexts along with the temporal changes and quality of contexts [7]. Dynamic spatial ontology was developed to represent snapshots of the geographical data and to support spatial queries [8]. Frederico T. Fonseca et al. [9] proposed ontology-based geographical knowledge system which can be developed using partial data.

Graphical modeling: Graphical modeling is used to represent the contexts as a conceptual model. Unified Modeling Language (UML) and ORM are the two major techniques used to represent the contexts. ContextUML, a UML-based language for model-driven context-aware services was proposed by Quan Z. Sheng et al. [10]. Henricksen et al. proposed a graphical context model which supports context classification, quality of contexts and temporal characteristics of contexts [11]. Their model uses timestamps to represent temporal contexts and additional relationships to represent the quality of contexts.

However, none of these models have proposed a native spatial model or a temporal model to represent history of events. In this paper, we present our object-role model which can be seen as an extended model of Henricksen's proposal. Our model overcomes the spatial and temporal modeling issues of existing models with alternative approaches.

3   Neo4j

Neo4j [12] is an open source NoSQL graph database with an expressive query language called Cypher query. Cypher query is an SQL-inspired language for describing patterns in graphs visually using an ASCII-art syntax [13]. Our model is built on top of Neo4j 2.3.0 and all the queries given in this paper follow the Neo4j 2.3.0 Cypher query syntax. Even though the model is built on Neo4j, it can be deployed on top of any graph databases with suitable changes in low level CRUD operations.

4   An ORM-Based Model

4.1   Design Considerations

A context-aware middleware must have the capability of processing, modeling, storing and distributing the context among various context-aware applications which are interested in a specific context. The context can be any information about relationships between users, physical objects, and applications. The interrelation of contexts helps to derive some high-level contexts which are not directly available from the raw sensors. For example, if Alice is in her office and Bob's mobile is connected to Alice's mobile via Bluetooth, we can conclude that Bob is closed to Alice. There are exceptions of course, for example, if Alice knows Bob, we cannot conclude that Bob knows Alice. Therefore, domain-specific rules on interrelationships of contexts are required to derive more contexts using existing knowledge.

Some contexts are inconsistent while some are not. For example, "Alice knows Bob" this relationship never changes once created, but "Alice is in city center" is not consistent with time. History of contexts which are changing with time must be available for some interested applications. For example, history of visited locations may be required for a tour guide application to decide on best places to visit. Again, a domain-specific rule is necessary on deciding which contexts to be stored with their past history.

4.2   Modeling Contexts

Our model is user oriented so the contexts are represented as the relationships of a user with other users, physical objects, and the environment. The wide range of contexts is classified into three major categories: social context, spatial context, and temporal context. Social context is the relationship of a user with

other people. Social context also includes the personal contexts like home location, work location, and user's device related information. Spatial context is the
relationship of a user with a location and the nearby physical objects. Temporal
context is the context changing with time and its history is required to derive
some other useful information. For example, the location data of the user which
are periodically collected and maintained as a temporal context can be used to
find the traveling pattern of the user and suggest him/her to adjust it based on
real-time traffic data and weather forecast.

All these three categories can be further classified into direct context and
indirect context based on the means by which the context is obtained. Direct
context is collected using the sensors connected to the middleware. This type
of contexts can be stored in the model without complex processing. Indirect
context is derived from direct context through aggregation and reasoning using
a processing engine. Indirect contexts can be stored in the context model or
immediately sent to the interested applications and discarded in the middleware
depending on the context type and its validity period.

All the contexts are modeled using ORM model because it is more expressive
to represent the contexts in various dimensions and modern graph databases
provide powerful processing support.

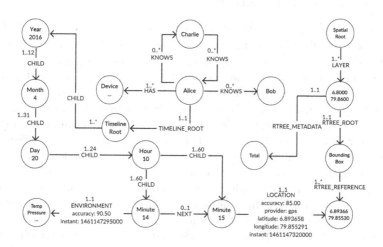

Fig. 1. A partial ORM model representing the contexts of Alice (Alice knows Bob but
Bob doesn't know Alice. Alice and Charlie know each other. Alice has a Device. On
20-04-2016 at 10.15, Alice was at 6.89366, 79.85530 location)

The Nodes: Person, Device, Environment, Location, Year, Month, Day, Hour,
Minute and WiFi represent the real world entities as their name suggest. Nodes
can have certain properties depending on their class. For example, Person node
has a name, email address and user_id and Device node has manufacturer
name, device_id, operating system version, Wi-Fi MAC address, Bluetooth MAC

address, last seen time, current battery level and a list of available sensors. The links: KNOWS, HAS, ACTIVE_DEVICE, ENVIRONMENT, LOCATION, LOCATED_AT, CHILD, NEXT, etc. represent the relationship between entities. All the links are directed links but the direction can be ignored during context reasoning depending on the domain and requirement. If a two-way direction is explicitly required, two links have to be used to achieve it. For example in Fig. 1, Alice knows Bob but Bob does not know Alice is represented by a directional link from Alice to Bob. Alice and Charlie know each other is represented by two directional links; one from Alice to Charlie and the other from Charlie to Alice. Links also can have properties based on their class. For example, the links ENVIRONMENT and LOCATION have a property 'accuracy' which represents the quality of the context. All devices which are with the user at the moment are linked using ACTIVE_DEVICE relationship. This link is useful to resolve contradicting contextual information reported by two devices. For example, if Alice has two phones and both are sending two different locations, our model stores the location reported by the ACTIVE_DEVICE only. If two active devices are reporting different locations, one with the highest accuracy will be stored in the model.

4.3   Modeling Spatial Contexts

R-Tree is a balanced tree data structure to store and process spatial objects in databases. It allows mapping geographical coordinates and polygons with high precision and acceptable performance. R-Tree does not guarantee a good worst-case performance but it works well on average cases for most kinds of data [14]. We use an existing R-Tree implementation for Neo4j database [15] which supports spatial queries like Contain, Cover, Covered By, Cross, Disjoint, Intersect, Intersect Window, Overlap, Touch, Within, and Within Distance. The R-Tree layer is a combination of geometries used to represent a collection of geometric objects with the same attribute. Our current model contains only one layer to represent the GPS coordinates of locations. It can be extended to include multiple layers with various geographical information. The layer has a bounding box and a metadata node to store the number of nodes connected to that layer and the range of the stored nodes. An ID is generated for Locations using approximated latitude and longitude values. The level of approximation is determined by the level of precision required by the application. Current model approximates the coordinates to 5 digits which provides a precision of 1.1 m [16]. Before storing a location, our model searches for an existing location with the same ID and if it is available, rather than creating a new Location node, existing node will be shared among the users in order to reduce the number of nodes in the model. The LOCATION link contains the accuracy reported by the GPS sensor and the exact latitude and longitude sent by the device. LOCATION link also contains an optional property 'provider' which stores the location provider used to derive the location. Currently, there are three location providers available in Android operating system which are GPS, network and passive. Location provider and the accuracy of the location can be used to define the quality of the context later in context reasoning process.

Nearby Wi-Fi terminals reported by devices are also associated with the location. The relationship 'LOCATED_AT' between Wi-Fi node and the location node contains a property named 'strength'. If a Wi-Fi terminal which is already available in the model, is available in another location with more than 500 m distance, that Wi-Fi terminal is considered as a portable terminal and the 'LOCATED_AT' relationship will be deleted. This information can be used to identify the location of a user with the help of available Wi-Fi networks instead of using GPS which consumes more power than Wi-Fi (Fig. 2).

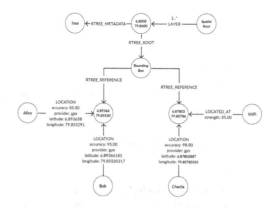

Fig. 2. Spatial model

4.4 Modeling Temporal Contexts

Even though modern smartphones synchronize the time with global time, there can be devices with wrong clock time. When multiple individual devices are sending contextual information to a central server, storing them using the device clock time will cause to event ordering problem due to the variation in devices time. As a solution, our model uses the server time to store time sensitive contextual information, ignoring network delays. The zero network delay assumption leads to another assumption that the HTTP requests sent by devices reach the server in the same order. In other words, we assume that if device A sent an event before device B, the request of device A reached the server before the request of device B. The time zone of a user is identified using his/her current location and stored in the TimelineRoot node. When an application requests a time sensitive contextual information, device local time is calculated using the time zone of the user and the server. Additional options are provided to override the user's time zone if required.

This model represents the time using a tree structure. Each user has a link to a unique TimelineRoot node. TimelineRoot node has CHILD links to Year nodes. Each year nodes can have 1–12 CHILD links to Month nodes. Similarly,

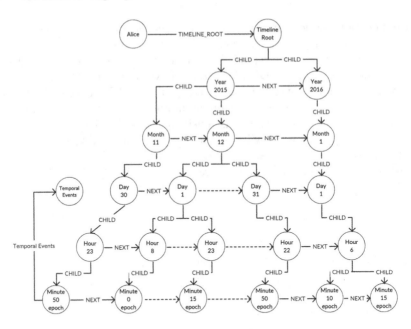

Fig. 3. Temporal model

the tree grows until Minute nodes. Nodes in the same depth have intermediate links named NEXT which points the next node if available. We stopped with the precision of minutes because of two reasons. First, the minimum time interval of mobile sensors to collect and report new data is 5 min if the battery level is 100% because frequent usage of sensors in a mobile device drains the power of the mobile device. We have ended with 5 min after trial and error experiments and this interval is dynamically adjusted based on the battery level of the device. Second, modeling with a precision of seconds leads to too many nodes and links in the database which needs more memory. The Minute nodes contain an extra property 'milliseconds' which is the number of milliseconds from Java epoch truncated to that specific minute. The actual instant in milliseconds is stored in the relationship which connects the Minute node and the context node (Fig. 3).

Since our model supports multiple devices and the precision is up to minutes, there is a possibility of two devices reporting the same context within a minute. If there are two different types of contexts reported by two active devices of the user within a minute, both will be linked to that specific time in this model. If the context types are same, the one with the highest accuracy is linked to the time.

5   Context Reasoning

Context reasoning is the process of deriving deduced contexts from raw contexts. It also provides a solution to resolve context inconsistency and conflict that caused by imperfect sensing [14]. Most of the modern graph databases provide query support to aggregate data and retrieve the interested information. Since our model is built on Neo4j, Cypher query of Neo4j is used to process the contexts and to derive the complex contexts based on the defined rules. Our middleware uses WSO2 Complex Event Processor [17] along with the database for realtime context processing. Combination of both CEP and database is used to derive high level contexts and to improve the quality of contexts as well.

For example, finding the visited locations of Alice from January 1st to April 15th in last five years can be done using the following Neo4j query.

```
MATCH (n:Person {name: 'Alice'})-[:TIMELINE_ROOT]->(:
TimelineRoot)-[:CHILD]->(y:Year)-[:CHILD]->(m:Month)-[:
CHILD]->(d:Day)-[:CHILD*]->(:Minute)-[:LOCATION]->(l:
Location) WHERE (y.value >= 2011 AND y.value < 2016)
AND (m.value < 4 OR (m.value = 4 AND d.value <= 30))
RETURN l
```

6 Evaluation

Five sample data sets were created using 100 to 500 users per sample along with 10 visited locations and 10 environmental conditions per user. Further, each model contain 100 known relationships among the users. The data sets were deployed on Neo4j server and tested through REST API of Neo4j. Therefore the time measured in these tests includes the delay in sending HTTP requests. The test has been done only for data retrieval because the behaviors of both writing to the model and reading from the model are identical in our context model. Testing the read-write performance of underlying database is out of the scope of this research. As shown in Fig. 4a, our model requires more nodes and relationships than the models suggested in existing works because of the temporal model we use. However, it does not heavily impact the overall performance of the model.

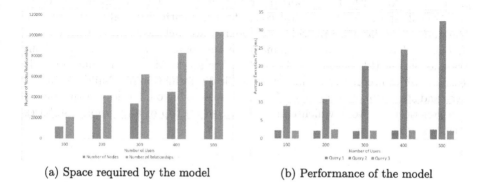

(a) Space required by the model   (b) Performance of the model

Fig. 4. Evaluation results

Three queries were used to test the performance of the model and the performance is compared in Fig. 4b. Query 1 searches for a given person using the user id to evaluate overall read performance of the model. The performance remains constant regardless of the number of nodes and the same result is expected for any entities searched using their indexed properties. Query 2 retrieves the nearby known people of a given user within a given interval to check the performance of spatial and temporal models. The query was purposefully designed to first retrieve the nearby locations using the R-Tree implementation and then search for known people in those locations within the given interval. Therefore the major impact on the performance is made by the spatial model. The R-Tree implementation provides more inbuilt features to the model but the performance is the limiting factor in using the spatial model. Performance decreases with the number of locations and the average time to retrieve the data is much higher than the time to retrieve other contextual information. However, the same information can be retrieved without using the advantage of the spatial model which is implemented in Query 3.

The exact information retrieved using the query 2 was retrieved using query 3 in another way. Query 3 starts from the known people and then searches for their location within the given interval. Once the visited locations were retrieved, it calculates the euclidean distance between those locations and the given location. Those who were within the given distance are returned as nearby known people. While both query 2 and 3 return the same result, the time taken to execute the queries significantly varies. As Fig. 4b shows, the performance of query 1 and 3 are quite similar which concludes that the performance of the model is not impacted by the temporal model we used. The spatial model does not provides better performance and should not be used if there are any other ways to retrieve the spatial information.

7   Conclusion

In this paper, we have presented an extensible ORM model to represent and process contexts with the support of graph database. Our context model represents social, spatial and temporal contexts along with the quality of contexts. The underlying database provides storage and also acts as a context processing engine. We have already used this model in our context-aware middleware Con-Tra and proved the validity of this model. We are looking at creating multiple R-Tree layers to represent various geographical information like buildings in one layer and streets in another layer. We are also focusing on developing this model as a generic framework which can be deployed on top of any graph databases with less or no effort.

References

1. Weiser, M.: The computer for the 21st century. SIGMOBILE Mob. Comput. Commun. Rev. **3**(3), 3–11 (1999)
2. Schilit, B., Adams, N., Want, R.: Context-aware computing applications. In: Proceedings of the 1994 First Workshop on Mobile Computing Systems and Applications. WMCSA 1994, pp. 85–90. IEEE Computer Society, Washington, DC (1994)
3. Abowd, G.D., Dey, A.K., Brown, P.J., Davies, N., Smith, M., Steggles, P.: Towards a better understanding of context and context-awareness. In: Gellersen, H.-W. (ed.) HUC 1999. LNCS, vol. 1707, pp. 304–307. Springer, Heidelberg (1999). doi:10. 1007/3-540-48157-5_29
4. Satyanarayanan, M.: Challenges in implementing a context-aware system. IEEE Pervasive Comput. **1**(3), 2 (2002)
5. Ejigu, D., Scuturici, M., Brunie, L.: An ontology-based approach to context modeling and reasoning in pervasive computing. In: Proceedings of the Fifth IEEE International Conference on Pervasive Computing and Communications Workshops. PERCOMW 2007, pp. 14–19. IEEE Computer Society, Washington, DC (2007)
6. Held, A., Buchholz, S., Schill, A., Schill, E.: Modeling of context information for pervasive computing applications (2002)
7. Gu, T., Wang, X.H., Pung, H.K., Zhang, D.Q.: An ontology-based context model in intelligent environments. In: Proceedings of Communication Networks and Distributed Systems Modeling and Simulation Conference, pp. 270–275 (2004)
8. Grenon, P., Smith, B.: Snap and span: towards dynamic spatial ontology. Spat. Cogn. Comput. **4**(1), 69–103 (2004)
9. Fonseca, F.T., Egenhofer, M.J.: Ontology-driven geographic information systems. In: Proceedings of the 7th ACM International Symposium on Advances in Geographic Information Systems. GIS 1999, pp. 14–19. ACM, New York (1999)
10. Sheng, Q.Z., Benatallah, B.: ContextUML: a UML-based modeling language for model-driven development of context-aware web services development. In: Proceedings of the International Conference on Mobile Business. ICMB 2005, pp. 206–212. IEEE Computer Society, Washington, DC (2005)
11. Henricksen, K., Indulska, J., Rakotonirainy, A.: Generating context management infrastructure from high-level context models. In: 4th International Conference on Mobile Data Management (MDM) - Industrial Track, pp. 1–6 (2003)
12. Neo4j: The world's leading graph database. http://neo4j.com. Accessed 07 Feb 2016
13. What is a graph database? A property graph model intro. http://neo4j.com/developer/graph-database/. Accessed 05 Jan 2016
14. Guttman, A.: R-trees: a dynamic index structure for spatial searching. In: Proceedings of the 1984 ACM SIGMOD International Conference on Management of Data. SIGMOD 1984, pp. 47–57. ACM, New York (1984)
15. Taverner, C.: Neo4j-contrib/spatial. https://github.com/neo4j-contrib/spatial. Accessed 05 Jan 2016
16. Hijmans, R.J., Guarino, L., Cruz, M., Rojas, E.: Computer tools for spatial analysis of plant genetic resources data: 1. DIVA-GIS. Plant Genetic Resources Newsletter, pp. 15–19 (2001)
17. Complex event processor - WSO2 inc. http://wso2.com/products/complex-event-processor. Accessed 03 May 2016

A Conceptual Framework for IS Project Success

Thanh D. Nguyen[1,2(✉)], Tuan M. Nguyen[2], and Thi H. Cao[3]

[1] Banking University of Ho Chi Minh City, Ho Chi Minh City, Vietnam
thanhnd@buh.edu.vn
[2] HCMC University of Technology, Ho Chi Minh City, Vietnam
n.m.tuan@hcmut.edu.vn
[3] Saigon Technology University, Ho Chi Minh City, Vietnam
thi.caohao@stu.edu.vn

Abstract. The global IT development is becoming ever more dominant. Notwithstanding, most of the projects of IS are not satisfied – the IS projects are still experiencing failure. This research reviews the IS project success with the multi-dimensional and multi-level approaches. Various works in academic journals and conferences from 1992 to 2016 were elaborated. The findings indicate that empirical studies are crucial. Interestingly, a mutual relationship between three themes of works (project success, IS success, and acceptance and use of technology) has been identified. Consequently, a conceptual framework provides the comprehensive explanation for IS project success is shown, which could be a promising avenue of IS research.

Keywords: IS success · IS project success · Acceptance and use of technology

1 Introduction

The global information technology (IT) development is becoming ever more dominant [43]. Notwithstanding, most of the information systems (IS) projects are not satisfied – a failure of the IS projects. There are roughly 60% of the projects of IS are a problem about cost and time [64]. According to highly cited CHAOS, the success rate of the IS project is only about 29% to 39% in the period of 2004–2013 [5]. This estimation provides the IS success rate should be ameliorated, inasmuch the majority of the projects of IS were not satisfied.

The works on the technology acceptance (Davis [16]); acceptance and use of technology (Venkatesh et al. [81, 84]); IS success (DeLone and McLean, [18–20]); and project success (Belassi and Tukel [3]; Pinto and Prescott [48, 49]), which have accommodated the theoretical models for the project management and IT/IS. There are several works on the project success, IS success, and acceptance and use of technology. However, the studies did not provide all factors which impact on the effectiveness of IS projects – the IS project success, the relationship between those factors and project success, especially, the discrimination among them (IS success, project success, acceptance and use of technology). Therefore, a work about the IS project success is the indispensable study.

© ICST Institute for Computer Sciences, Social Informatics and Telecommunications Engineering 2017
P. Cong Vinh et al. (Eds.): ICCASA 2016, LNICST 193, pp. 142–154, 2017.
DOI: 10.1007/978-3-319-56357-2_15

This research literatures articles from the academic papers in 3 research topics: (1) acceptance and use of technology (TRA [23], TPB [1], TAM [16], TAM2 [80], TAM2' [77], TAM3 [79], UTAUT [81], UTAUT2 [84]); (2) IS success (DeLone and McLean [18–20]); (3) project success (Belassi and Tukel [3]; Pinto and Prescott [48, 49]; Pinto and Slevin [50, 51]). A more correlated list of works (Hughes et al. [27]; Nguyen [40]; Petter et al. [45–47]; Rai et al. [53]; Seddon [60]; Tate et al. [69]). Correspondingly, the authors consistently synthesize scientific review of respectable papers for providing an entire list of sources of related works on the IS project success. Besides, a conceptual framework provides the comprehensive explanation for IS project success is shown, which could be a promising avenue of IS research.

2 Related Works

2.1 Literature Review

Acceptance and Use of Technology. Technology Acceptance Model (TAM) exculpates the acceptance of technology, and the elements can account for the system usage behavior [16]. TAM is extensively used in illuminating use intention and use behavior of IS users. Nevertheless, TAM requires convenient effusion, exposition, and prognostication is limited. Thus, usefulness on TAM2 [80] and ease of use on TAM2' [77], and both on TAM3 [79] which engraved immemorial the forces of prior works, evidently TAM to paraphrase use intention in the cognitive processes and social influence.

Venkatesh et al. [81] had proposed Unified Theory Acceptance and Use of Technology (UTAUT), explaining the IT/IS use intention and use behavior. This model cited from some theoretical frameworks, namely TAM [16]; Theory of Planned Behavior (TPB) [1]; Theory of Reasoned Action (TRA) [23]; TPB and TAM integrated model [70]; Diffusion of Innovations (DOI) [55]; Model of Personal Computer Utilization (MPCU) [71]; Motivation Model (MM) [17]; and Social Cognitive Theory (SCT) [9]. Venkatesh et al. [84] added more factors to UTAUT, called UTAUT2.

Investigation of theory based works revealed the acceptance and use of technology are divided into two branches that are TAM and UTAUT: (1) Based on TPB, TRA and the related theories (DOI, PMCU, MM, SCT) for building the technology acceptance model (TAM, TAM2, TAM2', TAM3...). (2) Unified theory of acceptance and use of technology (UTAUT, UTAUT2). A common trouble in the acceptance and use of technology work, the authors only cite the original models (TAM, UTAUT) without the extending frameworks [78] – a mark Venkatesh et al. [82] was commencement previous eight years. In the global, every day, enduring many studies on the acceptance and use of technology was jactitation, but they do not show any new theory. However, ideas necessitate the technology adoption works, e.g., the approach at TAM3's three levels (organization, team, and individual); adding more variables; considering new work contexts (managers and consumers); and proposing new mechanisms (hedonic motivation, habit, and net impact). Therefore, that accommodates the approaching works well-founded the technology adoption (project success and IS success).

IS Success. There are nearly as many measures as IS success; it is comprehensible when considering that *"information"*, a message or an IS output in a communication system, can be measured at 3 levels, including technical, semantic, and effectiveness [18]. In the communication, *technical level* as the system efficiency and propriety that information effectively; *semantic level* as the information success in promulgating intended meaning; and *effectiveness level* as the information impact on the receiver (Shannon and Weaver [63]). Thus, *"effectiveness"* as *"influence"* and information as *"event hierarchy take place at an information system receiving which may be used to identify the various approaches that might be used to measure output at the influence level"* (Mason [35, p. 227]). The events include the information application and information receipt, controlling a transform in system performance and recipient behavior [18].

DeLone and McLean [18, p. 88] propounded that *"the model of IS success clearly needs further validation and development before it could serve as a basis for the appropriate IS measure selection"* after proposing an original D&M model. Besides, some authors deprecated that the original IS success model is insufficient and recommended that more factors should be included in this model or presented other models. Then, Seddon [60]; Seddon and Kiew [61] advocated that the original D&M gaps comprehensiveness and further re-specified the IS success model by discriminating actual and expected influences, as well as by usefulness in TAM [16]. The correlated works contributed the general knowledge of the IS success theme. They construct that the works of IS success extensively reviewed the organizational and individual levels (Petter et al. [45]; Tate et al. [69]), not revised at the team level – these are theoretical gaps for developing other models on the IS success. Then, DeLone and McLean [19] updated the IS success design from the original D&M, and other authors also enhanced other IS success models from the D&M models (Gable et al. [25, 26]; Seddon [60]).

Besides, the IS success (DeLone and McLean [18–20]) and the acceptance and use of technology (TAM, UTAUT), there is the relationship among two theories. Distinctly, use intention and use appearing in both subjects [25, 60, 91]; the research on the sufficient model between the IS success and acceptance and use of technology [6, 57]. Also, the IS success works related to the success of project [22, 40].

Project Success. Schultz et al. [58] proposed the first efforts classify critical factors. The element groups at two accomplishment phases affecting project performance, top management support, project mission, project schedule. For each stage of works, Pinto and Slevin [50] invented success factors as Pinto and Prescott [48] provided the relative importance of once. That found the success factor correlation at different project periods. *"Success factors"* was proposed by Daniel [12]. The relationship between the project *"critical success factors"* (CSF) and the project success via the success criteria [12], e.g., Subiyakto and Ahlan [65] proposed the IS project success model from the project success criteria and project criteria. Rockart [56] had developed CSF as a management term for a factor indispensable for achieving its mission of the organization. CSF is a major factor in consolidating the organizational success, e.g., user involvement is one CSF for an IT/IS project success.

Accordingly, the scholars were only respected in the success of the project from the fundamentals of project management, e.g., infrastructure, project goal, top management support, team capabilities [10, 11]. Then, scholars were interested in the customer satisfaction, project quality, project economic [14, 39]. Thus, for a success of IS project, the study propensities related to IS success as well as acceptance and use of technology. The studies involved constituting the project success CSF list [3, 13, 48–50, 73], these are the criteria can increase project success's likelihood. Although the study has tried to propose many models that deputize the successful concepts [18–20, 24], but has not served all IS project success key factors. The authors also impale on testing the success standards in the context of the acceptance of project [2, 21, 29]. The project success or failure depends on the CSFs alignment for project implementation and the matching competence of the success criteria [27].

Furthermore, Ika et al. [30]; Westerveld [90] manifested, it has conspicuous between the project success and the CSFs. For instance, Subiyakto et al. [67] based on Davis [15]; DeLone and McLean [18–20]; Espinosa et al. [22]; Sudhakar [68] pointed out an IS project success model. Next, Putra et al. [52] inherited this model to suggest another IS project success model...

IS Project Success. Wateridge [87] cited from the Morris and Hough [38] and Turner [74] works to propose an IT project success model with the project factors (sponsor, manager, team, and user) can impact on the IT project success criteria (characteristics, time, cost, and user requirements). Wateridge [88] added some IS project success criteria (quality and user satisfaction). Espinosa et al. [22] inherited and built the IS project success from previous studies. For example, DeLone and McLean [18–20]; Ika et al. [30]; Pinto and Slevin [50]; Wateridge [87] with several factors: compliances (time and cost), success (economic and product), user satisfaction. Subiyakto and Ahlan [65] developed an IS project success model. Accordingly, the framework cited from the common collaboration and comparison. Davis [15] designated according to HIPO (process), the project success theory (Wateridge [87]), DeLone and McLean [18–20], the environmental projection theory (Lim and Mohamed [34]). A model is delegating the relationship among the CSF (user satisfaction, system use, and IS project success) and the IS project criteria (stakeholders, resources, and environment).

Besides, the project success works (Belassi and Tukel [3]; Pinto and Slevin [50, 51]); IS success (DeLone and McLean [18–20]). The IS project success works (Nguyen [40]; Subiyakto et al. [66]); the study inquired the relationship among these papers. Service quality, system use, user satisfaction, and net benefits emerging in both themes (Espinosa et al. [22]; Subiyakto et al. [67]). In addition, the works of project success also showed the studies of acceptance and use of technology. User satisfaction, acceptance of project emerging in both topics (Ika et al. [30]; Schultz et al. [58]).

2.2 Research Method

There are four phases of this work: (1) identifying a specific material item; (2) determining the particular period for searching scientific documents; (3) selecting the related studies; (4) proposing a conceptual framework.

Identifying a clear material item that was as discriminating, the academic journals published the papers of the leading authors. In addition, the top MIS journals [89] are considered. Besides, the MIS journals in the top rankings are also examined [59]. The best MIS international conferences are also examined. Determining the appropriate period for searching scientific documents. With the acceptance and use of technology, review from 1987 to 2016; with the IS success, the period between 1992 and 2016 was considered; with the project success, literature from 1987 and 2016. The research reviews the theoretical background will be searched for the theories' starting point. After that, from the variety of published sources in the period (up to 2016), choosing the articles related to 3 topics. All papers had been searched in *Google Scholar* selecting articles for the literature review. Completing the selection process, examining the paper list on the success of IS projects, remove unnecessary items. Based on related studies, the authors accentuate a conceptual framework for IS project success.

3   Research Results

3.1   Article Results

There are 169 re-selected items from roughly 200 papers were initially searching criteria (Sect. 2.2). The related sections are analyzed and reviewed in detail. There are 58 articles described in *"review study"* or *"none–empirical/conceptual study"* and 101 papers *"empirical study"*.

The works of *"none–empirical/conceptual study"* are disjointed on the left (Fig. 1), comprising *"speculation/commentary"*; *"review study"* *"conceptual/framework model"*. In 58 papers, there are 43 papers on framework/conceptual model (Davis [16]; DeLone and McLean [18–20]; Venkatesh et al. [81, 84, 85]), and 6 articles on commentary/ speculation (Gable et al. [25, 26]; Rai et al. [53]). Also, there are 8 papers on *"literature review"* (Hughes et al. [27, 28]; Urbach et al. [75]; Venkatesh [78]).

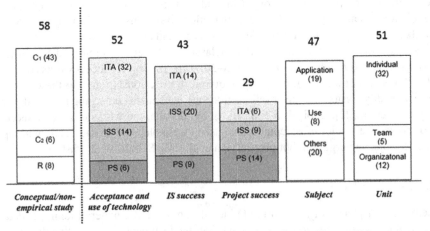

C1 & C2: Conceptual study; R: Review study; ITA: Acceptance and use of technology; ISS: IS success, PS: Project success

Fig. 1. The research approach summary of the success of IS project [44]

Moreover, the findings of this work externalized that, 47 papers on the application (Byrd et al. [4]; Wang and Yang [86]). Including, 19 papers on the application of IS, 8 articles on the implementation of organizational IS and success of organizational IS are specified, and other empirical works (Chu and Chen [7]; Nguyen et al. [41–43]). It has 32 papers on the individual level (Davis [14]; Petter et al. [45]; Tate et al. [69]), 5 papers on the team level (Jetu and Riedl [31]; Lee et al. [33]). It has 12 papers on the organizational level (Cserhati and Szabo [11]; Gable et al. [26]). Totally, the research results of the synthesis regard the success of IS project, thorough the theoretical basis understanding – acceptance and use of technology; project success criteria; project success; the relationship among 3 themes of the works (IS success, project success, and acceptance and use of technology).

The empirical studies disjointed on the right - 5 bars (Fig. 1). In which, 101 papers are approaching 3 topics of the works (acceptance and use of technology, IS success and project success). It has 52 papers on acceptance and use of technology (DeWit [21]; Putra et al. [52]; Venkatesh et al. [82]). There are 14 papers orderly to IS success (Sambasivan et al. [57]; Subiyakto et al. [67]; Wixom and Todd [91]), and 6 papers orderly to project success (Atkinson [2]; Coombs [10]; Subiyakto and Ahlan [65]). Besides, there are 52 papers on the IS success; there are 14 articles on the acceptance and use of technology (Sambasivan et al. [66]; Wixom and Todd [91]) and 9 papers on the project success (Muller and Jugdev [39]; Westerveld [90]). The research from the original D&M are 8 papers (Renzel et al. [54]) and updated D&M are 21 papers (Wixom and Todd [91]). There are 29 papers on the project success, it has 6 papers interested in the acceptance and use of technology (Atkinson [2]; Coombs [10]; Subiyakto and Ahlan [65]). There are 9 papers on the IS success (Ika [29]; Muller and Jugdev [39]; Westerveld [90]). Differently, there are 4 papers related to 3 themes of the works (acceptance and use of technology, IS success, and project success) (Putra et al. [52]; Subiyakto and Ahlan [65]).

3.2   IS Success, Project Success, and Acceptance and Use of Technology

The works of Belassi and Tukel [3]; DeLone and McLean [18–20]; Pinto and Prescott [48, 49]; Pinto and Slevin [50, 51]; Seddon [60]; Seddon et al. [62] are the distinctive work of the project success. Nguyen et al. [43]; Petter et al. [45–47]; Urbach and Muller [76]; Tukel and Rom [73] work on the success of IS. Espinosa et al. [22]; Nguyen et al. [42]; Putra et al. [52]; Subiyakto et al. [67]; Wateridge [87, 88] work on the IS project success. The studies of Ajzen [1]; Davis [16]; Fishbein and Ajzen [23]; Venkatesh et al. [81, 84] are the figurative works of the acceptance and use of technology. The works of Thong [72]; Venkatesh et al. [83] are the standard studies of IS acceptance.

In each topic, there are some gaps, e.g., authors have aggregated testing the acceptance and use of technology theoretical model (TPB, TAM) without propounding any appendage model, do not concentrate more theories. The majority of the related studies manipulated separately for a theme and fragment of research: (1) acceptance and use of technology (Fishbein and Ajzen [23]; Davis [16]; Venkatesh et al. [81, 83]). (2) IS success (DeLone and McLean [18–20]; Petter et al. [45–47]; Seddon and Kiew [61]; Seddon [60]). (3) Project success (Belassi and Tukel [3]; Cleland and King [8]; Pinto and Prescott [48, 49]; Pinto and Slevin [50, 51]) (Fig. 2). Meanwhile, Venkatesh et al. [82] recommended other authors can expand more theoretical models of acceptance and use of technology the initial model (TAM, UTAUT). Venkatesh [78] has repeated that issue after eight years, no new theoretical models based on TAM or UTAUT. Nevertheless, there are not anymore extend models contributing to the technology adoption [78].

Fig. 2. Acceptance and use of technology, IS Success and project success [46]

The findings of the review have been detailed in Table 1. In which, with acceptance and use of technology, called usefulness, ease of use in TAM [16, 79, 80]; hedonic motivation, facilitating conditions, social influence in UTAUT [81, 84]; attitude toward using in TPB [1], TAM [16, 79, 80]; behavioral intention, use behavior in TAM [16, 79, 80], UTATU [81, 84]; and new mechanisms as the newest recommendation of Venkatesh et al. [85]. With the success of IS, namely information quality, system quality, usage, individual impact, and organizational impact in original D&M model [18], and updated D&M model [19]; service quality, user satisfaction, use intention, and net benefits in the updated DeLone and McLean [23]; other elements in Gable et al. [25, 26]; Petter et al. [45]; Seddon [60]; and new mechanisms as the newest recommendation of Venkatesh et al. [85].

Table 1. Some related concepts of 3 themes of studies

Acceptance and use of technology	IS success	Project success
– Usefulness	– System quality	– *Critical success factors...*
– Ease of use	– Service quality	– Project performance
– Hedonic motivation	– Information quality	– IS project success[a]
– Social influence	– Use intention[a]	– Project success[a]
– Facilitating conditions	– User satisfaction[a]	– *New mechanisms*[a]
– Habit	– Usage[a]	
– Price value	– Individual impact[a]	
– Attitude toward using	– Organizational impact[a]	
– Use intention[a]	– Net benefits[a]	
– Use behavior[a]	– *New mechanisms*[a]	
– *New mechanisms*[a]		

[a]Appearing in the other topics

With the project success, called critical success factors, performance, project success in Belassi and Tukel [3]; Pinto and Prescott [48, 49]; Pinto and Slevin [50, 51]; and new elements in Davis [14]. Besides, with IS project success, there are related concepts in the studies of Espinosa et al. [22]; Hughes [27, 28]; Wateridge [87, 88].

Interestingly, the work related to others, e.g., use intention and usage appear in both of IS success and acceptance and use of technology. Project approval and user acceptance have exposed in the both of project success and IS success; user acceptance appears in the both of acceptance and use of technology and project success.

3.3   A Conceptual Framework for IS Project Success

Because the IS projects have seemingly had more complicated than those in other areas [36], it is evident that the related studies should take both multiple perspectives (technical, organizational, personal) as indicated in Mason [35]; Mitroff and Linstone [37]) and multiple levels (individual, team, organization) [32] approaches. Consequently, a conceptual framework is depicted in Figs. 3, 4, and 5. It should be noted that IS success could be both mediator and moderator in the relation between project success and acceptance and use of technology.

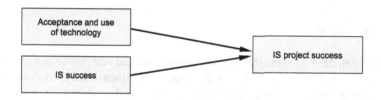

Fig. 3. Direct effect model

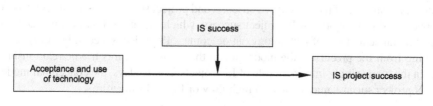

Fig. 4. Moderator effect model

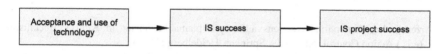

Fig. 5. Mediator effect model

In the author's conceptual framework, there are 3 effect models:

(1) *Direct effect model* (Fig. 3): acceptance and use of technology – independent dimensions (usefulness, ease of use, social influence, price value, habit and new mechanisms), and IS success – independent dimensions (service quality,

information quality, system quality, and new mechanisms). Project success – dependent dimensions (performance, IS project success, project success, and new mechanisms).

(2) *Moderator effect model* (Fig. 4): acceptance and use of technology – independent dimensions (ease of use, usefulness, social influence, price value, habit and new mechanisms). Project success – dependent dimensions (performance, IS project success, project success, and new mechanisms). IS success – moderator dimensions (service quality, information quality, system quality, user satisfaction, use intention, usage, and new mechanisms).

(3) *Mediator effects model* (Fig. 5): acceptance and use of technology – independent dimensions (ease of use, usefulness, social influence, price value, habit, and new mechanisms). Project success – dependent dimensions (performance, IS project success and new mechanisms). IS success – meditation dimensions (user satisfaction, use intention, usage, and new mechanisms).

The concepts of technology adoption are viewed as the independent dimensions. The concepts of IS success are viewed as the moderator dimensions and also viewed as the mediator dimensions on the relation to the concepts of IS project success – dependent dimensions. That will establish opportunities for work trends in the future.

4   Conclusions

This work synthesized the project success, IS success, and acceptance and use of technology studies as a review using the methods of multi-dimensional to explore the relationship among three theoretical key constructs. This work analyzed 200 articles from 1992 to 2016 in the top academic journals and conferences to identify the theoretical foundation and approaches to deal with the mutual relationship among three themes, as acceptance and use of technology, IS success, and project success. The findings propose a conceptual framework for IS project success, which maintains that the antecedent – the acceptance and use of technology, an outcome – IS project success, but IS success ranging from the precursor, the moderator to the mediator of this triadic relationship. Given the increasingly important role of IS projects in nowadays, the conceptual model for IS project success may indicate a high flow of IS works in entire.

References

1. Ajzen, I.: From intentions to actions: a theory of planned behavior. In: Kuhl, J., Beckmann, J. (eds.) Action Control, pp. 11–39. Springer, Heidelberg (1985)
2. Atkinson, R.: Project management: cost, time and quality, two best guesses and a phenomenon, its time to accept other success criteria. Int. J. Proj. Manag. **17**(6), 337–342 (1999)
3. Belassi, W., Tukel, O.: A new framework for determining critical success/failure factors in projects. Int. J. Proj. Manag. **3**(14), 141–151 (1996)
4. Byrd, T., Thrasher, E., Lang, T., Davidson, N.: A process-oriented perspective of IS success: examining the impact of IS on operational cost. Omega **34**(5), 448–460 (2006)

5. CHAOS: The standish group report (2014). https://www.standishgroup.com
6. Chen, J., Chang, J., Kao, C., Huang, Y.: Integrating ISSM into TAM to enhance digital library services: a case study of the Taiwan digital meta-library. Electron. Lib. **34**(1), 58–73 (2016)
7. Chu, T.H., Chen, Y.Y.: With good we become good: understanding e-learning adoption by theory of planned behavior and group influences. Comput. Educ. **92**, 37–52 (2016)
8. Cleland, D., King, R.: System Analysis and Project. McGraw-Hill, New York (1983)
9. Compeau, D., Higgins, C.: Application of social cognitive theory to training for computer skills. Inf. Syst. Res. **6**(2), 118–143 (1995)
10. Coombs, C.: When planned IS/IT project benefits are not realized: a study of inhibitors and facilitators to benefits realization. Int. J. Proj. Manag. **33**(2), 363–379 (2015)
11. Cserhati, G., Szabo, L.: The relationship between success criteria and success factors in organisational event projects. Int. J. Proj. Manag. **32**(4), 613–624 (2014)
12. Daniel, D.: Management information crisis. Harv. Bus. Rev. **39**(5), 111–121 (1961)
13. Davies, T.: The "real" success factors on projects. Int. J. Proj. Manag. **20**, 185–190 (2002)
14. Davis, K.: A method to measure success dimensions relating to individual stakeholder groups. Int. J. Proj. Manag. **34**(3), 480–493 (2016)
15. Davis, W.S.: HIPO hierarchy plus input-process-output. In: Davis, W.S., Yen, D.C. (eds.) The Information System Consultant's Handbook, Systems Analysis and Design, pp. 503–510. CRC, Boca Raton (1998)
16. Davis, F.D.: Perceived usefulness, perceived ease of use, and user acceptance of information technology. MIS Q. **13**(3), 319–340 (1989)
17. Davis, F.D., Bagozzi, R., Warshaw, P.: Extrinsic and intrinsic motivation to use computers in the workplace. J. Appl. Soc. Psychol. **22**(14), 1111–1132 (1992)
18. DeLone, W., McLean, E.: Information systems success: the quest for the dependent variable. Inf. Syst. Res. **3**(1), 60–95 (1992)
19. DeLone, W., McLean, E.: Information systems success: a ten-year update. J. Manag. Inf. Syst. **19**(4), 9–30 (2003)
20. Delone, W., McLean, E.: Measuring e-commerce success: applying the DeLone & McLean information systems success model. Int. J. Electron. Commer. **9**(1), 31–47 (2004)
21. DeWit, A.: Measurement of project success. Int. J. Proj. Manag. **6**(3), 164–170 (1988)
22. Espinosa, J., DeLone, W., Lee, G.: Global boundaries, task processes and IS project success: a field study. Inf. Technol. People **19**(4), 345–370 (2006)
23. Fishbein, M., Ajzen, I.: Belief, Attitude, Intention and Behavior: An Introduction to Theory and Research. Addison-Wesley, Reading (1975)
24. Fortune, J., White, D.: Framing of project critical success factors by a systems model. Int. J. Proj. Manag. **24**(1), 53–65 (2006)
25. Gable, G., Sedera, D., Chan, T.: Enterprise systems success: a measurement model. In: ICIS Proceedings, Seattle (2003)
26. Gable, G., Sedera, D., Chan, T.: Re-conceptualizing information system success: the IS-impact measurement model. J. AIS **9**(7), 377–408 (2008)
27. Hughes, D., Dwivedi, Y., Simintiras, A., Rana, N.: An analysis of the components of project success. In: Hughes, D., Dwivedi, Y., Simintiras, A., Rana, N. (eds.) Success and Failure of IS/IT Projects, pp. 27–43. Springer, London (2016)
28. Hughes, D., Dwivedi, Y., Rana, N., Simintiras, A.: Information systems project failure – analysis of causal links using interpretive structural modeling. Prod. Plan. Control **27**(16), 1313–1333 (2016)
29. Ika, L.: Project success as a topic in project management journals. Proj. Manag. J. **40**(4), 6–19 (2009)

30. Ika, L., Diallo, A., Thuillier, D.: Critical success factors for world bank projects: an empirical investigation. Int. J. Proj. Manag. **30**(1), 105–116 (2012)
31. Jetu, F., Riedl, R.: Determinants of information systems and information technology project team success: a literature review and a conceptual model. Commun. AIS **30**(1), 455–482 (2012)
32. Jones, A., Gallivan, M.: Toward a deeper understanding of system usage in organizations: a multilevel perspective. MIS Q. **31**(4), 657–679 (2007)
33. Lee, J., Park, J., Lee, S.: Raising team social capital with knowledge and communication in information systems development projects. Int. J. Proj. Manag. **33**(4), 797–807 (2015)
34. Lim, C., Mohamed, M.: Criteria of project success: an exploratory re-examination. Int. J. Proj. Manag. **17**(4), 243–248 (1999)
35. Mason, R.: Measuring information output: a communication systems approach. Inf. Manag. **1**(4), 219–234 (1978)
36. Metcalfe, M., Lynch, M.: Arguing for information systems project definition. In: Wynn, E.H., Whitley, E.A., Myers, M.D., DeGross, J.I. (eds.) Global and Organizational Discourse About Information Technology, pp. 295–321. Springer, New York (2003)
37. Mitroff, I., Linstone, H.: The Unbounded Mind: Breaking the Chains of Traditional Business Thinking. Oxford University Press, Oxford (1995)
38. Morris, P., Hough, G.: The Anatomy of Major Projects: A Study of the Reality of Project Management. Wiley, Chichester (1987)
39. Muller, R., Jugdev, K.: Critical success factors in projects: Pinto, Slevin, and Prescott – the elucidation of project success. Int. J. Manag. Proj. Bus. **5**(4), 757–775 (2012)
40. Nguyen, T.D.: A structural model for the success of information system projects. J. Sci. Technol. Dev. **18**(2Q), 109–120 (2015)
41. Nguyen, T.D., Nguyen, D.T., Cao, T.H.: Acceptance and use of information system: e-learning based on cloud computing in Vietnam. In: Linawati, Mahendra, M.S., Neuhold, E.J., Tjoa, A.M., You, I. (eds.) ICT-EurAsia 2014. LNCS, vol. 8407, pp. 139–149. Springer, Heidelberg (2014). doi:10.1007/978-3-642-55032-4_14
42. Nguyen, T.D., Nguyen, D.T., Nguyen, T.M.: Information systems success: the project management information system for ERP projects. In: Vinh, P., Alagar, V. (eds.) ICCASA 2015. LNCS (LNICST), vol. 165, pp. 198–211. Springer, Cham (2016). doi: 10.1007/978-3-319-29236-6_20
43. Nguyen, T.D., Nguyen, T.M., Cao, T.H.: Information systems success: a literature review. In: Dang, T.K., Wagner, R., Küng, J., Thoai, N., Takizawa, M., Neuhold, E. (eds.) FDSE 2015. LNCS, vol. 9446, pp. 242–256. Springer, Cham (2015). doi:10.1007/978-3-319-26135-5_18
44. Nguyen, T.D., Nguyen, T.M., Cao, T.H.: The relationship between IT adoption, IS success and project success. In: ICACCI Proceedings, pp. 1197–1203. IEEE (2016)
45. Petter, S., DeLone, W., McLean, E.: Measuring information systems success: models, dimensions, measures, and interrelationships. Eur. J. Inf. Syst. **17**(3), 236–263 (2008)
46. Petter, S., DeLone, W., McLean, E.: The past, present, and future of "IS Success". J. AIS **13**(5), 341–362 (2012)
47. Petter, S., DeLone, W., McLean, E.: Information systems success: the quest for the independent variables. J. Manag. Inf. Syst. **29**(4), 7–62 (2013)
48. Pinto, J., Prescott, J.: Variations in critical success factors over the stages in the project life cycle. J. Manag. **14**(1), 5–18 (1988)
49. Pinto, J., Prescott, J.: Planning and tactical factors in the project implementation process. J. Manag. Stud. **27**(3), 305–327 (1990)
50. Pinto, J., Slevin, D.: Critical success factors in effective project implementation. In: Project Management Handbook, pp. 479–512. Wiley, Hoboken (1988)

51. Pinto, J., Slevin, D.: Critical success factors in R&D projects. Res. Technol. Manag. **32**(1), 31–35 (1989)
52. Putra, S., Subiyakto, A., Ahlan, A., Kartiwi, M.: Coherent framework for understanding the success of an information system project. Telecommun. Comput. Electron. Control **14**(1), 302–308 (2016)
53. Rai, A., Lang, S., Welker, R.: Assessing the validity of IS success models: an empirical test and theoretical analysis. Inf. Syst. Res. **13**(1), 50–69 (2002)
54. Renzel, D., Klamma, R., Jarke, M.: IS success awareness in community-oriented design science research. In: Donnellan, B., Helfert, M., Kenneally, J., VanderMeer, D., Rothenberger, M., Winter, R. (eds.) DESRIST 2015. LNCS, vol. 9073, pp. 413–420. Springer, Cham (2015). doi:10.1007/978-3-319-18714-3_33
55. Rogers, E.: Diffusion of Innovations. Simon and Schuster, New York (1995)
56. Rockart, J.: Critical success factors. Harv. Bus. Rev. **57**(2), 81–91 (1979)
57. Sambasivan, M., Wemyss, G., Rose, R.: User acceptance of a G2B system: a case of electronic procurement system in Malaysia. Internet Res. **20**(2), 169–187 (2010)
58. Schultz, R., Slevin, D., Pinto, J.: Strategy and tactics in a process model of project implementation. Interfaces **17**(3), 34–46 (1987)
59. Scopus: Journal Rankings – Subject Category: Management Information Systems. Scimago Lab (2016). http://www.scimagojr.com
60. Seddon, P.: A respecification and extension of the DeLone and McLean Model of IS success. Inf. Syst. Res. **8**(3), 240–253 (1997)
61. Seddon, P., Kiew, M.: A partial test and development of the DeLone and McLean model of IS success. ICIS Proc. **4**(1), 99–110 (1994)
62. Seddon, P., Staples, S., Patnayakuni, R., Bowtell, M.: Dimensions of information systems success. Commun. AIS **2**(3), 5 (1999)
63. Shannon, E., Weaver, W.: Recent contributions to the mathematical theory of communication. Math. Theory Commun. **1**, 1–12 (1949)
64. Shenhar, A., Dvir, D.: Project management research - the challenge and opportunity. Proj. Manag. J. **38**(2), 93–99 (2007)
65. Subiyakto, A., Ahlan, A.: A coherent framework for understanding critical success factors of ICT project environment. In: ICRIIS Proceedings (2013)
66. Subiyakto, A., Ahlan, A., Putra, S., Kartiwi, M.: Validation of information system project success model. SAGE Open **5**(2), 1–14 (2015)
67. Subiyakto, A., Ahlan, A., Kartiwi, M., Sukmana, H.: Measurement of information system project success based on perceptions of the internal stakeholders. Int. J. Electr. Comput. Eng. **5**(2), 271–279 (2015)
68. Sudhakar, G.: Model of critical success factors for software projects. J. Enterp. Inf. Manag. **25**(6), 537–558 (2012)
69. Tate, M., Sedera, D., McLean, E., Jones, A.: Information systems success research: the twenty year update? Commun. AIS **34**(64), 1235–1246 (2014)
70. Taylor, S., Todd, P.: Understanding information technology usage: a test of competing models. Inf. Syst. Res. **6**(2), 144–176 (1995)
71. Thompson, R., Higgins, C., Howell, J.: Personal computing: toward a conceptual model of utilization. MIS Q. **15**(1), 125–143 (1991)
72. Thong, J.: An integrated model of information systems adoption in small businesses. J. Manag. Inf. Syst. **15**(4), 187–214 (1999)
73. Tukel, O., Rom, W.: Analysis of the characteristics of projects in diverse industries. J. Oper. Manag. **16**(1), 43–61 (1998)

74. Turner, J.: The Handbook of Project-Based Management: Improving the Processes for Achieving Strategic Objectives. McGraw-Hill, New York (1993)
75. Urbach, N., Smolnik, S., Riempp, G.: The state of research on information systems success. Bus. Inf. Syst. Eng. **1**(4), 315–325 (2009)
76. Urbach, N., Muller, B.: The updated DeLone and McLean model of information systems success. In: Dwivedi, Y.K., et al. (eds.) Information Systems Theory, vol. 28, pp. 1–18. Springer, New York (2012)
77. Venkatesh, V.: Determinants of perceived ease of use: integrating perceived behavioral control, computer anxiety and enjoyment into the technology acceptance model. Inf. Syst. Res. **11**(4), 342–365 (2000)
78. Venkatesh, V.: Technology acceptance model and the unified theory of acceptance and use of technology. In: Wiley Encyclopedia of Management. Wiley (2015)
79. Venkatesh, V., Bala, H.: Technology acceptance model 3 and a research agenda on interventions. Dec. Sci. **39**(2), 273–315 (2008)
80. Venkatesh, V., Davis, F.D.: A theoretical extension of the technology acceptance model: four longitudinal field studies. Manag. Sci. **46**(2), 186–204 (2000)
81. Venkatesh, V., Morris, M., Davis, G.B., Davis, F.D.: User acceptance of information technology: toward a unified view. MIS Q. **27**(3), 425–478 (2003)
82. Venkatesh, V., Davis, F.D., Morris, M.: Dead or alive? The development, trajectory and future of technology adoption research. J. AIS **8**(4), 267–286 (2007)
83. Venkatesh, V., Thong, J., Chan, F., Hu, P., Brown, S.: Extending the two-stage information systems continuance model: incorporating UTAUT predictors and the role of context. Inf. Syst. J. **21**(6), 527–555 (2011)
84. Venkatesh, V., Thong, J., Xu, X.: Consumer acceptance and use of information technology: extending the unified theory of acceptance and use of technology. MIS Q. **36**(1), 157–178 (2012)
85. Venkatesh, V., Thong, J., Xu, X.: Unified theory of acceptance and use of technology: a synthesis and the road ahead. J. AIS **17**(5), 328–376 (2016)
86. Wang, M.H., Yang, T.Y.: Investigating the success of knowledge management: An empirical study of small-and medium-sized enterprises. Asia Pac. Manag. Rev. **21**, 79–91 (2016)
87. Wateridge, J.: IT projects: a basis for success. Int. J. Proj. Manag. **13**(3), 169–172 (1995)
88. Wateridge, J.: How can IS/IT projects be measured for success? Int. J. Proj. Manag. **16**(1), 59–63 (1998)
89. Webster, J., Watson, R.: Analyzing the past to prepare for the future: writing a literature review. MIS Q. **26**(2), 13–21 (2002)
90. Westerveld, E.: The project excellence model: linking success criteria and critical success factors. Int. J. Proj. Manag. **21**(6), 411–418 (2003)
91. Wixom, B., Todd, P.: A theoretical integration of user satisfaction and technology acceptance. Inf. Syst. Res. **16**(1), 85–102 (2005)

Notes on Recognizing Echinocyte by the Top-Hat Transform

Hoang Manh Ha[(✉)]

Faculty of Information Technology, Thu Dau Mot University, 6 Tran Van On,
Phu Hoa, Thu Dau Mot City, Binh Duong, Vietnam
hahm@tdmu.edu.vn

Abstract. In diagnostic of hematology, one of a most important informations is to infer about echinocyte presence. The top-hat transform and its application on echinocyte detection were briefly introduced in [2]. This paper suggests a new improvement based on random method to reduce number of computation for above purpose. We explain the relation between an upper bound of number of the blood cells to perform top-hat transform and number of echinocyte in image.

Keyword: Blood cells · Echinocyte · Top-hat transform

1 Introduction

For many types of images, from satellite images to medical images, the interesting information is given by irregular structures of the objects such as texture. In images of blood cells [3–5], the contour of cells with thorn provides the location of an echinocyte which is particularly meaningful for recognition purpose [1, 6]. The detection of texture of the echinocyte is strongly motivated by purpose of this application. Until now, the top-hat transform is a main mathematical tool for extracting texture from a complex structure of objects in images. In our previous paper [2] an irregular structure of the echinocyte is typically detected by using the top-hat transform. In hospitals, the detection of echinocyte have to implement not only in large number of images but also in a thousand cells per each image. The method we mention above (see [2]) provides only performing top-hat transform all blood cells in image therefore it does not provide simple strategies for detecting an echinocyte presence in a blood cell image with very high density of cells. This is major motivation for studying random methods for collected echinocyte problem.

2 Extract an Irregular Structure by Using the Top-Hat Transform

Denote Gray – scale erosion by

$$(I \odot B)(x, y) = \min\{I(x + s, y + t) - B(s, t)\}, \tag{1}$$

© ICST Institute for Computer Sciences, Social Informatics and Telecommunications Engineering 2017
P. Cong Vinh et al. (Eds.): ICCASA 2016, LNICST 193, pp. 155–160, 2017.
DOI: 10.1007/978-3-319-56357-2_16

where I is a gray scale image. The domain of $I \odot B$ is the erosion of the domain of I by the domain of B.

Dilation of a grey-scale image $I(x, y)$ by a grey-scale structuring element $B(s, t)$ is denoted by

$$(I \oplus B)(x, y) = \max\{I(x - s, y - t) + B(s, t)\} \qquad (2)$$

The domain of $I \oplus B$ is the dilation of the domain of I by the domain of B. Dilation expands image set and erosion shrinks it. In closing process, erosion follows dilation. In opening process, dilation follows erosion. Opening generally smoothes the contour of an image, breaks narrow gaps. As opposed to opening, closing tends to eliminate small holes, and will gaps in the contours. The small feature of image I, denoted by $F_d(I)$, is defined as the difference set of the opening of an image $I(x, y)$ and the domain of I [7]. This is also known as dilation residue edge detector:

$$E_d(I) = (I \odot B) \oplus B - I$$

Figure 1(a) is an original blood cell image. There are some small features on all abnormal cells in this image. These are also morphological characters of blood cell image and these features make it possible to recognise a echinocyte.

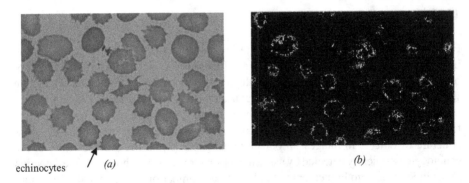

echinocytes   (a)   (b)

Fig. 1. Blood cells image

These features are extracted with the method suggested here. Morphological operations erode in Eq. (1) then morphological operations dilate in Eq. (2).

A difference between a dilated image and the original image makes it possible to extract the feature of echinocyte from the blood cells binary image [7]. An irregular feature of the echinocyte is reflected in Fig. 1(b). All of normal blood cells are disappeared in Fig. 1(b). This result will help observer focus on echinocyte. The extraction of feature of an echinocyte can be explained as follow (Fig. 2).

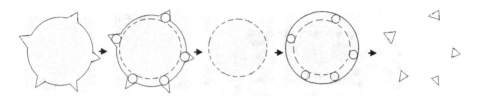

Fig. 2. A description of the irregular structure extraction using top-hat transform

In fact, the top-hat transform of blood cells image with large number of cells has a great computation, it has been shown that a present problem is how to detect echinocyte with minimum cost.

3 Determination of a Presence of an Echinocyte Using Random Texture Extraction Method

An important issue is to minimize time to collect an echinocyte. Suppose that there are n echinocyte in image, equally likely. The problem which have to solve: we need at least how many blood cells do you need to perform an irregular extracting on it to infer the presence of echinocyte. In following section, we show that: for detect all n echinocyte in image of blood cell, the maximum number of the extraction is $n\ln(n) + 13n$. This approach is based on the work of Weiyu Xu and A. Kevin Tang for solving a Generalized Coupon Collector Problem.

Let T be the time to recognize all n echinocyte, and let t_i be the time to recognize the *ith* echinocyte after $i - 1$ echinocyte have been recognized.

Think of T and t_i as geometric random variables. Observe that the probability of recognizing a new recognize given $i - 1$ echinocyte is $p_i = \dfrac{n - (i - 1)}{n}$. Therefore, t_i has geometric distribution with expectation $\dfrac{1}{p_i}$. By the linearity of expectations we have:

$$E[T] = E(t_1) + E(t_2) + \ldots + E(t_n) = \frac{1}{p_1} + \frac{1}{p_2} + \ldots + \frac{1}{p_n}$$
$$= n\left(1 + \frac{1}{2} + \ldots + \frac{1}{n}\right)$$
$$= nH_n$$

where $H_n = \sum_{k=1}^{n} \dfrac{1}{k}$

Using the independence of random variables t_i, we obtain: $Var[T] = \sum_{i=1}^{n} Var[t_i]$

$$\sum_{i=1}^{n} Var[t_i] \leq \sum_{i=1}^{n} \frac{1}{p_i^2}$$

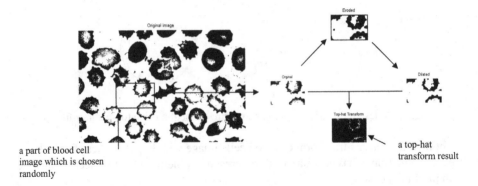

a part of blood cell
image which is chosen
randomly

a top-hat
transform result

Fig. 3. A description of the top-hat transform performing on a part of the blood cell image

$$\sum_{i=1}^{n} \frac{1}{p_i^2} = n^2 \sum_{i=1}^{n} \frac{1}{i^2}$$

$$n^2 \sum_{i=1}^{n} \frac{1}{i^2} \leq n^2 \sum_{i=1}^{\infty} \frac{1}{i^2} \quad \Rightarrow \quad Var[T] \leq \frac{n^2 \pi^2}{6}$$

Now we can use the Chebyshev inequality to bound the desired probability:

$$P\left(|T - nH_n| \geq cn\right) \leq \frac{2}{c^2}$$

$$\Rightarrow P\left(|T - nH_n| \geq \frac{c\sqrt{6}}{\pi}\sqrt{\frac{n^2 \pi^2}{6}}\right) \leq \frac{\pi^2}{6c^2}$$

For recognizing n echinocyte with probability of success is 0.9999 we need to perform $nH_n + 12.84n \approx n\ln(n) + 13n$ top-hat transform on blood cells. Following numerical example illustrate the mathematical results. The top-hat transform is performed on a part of the blood cells image which are chosen randomly as box in Fig. 3.

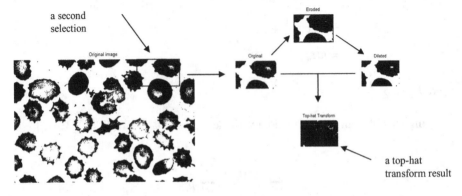

a second
selection

a top-hat
transform result

Fig. 4. A description of the top-hat transform performing on a second part of the blood cell image

In a top-hat transform result (Fig. 3), some of speckles reflect a echinocyte presence. The top-hat transform have a echinocyte detection in other part of that blood cell image (Fig. 4).

We performed these simulations over 25 images of blood cell with echinocyte for supporting results in the last section. Table 1 also show that there is much decreasing for computation to detect echinocyte when use our propose.

Table 1. The result of the echinocyte detection over 25 images with echinocyte

	Total of blood cells in image (estimate)	Number of Echinocyte in image n	Upper bound (Rounding of $n \ln(n) + 13n$)	The number of the extraction
1	1000	10	153	55
2	995	11	169	60
3	1005	15	236	45
4	1010	16	252	60
5	998	12	186	56
6	1500	20	320	45
7	1125	14	219	59
8	1229	22	354	15
9	800	5	73	55
10	1120	10	153	57
11	1525	9	137	60
12	1455	11	169	65
13	1112	9	137	45
14	1025	8	121	75
15	925	25	405	12
16	875	21	337	15
17	1002	10	153	30
18	1235	9	137	65
19	1225	10	153	58
20	1015	15	236	25
21	775	36	597	5
22	1300	6	90	80
23	885	40	668	5
24	773	45	756	5
25	1129	8	121	39

Following figure show that a needed extraction for detecting echinocyte always lower than the upper bound that i proposed in Sect. 3. The results in Table 1 and Fig. 5 are showed that the upper bound of the echinocyte $nH_n + 12.84n \approx n \ln(n) + 13n$ is good result for detection time decreasing.

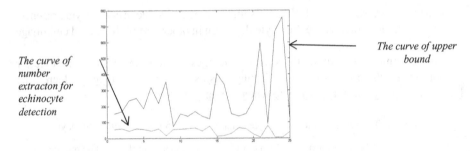

The curve of number extracton for echinocyte detection

The curve of upper bound

Fig. 5. A description of the distance between upper bound and number of extraction for echinocyte detection

4   Conclusion

This study provides a basis for designing an algorithm for detecting echinocyte from blood cells images. This result motivates a development of intelligent microscopes. Echinocyte or abnormal cells can be recognized not only with accuracy but also with low cost.

Acknowledgment. The authors are very grateful to Dr. Pham Canh Duong for his lectures on a PreTopo and Top-Hat transform.

References

1. Pierre, R.V.: Red cell morphology and the peripheral blood film. Clin. Lab. Med. **22**(1), 25–61 (2002)
2. Ha, H.M., Nga, T.T.: Extract an irregular structure of an echinocytes using morphological operations. In: Toi, V.V., Khoa, T.Q.D. (eds.) The Third International Conference on BioMedical Engineering in Vietnam. Springer, Heidelberg (2010)
3. Ranzato, M., et al.: Automatic recognition of biological particles in microscopic images. Pattern Recognit. Lett. **28**, 31–39 (2007)
4. Sonca, M., et al.: Image Processing, Analysis and Machine Vision. Chapman & Hall Computing, New York (1993)
5. Semmlow, J.L.: Biosignal and Biomedical Image Processing Matlab-Based Applications. Marcel Dekker Inc., New York (2004)
6. Mukhopadhyay, R., Gerald Lim, H.W., Wortis, M.: Echinocyte shapes: bending, stretching, and shear determine spicule shape and spacing. Biophys. J. **82**, 1756–1772 (2002)
7. Gonzalez, R.C., Woods, R.E.: Digital Image Processing. Addision-Wesley, Reading (2000)

Personalized Email User Action Prediction Based on SpamAssassin

Ha-Nguyen Thanh[1], Quan-Dang Dinh[2(✉)], and Quang Anh-Tran[3]

[1] Hanoi Department of Information and Communications, Hanoi, Vietnam
nguyenthanhha_sotttt@hanoi.gov.vn
[2] Faculty of Information Technology, Hanoi University, Hanoi, Vietnam
quandd@hanu.edu.vn
[3] Posts and Telecommunications Institute of Technology Hanoi, Hanoi, Vietnam
tqanh@ptit.edu.vn

Abstract. Email overload, even after spam filtering, causes waste of time and reduction of work efficiency to email users. Email prioritization is the general solution for the problem. The idea is to sort incoming emails in a decreasing order of importance so that the most important messages are read and processed first and less significant ones later, if there is enough time. This paper proposed a method to predict the action that a user would take on an email. The method is based on SpamAssassin, a famous spam filter framework. Instead of classifying emails as spam and ham (non-spam message), this method is used to predict amongst the three most common actions: reply, read and delete. Experiments are conducted to measure the effectiveness of the new method on a dataset built by the authors.

Keywords: Personalized email prioritization · Email user action · SpamAssassin

1 Introduction

Communication over the Internet has become crucial in every country and in every aspect of the modern society. Among the many applications of the Internet, email is one of the most used, most important. Email allows people to exchange information in a fast, reliable and cost-effective way. According to statistics reports, the number of emails sent per day in 2015 is approximately 205.6 billion and the figure is expected to be 246.5 billion in 2019 [14]. Along with email's increased usage volume come a great number of unwanted messages called spam (unsolicited bulk email). With a large number of spam, it takes more time for email users to process daily messages.

Spam's bad impacts led to the need for spam filtering. There have been many approaches to spam filtering which can be divided into two main categories: SMTP-based filtering and machine learning [1].

The SMTP-based filtering category addresses the weaknesses of SMTP – the protocol used for sending email. For instance, SMTP does not verify email senders [1], leading to the fact that it is trivial to fake email sender. Attackers can exploit this weakness to send spam or perform online phishing. To tackle that flaw, researchers have

P. Cong Vinh et al. (Eds.): ICCASA 2016, LNICST 193, pp. 161–171, 2017.
DOI: 10.1007/978-3-319-56357-2_17

introduced several methods to verify the sender including Sender Policy Framework (SPF), DomainKeys Identified Mail (DKIM) and SenderID. This category also includes methods such as Blacklisting, Greylisting and so on.

Approaches in the machine learning category focus on analyzing email content using a classifier. Many classifiers and their variations have been applied to detect spam [11, 15], e.g. Naïve Bayes, k-Nearest Neighbor (kNN), Support Vector Machines (SVM), Term Frequency-Inverse Document Frequency (TF-IDF) and so on. Methods in this category have been widely applied and the current state-of-the-art methods are based on Bayesian filters with filtering rates exceeding 99.5% [15].

The popularity of email also leads to the email overload, even after spam filtering. The problem tends to get more serious as Spira and Goldes stated in their study [6] that a typical office worker gets around 200 legitimate emails per day. High-level officers and managers receive even more emails. Emails of different levels of importance are mixed, making important emails easy to be missed.

The above issue can be solved with email prioritization – sorting incoming emails based on their importance. There are two different groups of email prioritization methods. The first group employed regression-based methods [3, 7, 8] because it assumes the linearity of email's importance. The second one considers it a multiclass classification problem. The number of classes is usually three [2, 4] or five [8–10]. User action prediction falls into this category. These studies have yet to achieve a practical performance. This field of study is a new, highly potential one. Therefore, it requires a lot more efforts to be made.

This paper proposes a new method which utilizes SpamAssassin to predict user action on an email. It involves automatic generation and optimization of different SpamAssassin rulesets in order to turn SpamAssassin into a multiclass classifier. Popular multiclass classifier building techniques (OVA, OVO and DAG) are tested against a self-built personal email dataset. Two experiments are conducted to test the prediction rate of the new method as well as its degree of personalization.

This paper's main contribution is as follows: A new method to predict user action on emails based on SpamAssassin is proposed; Experiments to compare different methods using different sets of personalized email data were conducted; Through our experiments, we evaluated the impact of personalized factors on the results of our method.

The remaining of this paper is organized as follows: Section 2 reviews papers related to the user action prediction problem; Section 3 explains the proposed method in details; Section 4 describes two experiments that we conducted and their results; Section 5 concludes our findings and suggests directions for future works.

2   Preliminaries

2.1   Studies on the User Action Prediction Problem

User action prediction aids users in processing daily emails by automatically determine the action that should be done on an email. If a user knows which email should be replied, read or deleted, he will be able to take suitable actions in order to save time. There have been a few studies to tackle this problem.

The problem was first introduced in 2005 [5]. Authors of [5] evaluated the factors that affect user's responses to incoming emails in order to produce a method to predict user action. Their study was done through an online survey in which questions are divided into three parts. The first part is to collect users' work environment information and the characteristics of their jobs. The second part asks about users' email usage and habits. The last part gathers information on content characteristics, level of importance, characteristics of the sender and associated actions on emails. The study used a self-built dataset with 1100 email messages. 124 persons took part of the survey. 10 features were used to predict the importance of an email. This study found that there is correlation between the importance/probability to get replied of an email and user's relationship with the sender as well as the email's content.

In [2], the authors proposed an email user action recommender system. The system is essentially a Bayesian multiclass classifier where each class represents a user action. There are three user actions: "reply", "read" and "delete".

2.2 SpamAssassin

SpamAssassin is a popular open-source spam filter which operates on multiple platforms. It uses a set of weighted (scored) rules to identify spam. Most of SpamAssassin rules are basically Regular Expressions used to find textual structures which indicate that a message is spam. Figure 1 shows an example of SpamAssassin's rule.

```
body       MONEY_BACK    /money back guarantee/i
describe   MONEY_BACK    Money back guarantee
score      MONEY_BACK    2.910
```

Fig. 1. A typical SpamAssassin body rule.

In Fig. 1, there is a body rule named MONEY_BACK. This rule checks if the body of an email contains a string that matches the RegEx "*/money back guarantee/i*" and adds a score of 2.910 to the total spam score of that email. The higher the total score, the more likely a message is spam. By default, all emails whose total score is equal to or higher than a threshold $T = 5.0$ are considered spam by SpamAssassin. The threshold T can be adjusted by user. Equation (1) shows how SpamAssassin calculates the total score for each message.

$$Score_R(m) = \sum_{i=1}^{k} Match(R_i, m) \times w_i \qquad (1)$$

where:

- $Score_R(m)$ returns the total score against ruleset R for the message m.
- R is a set consisting of k rules ($R_1 ... R_k$).
- $Match(R_i, m)$ returns 1 if m contains a string that matches rule R_i, 0 otherwise.
- w is a set of k scores ($w_1 ... w_k$) corresponding to k rules.

The score return by $Score_R(m)$ is compared to the threshold T to determine if m is spam using Eq. (2).

$$Spam_R(m) = \begin{cases} 1, & Score_R(m) \geq T \\ 0, & Score_R(m) < T \end{cases} \tag{2}$$

2.3   Automatic Generation of SpamAssassin Rules

The study in [12] proposed the method for automatic generation of SpamAssassin rules to detect spam in Vietnamese. That process can be summarized as follows:

Step 1 – Dataset preparation: According to data labels, separate the training set into two parts. The first part, called D_1, contains spam messages and the order part – D_2 – contains ham messages.

Step 2 – Extracting words: The Vietnamese tokenization tool vnTokenizer [13] is used to extract words from the email subjects in D_1 into the set WS_1. Similarly, words from the content of all emails in D_1 are extracted into the set WB_1.

Step 3 – Selecting keywords: The most frequent words from WS_1 and WB_1 are kept and put into two new sets, WS_2 and WB_2.

$$WS_2 = \forall w \in WS_1, freq_{WS_1}(w) > \alpha$$
$$WB_2 = \forall w \in WB_1, freq_{WB_1}(w) > \beta$$

The function $freq_{WS_1}(w)$ returns the times which the word w appears in WS_1. The two parameters, α and β, should be adjusted according to the size of the dataset. In our experiments (which are described later in Sect. 4), we use the value 2 and 6 for α and β respectively.

Step 4 – Building ruleset: A ruleset R_1 is build. Subject rules are generated from the keywords in WS_2 and body rules are generated from keywords in WB_2. Figure 2 shows the structure generated rules. In Fig. 2, *<word>* is replaced by the actual keyword from the two keyword sets.

```
header    ReplySubj_i  Subject ~= /\b<word>\b/i
describe  ReplySubj_i  Subject contains "word"
score     ReplySubj_i  0.1
```

Fig. 2.   The structure of auto-generated rules for SpamAssassin.

Step 5 – Rule selection: SpamAssassin's MassCheck tool is executed to see how the rules in R_1 are matched against emails in D_1 and D_2. Bad rules – rules with low hit rate or rules which match both spam and ham – are removed to create a new ruleset called R_2.

Step 6 – Weight (score) optimization: First, the MassCheck tool is executed again for the new ruleset (R_2). In R_2, each rule is initialized with a score value 0.1. A perceptron with a linear transfer function and a logsig activation function is built. Its weights are mapped to rule scores. It is then trained using the Stochastic Gradient Descent method to achieve highest spam recall and lowest ham error rate [18]. When training completes, the ruleset R_3 is created from R_2's rules and trained scores.

3   Email User Action Prediction Based on SpamAssassin

SpamAssassin, or more specifically, a SpamAssassin ruleset, is able to separate spam from ham. Therefore, it is a binary classifier. In this paper, we make SpamAssassin a multiclass classifier to predict user action (REPLY, READ, DELETE) on an email. Our proposed method can be easily configured to build a system which classifies emails into more than 3 classes. We apply three different approaches of building multiclass classifiers: OVA, OVO and DAG.

The authors of this paper observed that different generated SpamAssassin rulesets have different spam recall and ham error rates at different thresholds. This is not a problem when using a single ruleset. However, to perform multiclass with SpamAssassin, multiple rulesets are required. Therefore, in addition to 6 steps of rule generation described in Sect. 2.3, we add one more step to find the best threshold for each ruleset created. The best threshold for a ruleset is defined as one which achieves the highest *spam recall* while *ham error* remains lower than 1%.

3.1   OVA (One vs. All)

Assume that we have N classes called X_i ($i = 1, 2...N, N > 2$). N binary classifiers called C_i ($i = 1, 2...N$) are needed to build a classifier for N classes using OVA method. Each classifier C_i is able to separate data of class X_i (One) from data of the other ($N - 1$) classes (All). As mentioned before, a SpamAssassin ruleset is equivalent to a binary classifier. Therefore, we need to build N rulesets for OVA to work. The algorithm for the prediction process of the OVA method is described in Fig. 3.

> *Input:*   An email message m
> N rulesets RS_i ($i = 1, 2...N$)
> N thresholds for the rulesets T_i ($i = 1, 2...N$)
> A default class (in case all rulesets return 0)
> *Output:*   An integer indicating the class for the message m
> 1.   **Set** $S = new\ Array()$, $max = 0$, $class = defaultClass$
> 2.   **For** $i = 1 \rightarrow N$
> 3.   **Set** $S_i = Score_{RS_i}(m) \div T_i - 1$
> 4.   **If** $(S_i > max)$ **then** { Set $class = i$, $max = S_i$ }
> 5.   **Return** ($class$)

Fig. 3.   OVA prediction algorithm.

When building the ruleset for class X_i using the process described in Sect. 2.3, the D_1 should consist of emails marked as X_i and D_2 should contain the emails from all other classes. After the process, a ruleset RS_i should be created and there should be N rulesets ($RS_1, RS_2...RS_N$).

3.2   OVO (One vs. One)

In this method, there exists a binary classifier between any pair of different classes. The input data is tested against all classifiers and results them are aggregated to produce the final prediction. However, there are many aggregation models for OVO. In this paper, we adapt three most popular models which are MS (Max Sum, also called "Weighted Voting") [17], MV (Majority Voting) [16] and MC (Most Confident) [8].

For N classes, the number of binary classifiers needed is $N_R = N \times (N-1) \div 2$. For instance, when $N = 2, 3, 4$, $N_R = 1, 3, 6$. This means N_R rulesets $RS_{i,j}$, in which i and j represents two different classes among N classes, should be built. When building $RS_{i,j}$ using the method described in Sect. 2.3, the set D_1 should contain emails from class X_i and D_2 should contain emails from class X_j. The threshold for $R_{i,j}$ is $T_{i,j}$. To predict using the OVO-MS aggregation model, we use the algorithm shown in Fig. 4.

> *Input:*   An email message m
> N_R rulesets $R_{i,j}$ ($1 \le i \le N$, $1 \le j \le N$, $i < j$)
> N_R corresponding thresholds $T_{i,j}$
> A default class (in case all classes get equal weight)
> *Output:*   An integer indicating the class for the message m
> 1. **Set** $S = new\ Array()$
> 2. **For** $i = 1 \to N$ { **Set** $S_i = 0$ }
> 3. **For** $i = 1 \to N - 1$
> 4.   **For** $j = i + 1 \to N$
> 5.   **Set** $tmp = Score_{R_{i,j}}(m) \div T_{i,j} - 1$
> 6.   **Set** $S_i = S_i + tmp$, $S_j = S_j - tmp$
> 7. **Set** $equalCheck =$ true, $class = 1$, $max = S_1$
> 8. **For** $i = 2 \to N$
> 9.   **If** $S_i \ne S_{i-1}$ **then** { **Set** $equalCheck =$ false }
> 10.   **If** $S_i > max$ **then** { **Set** $class = i$, $max = S_i$ }
> 11. **Return** ($equalCheck$? $defaultClass$: $class$)

Fig. 4.   The algorithm for OVO-MS prediction model.

OVO-MV predicts the class similarly to OVO-MS. The only difference is that OVO-MV counts the votes from classifiers instead of adding up their scores (see Fig. 5).

A binary classifier gives a score to indicate its level of confidence. OVO-MC selects the class that receives the *highest confidence* from any classifier (Fig. 6).

Input: An email message m

N_R rulesets $R_{i,j}$ ($1 \leq i \leq N$, $1 \leq j \leq N$, $i < j$)

N_R corresponding thresholds $T_{i,j}$

A default class (in case all classes get equal vote)

Output: An integer indicating the class for the message m

1. **Set** $S = new\ Array()$, $max = 1$, $class = defaultClass$
2. **For** $i = 1 \rightarrow N$ { **Set** $S_i = 0$ }
3. **For** $i = 1 \rightarrow N - 1$
4.   **For** $j = i + 1 \rightarrow N$
5.   **If** $Score_{R_{i,j}}(m) \div T_{i,j} \geq 1$ **then**
6.   **Set** $S_i = S_i + 1$
7.   **Else**
8.   **Set** $S_j = S_j + 1$
9. **For** $i = 1 \rightarrow N$
10.   **If** $S_i > max$ **then** { **Set** $class = i$, $max = S_i$ }
11. **Return** ($class$)

Fig. 5. The algorithm for OVO-MV prediction model.

Input: An email message m

N_R rulesets $R_{i,j}$ ($1 \leq i \leq N$, $1 \leq j \leq N$, $i < j$)

N_R corresponding thresholds $T_{i,j}$

A default class (in case all scores are equal)

Output: An integer indicating the class for the message m

1. **Set** $S = new\ Array()$
2. **For** $i = 1 \rightarrow N$ { **Set** $S_i = 0$ }
3   **For** $i = 1 \rightarrow N - 1$
4.   **For** $j = i + 1 \rightarrow N$
5.   **Set** $tmp = Score_{R_{i,j}}(m) \div T_{i,j} - 1$
6.   **If** $tmp > S_i$ **then**
7.   **Set** $S_i = tmp$
8.   **Else If** $1 - tmp > S_j$ **then**
9.   **Set** $S_j = 1 - tmp$
10. **Set** $equalCheck = $ true, $class = 1$, $max = S_1$
11. **For** $i = 2 \rightarrow N$
12.   **If** $S_i \neq S_{i-1}$ **then** { **Set** $equalCheck = $ false }
13.   **If** $S_i > max$ **then** { **Set** $class = i$, $max = S_i$ }
14. **Return** ($equalCheck$? $defaultClass$: $class$)

Fig. 6. The algorithm for OVO-MC prediction model.

3.3   DAG (Directed Acyclic Graph)

Similar to OVO, DAG requires a binary classifier for each pair of different classes. However, DAG reduces the number of classifiers invoked in the prediction phase to ($N - 1$) by making use of a binary decision tree. N_R classifiers are arranged in the order given in

Fig. 7. At each level, the prediction process follows either the left or right branch from the current node depending on the outcome of the classifier at that node.

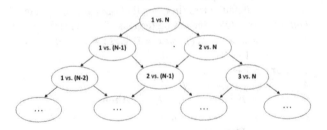

Fig. 7. The binary decision tree for the DAG model.

To apply DAG for the user action prediction problem, we repeat the rule creation part of OVO to build N_R rulesets. After that, we apply the algorithm described in Fig. 8 for prediction.

> *Input:*   An email message m
> N_R rulesets $R_{i,j}$ $(1 \leq i \leq N, 1 \leq j \leq N, i < j)$
> N_R corresponding thresholds $T_{i,j}$
> *Output:* An integer indicating the class for the message m
> 1. **Set** $i = 1$, $j = N$, *class* $= 0$
> 2. **While** $i < j$ **do**
> 3.   **If** $Score_{R_{i,j}}(m) > T_{i,j}$ **then**
> 4.   **Set** $j = j - 1$, *class* $= i$
> 5.   **Else**
> 6.   **Set** $i = i + 1$, *class* $= j$
> 7. **Return** (*class*)

Fig. 8. The prediction algorithm for DAG.

4   Experiments

4.1   Dataset

Our dataset consists of 1408 emails in both English and Vietnamese collected from a personal mailbox. For this same set, 3 different sets of labels are collected. The first label set is directly extracted from the email owner's real data. Two more sets of label are done independently by 2 volunteers. The numbers of emails labeled by 3 users are shown in Table 1.

4.2   Experiment 1

This experiment is conducted to compare 5 multiclass classification models used in our study: OVA, OVO-MS, OVO-MV, OVO-MC and DAG. The authors used 2 measures

Table 1. Number of emails labeled by 3 different users.

User	Reply	Read	Delete	Total
1	183	704	335	1408
2	316	504	402	1408
3	270	402	550	1408

for evaluation: Accuracy and Delete FPR (False Positive Rate, also called "Fall-out"). Accuracy is a common measure used to evaluate multiclass classifiers [2, 15]. In the email user action prediction problem, marking a READ or REPLY email as DELETE is obviously more serious than marking a DELETE email as READ or REPLY. Therefore, the authors decided to include the FPR measure for the DELETE class to more accurately evaluate the methods. Regarding the user action prediction problem, FPR for DELETE can be interpreted as "*How many important messages are mistakenly classified as DELETE?*". Equation (3) shows the formula for Accuracy and Eq. (4) illustrates the FPR measure.

$$Accuracy = \frac{\#\,of\,correct\,predictions}{total\,\#\,of\,tests} \tag{3}$$

$$FPR = \frac{false\,positives}{false\,positives\,+\,true\,negatives} \tag{4}$$

- *false positives*: the number of REPLY and READ messages marked as DELETE.
- *true negatives*: the remaining number of REPLY and READ messages.

From the test results (see Table 2), OVA has the highest overall Accuracy but also the highest FPR. OVO-MC produces lowest FPR but has poor Accuracy. DAG seems to be the most balanced model with high Accuracy and reasonably low FPR.

Table 2. Accuracy and Delete FPR measured from testing with 5 different methods on 3 users. Shown values are 10-fold cross validation average, represented in percentage (%).

User	OVA		OVO-MS		OVO-MV		OVO-MC		DAG	
	Acc.	FPR	Acc.	FPR	Acc.	FPR	Acc.	FPR	Acc.	FPR
1	85.04	2.36	78.86	2.44	75.14	2.21	70.18	0.51	82.82	0.88
2	69.96	6.40	69.39	4.78	65.25	4.27	58.64	1.47	70.03	2.28
3	72.80	7.09	72.56	4.31	65.11	4.31	54.74	1.48	66.54	2.01

4.3 Experiment 2

This experiment is done to see if a user's rulesets can be effectively applied to other users. We get the rulesets from user 1 for the test because it gives the best results. These rulesets are tested on user 2 and user 3's data. In this experiment, only the Accuracy measure is used (Table 3).

Table 3. Accuracy measured from using user #1's rulesets to test against the other users' test data. Shown values are 10-fold cross validation average, represented in percentage (%).

User	OVA	OVO-MS	OVO-MV	OVO-MC	DAG
1	85.04	78.86	75.14	70.18	82.82
2	63.60	60.49	56.98	55.03	61.08
3	49.72	47.98	47.21	44.67	47.40

Accuracy is decreased dramatically in all 5 methods. This means the rulesets built for a user are personalized and it is not feasible for other users to use those rulesets.

5 Conclusion

In this paper, we proposed a method to predict user action on email using SpamAssassin. From our experiments, a few conclusions can be made. Firstly, among five prediction models that we studied, DAG has the highest overall performance. Second, the rate of false positives for the Delete action is still not practical. We should attempt to repeat the experiments using different parameters to reduce Delete FPR. Finally, our new method is intended for personal email data and experiment result has proven so. For future studies, we would like to consider experimenting on a large dataset and apply more features besides email content.

References

1. Caruana, G., Li, M.: A survey of emerging approaches to spam filtering. ACM Comput. Surv. (CSUR) **44**(2), 9 (2012)
2. Ha, Q.M., Tran, Q.A., Luyen, T.T.: Personalized email recommender system based on user actions. In: Asia-Pacific Conference on Simulated Evolution and Learning, pp. 280–289 (2012)
3. Hasegawa, T., Ohara, H.: Automatic priority assignment to E-mail messages based on information extraction and user's action history. In: International Conference on Industrial, Engineering and Other Applications of Applied Intelligent Systems, pp. 573–582 (2000)
4. Dabbish, L.A., Kraut, R.E., Fussell, S., Kiesler, S.: Understanding email use: predicting action on a message. In: Proceedings of the SIGCHI Conference on Human Factors in Computing Systems, pp. 691–700 (2005)
5. Bennett, P.N., Carbonell, J.: Detecting action-items in e-mail. In: Proceedings of the 28th Annual International ACM SIGIR Conference on Research and Development in Information Retrieval, pp. 585–586 (2005)
6. Spira, J.B., Goldes, D.M.: Information overload: We have met the enemy and he is us. Basex Inc. (2007)
7. Neustaedter, C., Brush, A.B., Smith, M.A., Fisher, D.: The social network and relationship finder: social sorting for email triage. In Proceedings of 7th Annual Collaboration, Electronic messaging, Anti-Abuse and Spam Conference (CEAS) (2005)
8. Yoo, S., Yang, Y., Carbonell, J.: Modeling personalized email prioritization: classification-based and regression-based approaches. In: Proceedings of the 20th ACM International Conference on Information and Knowledge Management, pp. 729–738 (2011)

9. Yang, Y., Yoo, S., Lin, F., Moon, I.C.: Personalized email prioritization based on content and social network analysis. IEEE Intell. Syst. **25**(4), 12–18 (2010)

10. Yoo, S., Yang, Y., Lin, F., Moon, I.C.: Mining social networks for personalized email prioritization. In: Proceedings of the 15th ACM SIGKDD International Conference on Knowledge Discovery and Data Mining, pp. 967–976 (2009)

11. Blanzieri, E., Bryl, A.: A survey of learning-based techniques of email spam filtering. Artif. Intell. Rev. **29**(1), 63–92 (2008)

12. Dinh, Q.D., Tran, Q.A., Jiang, F.: Automated generation of ham rules for Vietnamese spam filtering. In: the 2014 Seventh IEEE Symposium on Computational Intelligence for Security and Defense Applications (CISDA), pp. 1–5 (2014)

13. Huyen, N.T.M., Roussanaly, A., Vinh, H.T.: A hybrid approach to word segmentation of Vietnamese texts. In: International Conference on Language and Automata Theory and Applications, pp. 240–249 (2008)

14. The Radicati Group. Email Statistics Report, 2015–2019. Palo Alto, CA, USA (2015)

15. Carpinter, J., Hunt, R.: Tightening the net: A review of current and next generation spam filtering tools. Comput. Secur. **25**(8), 566–578 (2006)

16. Friedman, J.: Another approach to polychotomous classification, vol. 56. Technical report, Department of Statistics, Stanford University (1996). http://statweb.stanford.edu/~jhf/ftp/poly.pdf

17. Hastie, T., Tibshirani, R.: Classification by pairwise coupling. The annals of statistics **26**(2), 451–471 (1998)

18. Stern, H.: Fast SpamAssassin Score Learning Tool (2004). https://svn.apache.org/repos/asf/spamassassin/trunk/masses/README.perceptron

Deadlock Avoidance for Resource Allocation Model V VM-out-of-N PM

Ha Huy Cuong Nguyen[1(✉)], Hoang Dung Tran[2], Van Thang Doan[3], and Vu Thi Phuong Anh[4]

[1] Department of Information Technology, Quangnam University, Tam Ky, Vietnam
nguyenhahuycuong@gmail.com
[2] College of Food Industry, Danang City, Vietnam
dungdnt@gmail.com
[3] Ho Chi Minh City Industry and Trade College, Ho Chi Minh City, Vietnam
vanthangdn@gmail.com
[4] Quangnam University, Tam Ky, Vietnam
vuphuonganhdbqh@gmail.com

Abstract. This paper, presents an deadlock avoidance for model V VM-out-of-N PM. Algorithm used to reschedule the policies of resource supply for resource allocation on heterogeneous distributed platform. In the current scenario, deadlock avoidance for model V VM-out-of-N PM algorithm using Two - Way search method has created the problem of taking higher time complexity of $O(m*(n − 1)/2 + 2e)$ where e is the number of edges, for m processes at n sites. This paper proposes the algorithms for allocating multiple resources to competing services running in virtual machines on a heterogeneous distributed platform. We have implemented and performed our algorithm proposed by using *CloudSim* simulator. The experiments results show that our algorithm can quickly avoid deadlock and then resolve the situation of approximately orders of magnitude in practical cases.

Keywords: Cloud computing · Resource allocation · Heterogeneous distributed platforms · Deadlock avoidance

1 Introduction

In the past, grid computing and batch scheduling have both been commonly used for large scale computation. Cloud computing presents a different resource allocation paradigm than either grids or batch schedulers [1,3,4]. Infrastructure as a Service (IaaS) is the concept of resource allocation hardware as a service. It allocation the required hardware resources offers CPU, RAM, HDD and software resources. Infrastructure as a Service is the Virtual Machine (VM) in heterogeneous. The introduction of heterogeneity allows clouds to be competitive with traditional distributed computing systems, which often consist of various types of architecture as well. Recently, reports have appeared that many of the studies provide cloud computing resources, the majority of this research to deal with

© ICST Institute for Computer Sciences, Social Informatics and Telecommunications Engineering 2017
P. Cong Vinh et al. (Eds.): ICCASA 2016, LNICST 193, pp. 172–182, 2017.
DOI: 10.1007/978-3-319-56357-2_18

variability in resource capacity for infrastructure and application performance in the cloud. In this paper, we develop a method to avoid a deadlock occurs in the process of providing resources in class infrastructure as a service. Our rating indicates that the deadlock avoidance method using Two-Way search algorithm may improve the effectiveness and efficiency of resource allocation for heterogeneous distributed platforms.

In this work, we propose a deadlock avoidance algorithm, to avoid deadlock in resources allocation for model V VM-out-of-N PM. More specifically, our contributions are as follows:

1. Based on the resource model provides P-out-of-Q. We develop the resource model provides multiple virtual machines on multiple physical machines scattered V VM-out-of-N PM.
2. We provide an algorithmic to request and to avoid deadlock in resource allocation for model V VM-out-of-N PM. This algorithm is, in fact, more generally, even for heterogeneous distributed platforms, and only allows allocating minimal resources to meet QoS (*Quality of Service*) arbitrary force.
3. We have studied the effects not effective in resources allocation, predict failures may occur in the system heterogeneous and suggest different approaches to mitigate this problem, followed by set out a strategy of automation in providing resources.

The work is organized as follows: Section 2 describes existing models; Section 3 provides the related works; Section 4 presents algorithm; Section 5 experiments and results and Sect. 6 presents our conclusions and suggestions for future work finally.

In this paper, we consider the proposed model resources allocation V VM-out-of-N PM. From this model, we propose two algorithms to solve the problem. That algorithm resource requirements and algorithms avoid deadlock in resource allocation.

2   System model resource allocation in heterogeneous distributed platforms

2.1   The V VM-out-of-N PM model

A heterogeneous distributed platforms are composed of a set of an asynchronous processes $(p_1, p_2, \ldots, p_n)$ that communicates by message passing over the communication network [4]. Based on the basic work of the authors Kshemkalyani-Singhal, and other works such as Menasce-Muntz, Gligor - Shattuck, Ho - Ramamoorthy, Obermarck, Chandy, and Choudhary [10]. They have the same opinions that the requested resource model of distributed system is divided into five model resource requirements. It's simple resource models, resource models OR, AND resource models, models AND/OR, and model resource requirements P-out-of-Q. Through this model, the researchers have discovered a technical proposal deadlock corresponding to each model. In this work, we use model

P-out-of-Q as a prerequisite for developing research models provide resources in the cloud. The V VM-out-of-N PM problem depicts on-demand resource allocation to V VMS residing in N servers, where each VM may use resources in more than one server concurrently. Thus, we model it to guide the design of algorithm avoid deadlock in resource allocation among VMs each of which may use the resource in various servers concurrently.

E_{ijt} is the amount of resources allocated to VM_{ij} at time t, where

$$\sum_{i}^{N} E_{ij} = \sum_{i}^{N} (A_{ij} + \sum_{i=1}^{V} C_{ij}) \tag{1}$$

E_{ijt} obeys the rules as follows:

$$E \geq \sum_{i=1}^{N} \sum_{j=1}^{V_N} E_{ijt} \tag{2}$$
$$E_{ijt} \geq C_{ij} \geq 0 (i = 1, ..., N; j = 1, ..., V_N)$$

The resource allocation problem is how to control the resource allocation to VMs with the goal of minimizing the function F_t, giving the limited resources. We get the following formulation:

$$F_t = min \sum_{i=1}^{N} \sum_{i=1}^{V_i} \frac{f_{ij}(EN_{ijt}, \sum_{x=1}^{V} EO_{ijt}^x, D_{ijt})}{\Phi_{ij}} \times SP_{ij}$$
$$\begin{cases} \sum_{i=1}^{N} \sum_{i=1}^{V_i} E_{ijt} \leq E \\ E_{ijt} \geq C_{ij} \ (i = 1, 2, ..., V; j = 1, 2, ..., N) \\ \sum_{i=1}^{V_i} EN_{ijt} + \sum_{j=1}^{V_i} EO_{ijt}^i \leq E_i \\ E_{it} \geq C_{ij} \ (i = 1, 2, ..., V; j = 1, 2, ..., N). \end{cases} \tag{3}$$

We can use methods to avoid deadlock to solve optimal resource model provides V VM-out-of- N PM. Our algorithm is based on wait-for graphs (WFG) algorithm is presented in Sect. 4.

2.2   Problem with Definitions

The clustering is the subdivision of graph node set into groups. It partitions the graph into a smaller subdivision of connected sub graph called clusters. The techniques use the tree data structure to store the information about the graph edges and nodes [10].

In heterogeneous distributed platforms, the state of the system can be modeled by a directed graph, called a wait for graph (WFG). In a WFG, nodes are processes and there is a directed edge from node P_1 to node P_2 if P_1 is blocked and is waiting for P_2 to release some resources. A system is deadlocked if and only if there exists a directed cycle or knot in the WFG [10].

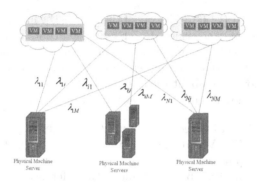

Fig. 1. A simple model V VM-out-of-N PM

An allocation of resources to a virtual machine specifies the maximum amount of each individual element of each resource type that will be utilized, as well as the aggregate amount of each resource of each type (Fig. 1).

In heterogeneous environment, resource allocation is thus represented by two vectors, a maximum elementary allocation vector and an aggregate allocation vector.

Resource allocation graphs are used to detect and avoid deadlock in heterogeneous system. Creating resource allocation graph for IaaS is very difficult due to dynamic nature of cloud user and their respective requirements.

2.3 Resources Allocation Based on Approaches Fuzzy

The current, we know only a few research apply Fuzzy Logic to resource allocation. Fuzzy logic [5] is a tool that deals with uncertain, imprecise, or qualitative information, as well as with precise information in heterogeneous system. Which are not defined with formal mathematical the model V VM-out-of-N PM. In Boolean logic, an element x can or cannot belong to a set A, with a membership degree equal to 1 or 0. Instead, in fuzzy logic, the membership degree of x to a fuzzy set F has a value in a continuous interval between 0 and 1. A fuzzy subset A of a set X can be defined as a set of ordered pairs, each with the first element from X and the second from the interval [0,1], with exactly one ordered pair for each element of X. Unlike classical set theory, Fuzzy theory allows an element to have partial membership degree in one or more fuzzy sets. This membership degree is obtained through membership functions that map elements into the interval [0,1]:

$$\mu A : X \rightarrow [0, 1] \tag{4}$$

The value zero and one represent complete non-membership and complete membership respectively, whereas values in the interval [0, 1] represent intermediate degrees of membership. Fuzzy logic can be used for the design of control dynamic allocation resource in heterogeneous systems. In this case, the controller is called

Fuzzy Logic Controller (FLC). The core of the FLC is the inference engine, whose role is to apply the inference rules (IF-THEN rules) contained in the rule base. IF-THEN rules are made by antecedents, consequence and embody the system control dynamic. These rules are implemented by fuzzy implications and represent the expert knowledge about the systems behavior.

The FLC main modules are the following [9]:

- Inputs fuzzification: FLC receives as input the differences between the IaaS resources values. The VM request parameters, which will be fuzzified using membership functions.
- Inference engine and Rule base: the role of the Inference engine is to infer the fuzzy implication contained in the Rule base.
- Defuzzification method: center of gravity has been used as defuzzification algorithm for the aggregated fuzzy subset.

The inputs fuzzification process includes the definition of fuzzy sets for inputs classification and the corresponding membership functions, thus determining the inputs membership degrees, always included by definition in the interval [0, 1].

3 Related Works

Resource allocation in cloud computing has attracted the attention of the research community in the last few years. In 2015, Nguyen [1] used an anlytical model to estimate completion time, and they used the result to determine right size of resources. In previous articles we have published two algorithms. Which were used to detect deadlock in resources allocation heterogeneous distributed platforms [1,3]. We provide deadlock detection algorithms and resolve the optimization problems of resources based the recovery of resources allocated. In [3], we provide deadlock detection algorithms and resolve optimal problems according to groups of users. To maximize performance, these scheduling algorithms tend to choose free load servers when allocating new VMs. On the other hand, the greedy algorithm can allocate a small lease (e.g. with one VM) to a multi-core physical machine. In this study, we propose solutions to avoid deadlock in resource supply, then proceed to build the resource supply automatically detects and avoid deadlock occurs. This issue is also effective in allocation resources. The mathematical model computes the optimal number of servers and the frequencies at which they should run in [5,6,9].

In [6], the authors build a fuzzy set for only 7 cases. However, in actual, the value of fuzzy sets is more. In addition, the authors use fuzzy logic to build value for each member of the fuzzy sets. In the next study, we will propose a new model for VM resource allocation based on Hedge Algebras. We will use hedge algebras for building value for each member in the fuzzy sets and fuzzy membership function.

Based on the advantages of the structure of hedge algebra (HA), the authors studied and apply in the models (fuzzy relational database and fuzzy object-oriented database model) and there have been many results [5,6].

Approached in hedge algebra, in which linguistic semantics be quantified by quantitative semantic mapping of hedge algebra. In this approach, language semantics can be expressed in a neighborhood of intervals determined by the fuzziness measure of linguistic values of an attribute as a linguistic variable.

On this basis, we will consider domain of fuzzy value is hedge algebra and transformer interval values into subsegment [0, 1], and thereby providing resource allocation for virtual machine with fuzzy information and uncertainty become effective.

4   Our Algorithm

In this paper, we will proposed algorithm for deadlock avoidance maintains property of n-vertex directed graph when the new is added in the graph using two-way search.

The time bound for the incremental cycle algorithm for deadlock avoidance take $O(m^*(n-1)/2 + 2e)$ time bound for the e edge insertion in the directed graph. It reports the cycle when the algorithm detects for edge (v,m) that there exist a path from vertex w to v.

As can be considered here is the case where a process p_i requires the resources it needs for its session one after the other, hence the name incremental requests. The main issue that has to be solved is the avoidance of deadlocks.

As a matter of fact that deadlock avoidance would help in providing resources as good as possible.

As it is commonly known, process must wait for the resources as deadlock occurred since they are being occupied by other processes.

Therefore, when process in a wait-for the dependency is broken, the corresponding information must be instantly restored from the system, otherwise, deadlock would be happening.

Let r_1, r_2, ...,r_n be the whole set of resources accessed by the processes, each process accessing possibly only a subset of them.

Let < be a total order on this set of resources. The processes are required to obey the following rule:

- During a session, a process may invoke request resource(r_k) only if the it has already obtained all the resources r_j it needs which are such $r_j < r_k$.
- As p_1 is owning the resource r_a and waiting for the resource r_b, it invoked first request resource(r_a) and then a request resource(r_b).
- As p_2 is owing the resource x_b and waiting for the resource r_a, it invoked first request resource(r_b) and then request resource(r_a).

Algorithm 1. Deadlock Avoidance Algorithm (DAA)

Input: $P_i^{j(CPU)^*}$, $P_i^{j(RAM)^*}$ from IaaS provider i;
Output: new resource $r_j^{CPU^{(n+1)}}$, $r_j^{RAM^{(n+1)}}$;

BEGIN
Operation request resource (r_i) in the critical section is
$csstate_i \longleftarrow$ trying;
$lrd_i \longleftarrow clock_i + 1$;
for each $j \in R_i$ do
if $(usedby_i[j] = 0)$ the send request (lrd_i, i) to p_j end for;
$sentto_i$ [j] $\longleftarrow$ true;
$usedby_i[j] \longleftarrow$ R
else $sentto_i[j] \longleftarrow$ false
end if
end for;
$usedby_i[i] \leftarrow k_i$;
wait $(\sum\limits_{j=1}^{V} usedby_i[j] \leq NPM)$;
$csstate_i \longleftarrow$ in;
When REQUEST(i,j,k) is received from p_j do
$clock_i \leftarrow$ max$(clock_i, n)$;
$prio_i \leftarrow (csstate_i = in) \vee ((csstate_i = trying) \wedge ((lrd_i, j, k) < (n, j, k)))$;
$if(prio_i)$ then send USED(N PM) to p_j else if$(n_i \neq N$ PM) then send USED(N PM - n_i)
to p_j end if
$permdelayed_i \leftarrow permdelayed_i \cup$ j
end if.
When permission(i,j,k) is received from p_j do
$NPM_i \leftarrow NPM_i \setminus$ j;
When USED(x) is received from p_j do $usedby_i[j] \leftarrow usedby_i[j] - x$;
$if((csstate_i = trying) \wedge (usedby_i[j] = 0) \wedge (notsentto_i[j])$
then send RELEASE(lrd_i, j, k) to p_j
$sentto_i[j] \leftarrow$ false;
$usedby_i[j] \leftarrow N$ PM;
end if.
END.

In many systems, a heterogeneous environment is preferable to one that is homogeneous. However, it provides better performance particular systems and workload. Even if the workload itself is more suitable to a heterogeneous distributed platforms, the systems rescheduling algorithm should exploit heterogeneity well to benefit from it (Table 1).

Table 1. The description of notations

Notations	Meanings
$csstate_i = $ out	mean that p_i is not interested in executing the statemment critical section
$csstate_i = $ in	mean that p_i is executing the statemment critical section
$csstate_i = $ trying	mean that p_i is executing the operation requests resource
$clock_i$	mean that is a scalar clock initialized to 0
lrd_i	mean that is a local variable used by p_i to save the logical date of its
$prio_i$	mean that is an auxiliary Boolean when it receives a request message
$permdelayed_i$	mean that is a set used by p_i to contain the identities of the processes
$usedby_i$	mean that is the identities of the processes

5 Experiments and Results

In this paper, the solution provides effective resources is done through two algorithms. Algorithm resource requirements and algorithms avoid deadlock in resource supply. Based on the resource model provides V VM-out-of-N PM. Methods of optimizing the use of functions in the formula 3. Optimal recovery method in materials allocated because the process still holds resources when finishing requirements (Table 2).

The comparative analysis of experimental result can be seen in many times, apter task execution, although there were individual time improved PDA algorithm response time was not significantly less than an optimal time algorithm. In most cases, improved algorithm is better than the optimal time algo-

Table 2. Comparison the optimal time of our algorithm DAA to PDDA Improved [3] algorithm

Cloudlet ID	Data center ID	VM ID	PDDA Improved			DAA			Improved (%)
			Start	End	Time	Start	End	Time	
0	1	1	0.1	100.1	100	0.1	70.1	70	22.22%
1	2	2	0.1	110.1	110	0.1	80.1	80	20.00%
2	3	3	0.1	132.1	132	0.1	80.1	80	27.27%
3	3	4	0.1	145.1	145	0.1	90.1	90	43.75%
4	1	5	0.1	147.1	147	0.1	100.1	100	39.39%
5	2	6	0.1	145.1	145	0.1	110.1	110	36.05%
6	1	7	0.1	152.1	152	0.1	110.1	110	42.86%
7	2	8	0.1	153.1	153	0.1	100.1	100	44.44%
8	3	9	0.1	163.1	163	0.1	90.1	90	50.55%
9	2	10	0.1	168.1	168	0.1	65.1	65	64.86%

Table 3. Comparison the optimal time of our algorithm DAA to PDA [2] algorithm

Cloudlet ID	Data center ID	VM ID	PDA [2]			DAA			Improved (%)
			Start	End	Time	Start	End	Time	
0	1	1	0.1	60.1	60	0.1	70.1	70	10.00%
1	2	2	0.1	67.1	67	0.1	80.1	80	13.00%
2	3	3	0.1	74.1	74	0.1	80.1	80	16.00%
3	3	4	0.1	82.1	82	0.1	90.1	90	8.00%
4	1	5	0.1	83.1	83	0.1	100.1	100	23.00%
5	2	6	0.1	95.1	95	0.1	110.1	110	16.00%
6	1	7	0.1	90.1	90	0.1	110.1	110	20.00%
7	2	8	0.1	89.1	89	0.1	100.1	100	11.00%
8	3	9	0.1	72.1	72	0.1	90.1	90	18.00%
9	2	10	0.1	50.1	50	0.1	65.1	65	15.00%

rithm, thus validated the correctness and effectiveness. The process of rescheduling parallel tasks determines the order of task execution and the processor to which each task is assigned.

Typically, an optimal reschedule is achieved by minimizing the completion time of the message request.

Finding the optimal reschedule has long been known as an NP-hard problem in both heterogeneous distributed platforms and homogeneous.

The experiments were conducted in an environment CloudSim, test data are as follows: Table 3 [11].

The experiment results show that our technology resource allocation used algorithms avoid deadlock can reduce completion time by up 20% when compared to simple algorithm allocation (Fig. 2).

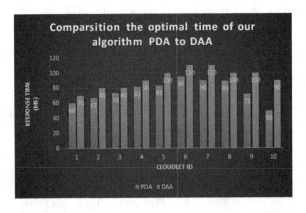

Fig. 2. Comparison the optimal time of algorithms PDA and DAA

6 Conclusion and Future Works

A wait-for graph in model V VM-out-of-N PM is a directed graph used for detection and avoidance deadlock. The comparative analysis of experimental result can be seen in many times, apter task execution, although there were individual time DDA algorithm response time greater than an optimal time algorithm, in most cases, improved algorithm is better than the optimal time algorithm, thus validated the correctness and effectiveness. In summary, there have been a body of researches in cloud computing systems that take either heterogeneous.

In paper, we attempt to exploit heterogeneity and ensure fairness at the same time. A deadlock avoidance algorithm is implemented for resource allocation on heterogeneous distributed platforms. The avoid deadlock algorithm has $O(m^*(n - 1)/2 + 2e)$ time complexity, an improvement of approximate orders of magnitude in practical cases.

In this way, programmers can quickly avoid deadlock and then resolve the situation, e.g., by releasing held resources. Through this research, we found that the application of appropriate avoid deadlock algorithms would give optimal performance to distributed resources of virtual server systems.

References

1. Nguyen, H.H.C., et al.: A new technical solution for resource allocation in heterogeneous distributed platforms. In: Mizera-Pietraszko, S.F.J. (ed.) Advances in Digital Technologies, pp. 184–194. IOS Press, The Netherlands: The University of Macau, Macau (2015)
2. Nguyen, H.H.C., et al.: Deadlock prevention for resource allocation in heterogeneous distributed platforms. In: Mizera-Pietraszko, S.F.J., Chung, Y.-L., Pichappan, P. (eds.) Advances in Digital Technologies, pp. 40–49. IOS Press, The Netherlands: The University of Macau, Macau (2016)
3. Nguyen, H.H.C., Dang, H.V., Pham, N.M.N., Le, V.S., Nguyen, T.T.: Deadlock detection for resource allocation in heterogeneous distributed platforms. In: Unger, H., Meesad, P., Boonkrong, S. (eds.) Recent Advances in Information and Communication Technology 2015. AISC, vol. 361, pp. 285–295. Springer, Cham (2015). doi:10.1007/978-3-319-19024-2_29
4. Nguyen, H.H.C., Le, V.S.: Detection and avoidance deadlock for resources allocation in heterogenenous distributed plaforms. Int. J. Comput. Sci. Telecommun. (IJCST), English **6**(2), 1–6 (2015)
5. Adami, D., Gabbrielli, A., Giordano, S., Pagano, M., Portaluri, G.: A fuzzy logic approach for resources allocation in cloud data center. In: Proceedings 2015 IEEE Globecom Workshops (GC Wkshps), pp. 1–6 (2015)
6. Thang, D., Quoc, D.C.: Defining membership functions in fuzzy object-oriented database model. In: Dang, T.K., Wagner, R., Küng, J., Thoai, N., Takizawa, M., Neuhold, E. (eds.) FDSE 2015. LNCS, vol. 9446, pp. 314–322. Springer, Cham (2015). doi:10.1007/978-3-319-26135-5_23
7. Sotomayor, B.: Provisioning computational resources using virtual machines and leases. Ph.D. thesis, University of Chicago (2010)

8. Sotomayor, B., Keahey, K., Foster, I.T.: Combining batch execution and leasing using virtual machines. In: HPDC, pp. 87–96 (2008)
9. Warneke, D., et al.: Exploiting dynamic resource allocation for efficient parallel data processing in the cloud. IEEE Trans. Parallel Distrib. Syst. **22**(6), 985–997 (2011)
10. Kshemkalyani, A.D., Singhal, M.: Distributed Computing Principles, Algorithms, and Systems. Cambridge University Press, UK (2008)
11. www.cloudbus.org/cloudsim/

Enhance Performance of Action Evaluation Functions with Stochastic Optimization Algorithms

Nguyen Quoc Huy[1,2(✉)], Dao Duy Nam[1,3], and Dang Cong Quoc[4]

[1] SaigonTech, SaigonTech Tower, Lot 14, Quang Trung Software City,
District 12, Ho Chi Minh City, Vietnam
{huy.nq,namdd}@saigontech.edu.vn
[2] Saigon University, District 5, Ho Chi Minh City, Vietnam
[3] High school for the gifted, VNUHCM, 153 Nguyen Chi Thanh, District 5,
Ho Chi Minh City, Vietnam
[4] Hue University, 03 Le Loi, Hue City, Vietnam
dangcongquoc@hitu.edu.vn

Abstract. In this paper, we describe how to optimize the weights of board cells from data set of game records, the weights of board cells are applied in the action evaluation function which usually uses to enhance Monte Carlo Tree Search programs. The general optimization process is introduced and discussed, and one specific method is implemented. We use Othello as a testing environment, and experiment results is better if the action evaluation function is better.

1 Introduction

The emergence of Monte Carlo Tree Search (MCTS) has led to considerable result in resolving the difficult problems of board games with a very large search space as well as the games that are difficult to build a board evaluation function. MCTS need not a board evaluation function, but it needs a good action evaluation function to enhance its performance. Static knowledge combined with an action evaluation function is a popular method when implementing a Monte Carlo framework in order to improve the quality of the simulated games of simulation phase as well as for knowledge bias of selection phase. Many such systems have been developed, and used domain knowledge encoded from game records to provide a good probability distribution for random games. Weighting of board cells is one of many methods to incorporate domain knowledge into board game programs. Historically, Artificial Intelligence game programmers learned the target game, and weighted the board cells by their experience. Today, the weighting of cells can be optimized automatically by many methods, if game records are available.

The optimization process has three main elements: variables to be optimized, the objective function, and the optimization method. This process will optimize the variables, the optimized variables will be applied in an action evaluation function. There are many representations of variables, many kinds of objective functions, many optimization methods. The optimization process is introduced detail in Sect. 3.

© ICST Institute for Computer Sciences, Social Informatics and Telecommunications Engineering 2017
P. Cong Vinh et al. (Eds.): ICCASA 2016, LNICST 193, pp. 183–192, 2017.
DOI: 10.1007/978-3-319-56357-2_19

In this paper, the variables that we want to optimize are the weights of board cells. There are many board cells in a game board, and each cell has an important degree for game players. How to find the best weights of board cells based on the huge game records is an interesting problem. Evolutionary computing is an option of solving effectively for the optimization problems. From that, our problem can be formulated as finding a solution maximizing a criterion among a number of candidate solutions.

Othello is a popular game, its rules are simple. Moreover, we have already the high quality Othello game records. Thus, we select Othello as a testing environment for our research. Because of the symmetry of game board, so we need to find the weights of nine positions {A1, B1, C1, D1, B2, C2, D2, C3, D3} such that the winning probability of a selected move from data set of game records is maximal (see Fig. 1(b)), instead of weighting the board cells by experts (see Fig. 1(a)) [9]. Because the weighting by experts is not precise in complex board such as Shogi, Go. Besides, we have many levels of game records, the automatic weighting is very comfortable in adjusting the strong level of board game program.

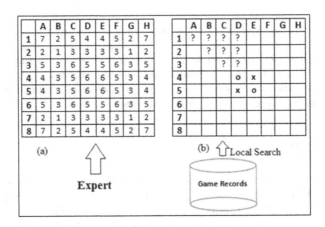

Fig. 1. The board cells to be optimized

This paper is organized as follows: Section 2 discusses related work about MCTS and knowledge encoding, Sect. 3 explains the problem description and our method in details, Sect. 4 presents experimental results and evaluating them, and Sect. 5 presents our conclusions and future work.

2   Related Works and Background

This section introduces some related works, and we focus on three things: (1) What is MCTS, (2) how to obtain knowledge from game data before adding it into MCTS, and (3) how an action evaluation function improve MCTS.

2.1   Learning from Game Records

There are many methods to extract knowledge from professional game records. A popular approach to automatically generate patterns is supervised learning such as a pattern extraction scheme for efficiently harvesting patterns of a given size and shape [3], using the relative frequencies of local board patterns observed in game records to generate a ranked list of moves [2], using a neural network approach to generate local moves [6], using the K nearest-neighbor representation to generate local moves [1], or automatic acquisition of tactical patterns for eyes or connections [7]. In this approach, expert knowledge is used to choose some relevant pattern shapes and pattern features, and then a machine-learning algorithm is used to find the patterns corresponding to these shapes and features, and then to evaluate them. The advantage of automatic pattern learning over hand-made patterns is that thousands of patterns may be generated and evaluated with little effort, and little domain expertise [4]. Also, Michael Buro proposed a Generalized Linear Evaluation Model (GLEM) [10] for building pattern-based evaluations. In this model, feature weights are optimized by using linear regression, and then GLEM combines automatic feature space exploration with fast numerical parameter tuning by building patterns from atomic features and assign pattern weights by linear regression. This model is suitable for algorithms that need an evaluation function such as minimax, alpha-beta, and negamax. In this paper, the knowledge to apply into the action evaluation function to enhance MCTS programs is the weight of board cells. The weight will be optimized by optimization process. It will search the best value of each cell such that all values of cells will be the most matching with the data set of game records.

2.2   Improving the MCTS with Static Knowledge

Monte Carlo Tree Search is a method of finding optimal decisions by taking random samples in the decision space. With static knowledge, MCTS can use an action evaluation function to enhance the quality of simulated games better than that of random simulations as well as the accuracy of selection policy.

Simulation Improvement: Probabilities and selections are two characteristics this step for the quality of simulated game. The selection in simulation phase is different with the selection step of MCTS, we can choose one of approaches such as Roulette-wheel, tournament selection, Reward-based selection, stochastic universal sampling, and Rank-base selection.

Progressive Strategy: The UCB + MCTS will be done accurately if the number of playouts is high. In case of the branching factor is high but the number of playouts is low, the UCB + MCTS will be inaccurate. Using a probability model with static knowledge to improve the move search more efficient is called progressive strategy. There are two progressive strategies: (1) Progressive widening first reduces the branching factor, and then increases it gradually to limit the number of search moves. (2) Knowledge bias uses knowledge to direct the search to give a bonus to make UCT be more accurate if the number of playouts is low. Adding a bias in UCB formula is applied in several MCTS programs such as Erica and Zen. Our paper is based on the integration between knowledge action evaluation function with UCB formula [11]. There are many formulas, but the following formula is the sophisticated one.

$$UCB_{bias}(i) = \frac{w_i}{n_i} + C \times \sqrt{\frac{\ln n}{n_i}} + C_{BT} \times \sqrt{\frac{K}{n+K}} \times P(m_i) \qquad (1)$$

where CBT is the coefficient to tune the effect of bias, and K is a parameter that tunes the rate at which the effect decreases. $P(m_i)$ is the action evaluation function [11].

3   Problem Description and Our Method

The main purpose of this paper is finding the optimized weights of board cells. This is an optimization problem, and has three elements: (1) variables to be optimized, (2) the objective function, and (3) the optimization method. Figure 2 shows the optimization process of variables following an objective function.

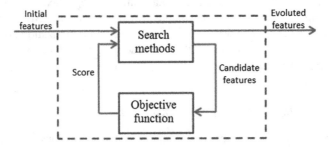

Fig. 2. Process of variables optimization.

3.1   Variables to be Optimized

In board games, the board cells have the different weights following the board game experts. However, the weighting from experts may be not optimal. Thus, we need an optimization method to find the optimal weights of board cells based on the game records. Beside the weights of board cells, there are many kids of other features such as patterns, local shapes, pattern shapes, etc. As the board of Fig. 1(b), we consider nine cells A1, B1, C1, D1, B2, C2, D2, C3, D3, these cells are the variables that need to be optimized in this paper. Let $x = \{x_1, x_2... x_m\}$ be the set of cell weights in the considered part of board. Element x_1 is the weight of board cell A1, element x_2 is the weight of board cell B1,.., element x_9 is the weight of board cell D3. The elements of x is called the variables that need to be optimized.

3.2 Objective Functions

To select the best move from legal moves based on the game records, we usually use some following formulas.

$f_1(H,x) = \dfrac{\sum\limits_{i}^{\|H\|} prob(a_i^*)}{\|H\|}$	$f_2(H,x) = \dfrac{\|\{s,a^* \| prob(a^* < 0.1\}\|}{\|H\|}$
$f_3(H,x) = \dfrac{\sum\limits_{i}^{\|H\|} rank(a_i^*)}{\|H\|}$	$f_4(H,x) = \dfrac{\sum\limits_{i}^{\|H\|} \sum\limits_{a \neq a^*} sigmoid(prob(a_i) - prob(a_i^*))}{\|H\|}$

where $prob(a_i^*) = \dfrac{value(a^*)}{\sum\limits_{a \in A} value(a)}$ is a probability of a move on all legal moves in a state

of board. In Fig. 1(a), we can calculate the probability of a move from the legal moves (B4, C1, F3, G2) in the state of board. The result are $prob(C1) = \frac{4}{3+4+6+1} = 28.57\%$, $prob(B4) = 21.42\%$, $prob(F3) = 42.85\%$, $prob(G2) = 7.14\%$

Then, probability of F3 is the highest, and the action evaluation function will select move F3.

Let H be a set of game records, $| H |$ be the number of moves in set H. The move i^{th} is represented by a pair (s_i, a_i^*), where si is state of board at the move i^{th}. Let A be a set of legal moves in state s, $a \in A$ is a legal move, $a^* \in A$ is a selected move. We see that the Eq. 2 is the most natural one, so it is selected in our method. From that, we can try can compare with other objective function by using Eqs. 3, 4, 5.

3.3 Optimization Method

Some following optimization methods can be used.

Random Search. Given a current solution x, if a new random solution x' is better than current solution x, then $x = x'$. After many iterations, the solution is much better than the initial solution. The cost of this method is low, but the expected performance is not high.

Hill-Climbing. Given a current solution x, the new solutions are in neighborhood region of the current solution. If a new solution x' is better than current solution x, then $x = x'$. After many iterations, the solution is much better than the initial solution. The cost of this method is higher than that of random search, and the expected performance is also higher. This method is always achieved the local optimum.

Simulated Annealing (SA). This method spends more cost than LS to overcome some traps of LS, then the global optimum can be achieved.

Genetic Algorithm (GA). It is difficult to compare the performance between SA and GA, but we can see the cost of SA is lower than GA in generating and evaluating the new solutions.

Brute Force. This method is useful if the search space is small. It is difficult to be used if the search space is large, and the cost of this method is always the highest.

3.4   Our Method

From three elements of optimization process, we can see that there are many methods that are combined by these elements. With the variables are vector x, our method uses the Eq. 2 as the objective function, Hill-Climbing or Simulated Annealing as an optimization method. We select Hill-Climbing or Simulated Annealing to balance between the cost and performance. Figure 3 shows the selected elements of our method.

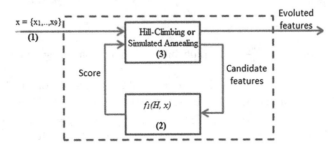

Fig. 3. Process of variables optimization.

Hill-Climbing procedure
Input: set the initial value of vector x, a set of game records H.
Output: the optimized value of vector x
1) The best value of x is the initial value
2) **repeat**
   a) Generate a neighbor x from x
   b) **if** $f_1(H, x) > f_1(H, x')$ **then**
   c) $x = x'$
3) **until** k iterations but no any x' be better than x
4) **return** x

Let $x = \{x_1 \ldots x_9\}$ be the variables to be optimized, $D = \{d_1 \ldots d_9\}$ be the neighborhood region of x, cho $d_i = x_i/10$. Let $x' = \{x'_1 \ldots x'_9\}$, such that $x_i - d_i \leq x'_i \leq x_i + d_i \cdot |H|$ is the number of moves in set of game records H. Each Riversi game record has maximum 60 moves, suppose that the average of each game records is 59 moves, set H has 1000 game records, so the total number of moves is 59000. Each selected move $a*$ leads to a new state of board, the board state includes the set of legal moves A. From that, we can calculate the probability for a selected move $prob(a*)$ based on the weights of board cells. Average of 59000 probabilities is the value of objective function. After many iterations, the value of objective function is increased as the Fig. 4.

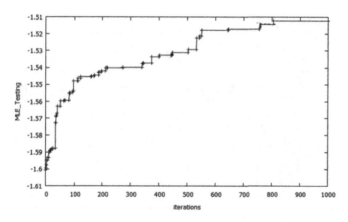

Fig. 4. An evolutionary behavior of Hill-Climbing.

Simulated Annealing Procedure

Input: Set the initial value of vector x, a set of game records H, T_{init}, T_{stop}, *gamma*

Output: the optimized value of vector x

1) $T = T_{init}$;
2) The best value of x is the initial value
3) **while** $T < T_{stop}$
    a) Generate a neighbor x' from x
    b) $\Delta = f_1(H,x) - f_1(H,x')$
    c) **if** $\Delta \le 0$ **then**
    d) x = x'
    e) **else** x = x' with probability $e^{\Delta/T}$
    f) $T = T \times gamma$
4) **return** x

In Simulated Annealing, select randomly a state x' in the neighborhood region of x. If x' is better than $x(cost(x') > cost(x))$, then x' is selected. On the contrary, the state x' is selected with some probability. The probability is decreased by the "badness of state x'. The probability depends on the temperature T. The higher the temperature T is, the more the bad state is selected. In searching process, temperature T decreases gradually to zero. When T is close zero, the behavior of Simulated Annealing looks like that of Hill-Climbing. The probability of selecting the bad state between x' and x is $e^{\Delta/T}$, where $\Delta = \cos t(x') - \cos t(x)$. Figure 5 is the evolutionary behavior of Simulated Annealing, it differs with evolutionary behavior of Hill-Climbing.

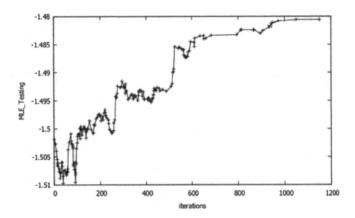

Fig. 5. An evolutionary behavior of Simulated Annealing.

4 Experiments and Evaluation

This section presents the experiments of Hill-Climbing, and Simulated Annealing. From that, we selected the best vector of weights, and applied it into the action evaluation function. The performance of Riversi MCTS is enhanced with the action evaluation function. The process of optimization was performed on game records played by strong players on a site of Michael Buro [5], author of Logistello program.

A. Experiment Results of Hill-Climbing
The parameters for Hill-Climbing:

- Initially, x = {496, 22, 161, 111, 4, 58, 39, 38, 89}
- The maximum iterations but no any candidate were found: 2000
- Number of game records: 480.000

Table 1. The evolutionary process of vector x

Iter	A1	B1	C1	D1	B2	C2	D2	C3	D3	$f_1(H,x)$
init	496	22	161	111	4	58	39	38	89	0.170907
1	503	17	161	88	8	44	59	61	114	0.172096
2	484	27	141	89	16	53	54	43	108	0.175772
4	507	13	149	86	18	43	49	35	92	0.177810
63	508	13	143	114	12	40	61	37	105	0.178249
162	506	23	138	112	17	35	52	39	108	0.178436
179	517	17	142	102	17	37	52	36	93	0.178454
631	510	26	148	113	10	35	60	36	108	0.178508
645	505	31	155	100	16	35	61	38	107	0.179525
967	498	20	144	90	17	38	64	36	103	0.180125
1350	502	16	153	106	18	36	64	35	106	0.180930
...										
3350	502	16	153	106	18	36	64	35	106	0.180930

Table 1 shows the evolutionary process of function f1. The value is evolved by Hill-Climbing method and stop at iteration 1350. We implement Hill-Climbing method many times, and Table 1 is the best one.

B. Experiment Results of Simulated Annealing The parameters for Simulated Annealing:

- Initially, x = {496, 22, 161, 111, 4, 58, 39, 38, 89}
- Number of game records: 480.000
- Initial temperature: T_{init} = 0.001
- Stop temperature: T_{stop} = 0.0001
- Coefficient of temperature decreasing: gamma = 0.999
- Number of iterations (for these parameters): 2301

The neighborhood candidate in Simulated Annealing procedure is changed two random elements in nine elements of vector x. The Simulated Annealing is implemented many times, and Table 2 is the top-4 data of many times.

Table 2. Top-4 Data of Simulated Annealing

Stop at	A1	B1	C1	D1	B2	C2	D2	C3	D3	$f_1(H,x)$
2301	458	416	255	196	10	73	73	38	97	0.182423
2301	464	459	277	212	11	66	69	36	85	0.182348
2301	501	317	302	144	7	55	68	74	96	0.181988
2301	492	343	449	222	4	77	98	81	63	0.181574

C. Applying Monte Carlo Tree Search Program The Monte Carlo Tree Search program in this paper is Riversi MCTS, we implemented a Riversi program based on Monte Carlo Tree Search instead of Alpha-Beta. Besides, we also have the other strong Riversi which is implemented by Alpha-Beta. The Riversi is downloaded from the Internet (http://www.codeproject.com/Articles/4672/Reversi-in-C), we use it for comparing with our program Riversi MCTS.

The best set of weights x = {458, 416, 255, 196, 10, 73, 73, 38, 97} is selected, this set is the variables that make the objective function have the highest value $f_1(H, x)$ = 0.182423. Apply the weights into the action evaluation function $prob(a_i^*) = \dfrac{value(a^*)}{\sum\limits_{a \in A} value(a)}$, the Riversi_MCTS program is improved, Table 3.

Table 3. Performance of Riversi_MCTS before/after using action evaluation function

	Before	After
Riversi_MCTS	343	432
Riversi (expert level)	657	568
Result	657/1000 = 34.3%	568/1000 = 43.2%

5 Conclusion

This section reviews our work, summaries the experiment results, and discusses the future work. The first, we introduce a process of optimization which has three important elements: Variables to be optimized, the objective function, and the optimization method. This process is used to optimize the features from a given set of data. The feature is considered in our paper is the weights of board cells. These weights are applied in the action evaluation function to enhance the MCTS program.

In experiment, we use Hill-Climbing and Simulated Annealing as the optimization methods to balance the cost and the performance of experiments. From that, the best set of weights is found out. These weights are applied into the action evaluation function of our Riversi MCTS program. Performance of MCTS program is improved in comparing with other strong Riversi. However, the performance of Riversi MCTS is still not better than that of Riversi. We have a plan to study in other features instead of the weights of board cells. Besides, this method can be applied in other board games.

References

1. Araki, N., Yoshida, K., Tsuruoka, Y., Tsujii, J.: Move prediction in Go with the maximum entropy method. In: Proceedings of the IEEE Symposium on Computational Intelligence and Games (2007)
2. Stern, D., Herbrich, R., Graepel, T.: Bayesian pattern ranking for move prediction in the game of Go. In: Proceedings of the 23rd international conference on Machine learning, Pittsburgh, pp. 873–880 (2006)
3. Coulom, R.: Computing Elo ratings of move patterns in the game of Go. In: Computer Games Workshop, Amsterdam, Netherlands (2007)
4. http://skatgame.net/mburo/ggs/game-archive/Othello (2012)
5. Werf, E., Uiterwijk, J.W.H.M., Postma, E., Herik, J.: Local move prediction in Go. In: Schaeffer, J., Müller, M., Björnsson, Y. (eds.) CG 2002. LNCS, vol. 2883, pp. 393–412. Springer, Heidelberg (2003). doi:10.1007/978-3-540-40031-8_26
6. Cazenave, T.: Automatic acquisition of tactical go rules. In: 3rd Game Programming Workshop in Hakone, Japan, pp. 10–19 (1996)
7. Chaslot, G., Bakkes, S., Szita, I., Spronck, P.: Monte-Carlo tree search: a new framework for game AI. AIIDE 2008
8. http://www.apld.co.uk/riscworld/volume3/issue5/agrm/chap09.htm
9. Buro, M.: From simple features to sophisticated evaluation functions. In: Herik, H.J., Iida, H. (eds.) CG 1998. LNCS, vol. 1558, pp. 126–145. Springer, Heidelberg (1999). doi:10.1007/3-540-48957-6_8
10. Ikeda, K., Viennot, S.: Efficiency of static knowledge bias in monte-carlo tree search. Computers and Games 2013 (2013)

A Method for Mobility Management in Cellular Networks Using Data Mining

Giang Minh Duc[1(✉)], Le Manh[2], and Do Hong Tuan[1]

[1] HCM City University of Technology, Ho Chi Minh City, Vietnam
ducgm.bdg@vnpt.vn, do-hong@hcmut.edu.vn
[2] Van Hien University, Ho Chi Minh City, Vietnam
manhle@uit.edu.vn

Abstract. The Mobility prediction is one of the important issues in mobile computing systems. The moving logs of mobile users in mobile computing environment are stored in the Home Location Registry (HLR). The generated moving logs are used for mining mobility patterns. The discovered location patterns can be used to provide various location based services to the mobile user by the application server in mobile computing environment. Currently, some papers have written about mobility data mining methods of mobile users in cellular communications networks. In this paper, we propose a method which decrease time to compute the mobility patterns.

Keywords: Data mining · Mobility rules · Mobility prediction · Cellular networks

1 Introduction

Currently, with rapid development of cellular communication networks, many people use their mobile devices to search for information on the internet. Almost everyone has a mobile device such as mobile phones, mobile tablets, notebook, etc. Many people also search for information as traveling all over the world. At about 7 billion mobile phones are used around the world in 2015 at the rate of 95, 56% of the world population[1]. Therefore, the aim of the issue is how to ensure the quality of service of mobile networks.

In cellular communication networks, a mobile user can move from one location to another one, which neighbors' cell in the network. When mobile users move like that, the location of mobile users will be constantly updated to Visitor Location Register (VLR) of the system. VLR is an intermediate database to store temporary information about mobile users in the service area of Mobile Switching Center (MSC). Mobile users' location information then is transferred to home location register (HLR). The HLR is a database which is a long-term storage of mobile users' information. The movement history of mobile users is extracted from the log files and stored in the HLR of the MSC. The historical data is used to predict the mobility of mobile users [1, 7].

---

[1] B. Sanou. (2015, May) www.itu.int/ict. [Online]. https://www.itu.int/en/ITU-D/Statistics/Documents/facts/ICTFactsFigures2015.pdf.

© ICST Institute for Computer Sciences, Social Informatics and Telecommunications Engineering 2017
P. Cong Vinh et al. (Eds.): ICCASA 2016, LNICST 193, pp. 193–204, 2017.
DOI: 10.1007/978-3-319-56357-2_20

In addition, the mobility prediction of the mobile users is used to increase the efficiency of the cellular networks [10, 11]. Many application areas including:

- The service providers can calculate in an optimal way when they design structure and bandwidth of mobile networks [12].
- The telecommunications service providers can reduce the number of unnecessary handover in hierarchical macro/femto-cell networks [13].
- Location Based Services (LBS).
- Etc...

2   Problem Definition

Some researchers applied the data mining techniques and other methods with the aim of solving the problem of cell communication networks, such as mobility, disconnect, long delay time, handover, bandwidth continuously changing... However, these methods have a long execution time. Therefore, to improve further the quality of service of the mobile networks, we propose a new contribution as follows: we redefine the CandidateGeneration() function in the UMPMining algorithm in [7] to reduce running time of the algorithm. Results of our experiment show that our proposed algorithm outperforms the UMPMining algorithm in terms of the execution time.

3   Related Work

The techniques which mine the movement patterns of mobile users is mentioned in the article [3, 4].

Mobility Prediction Method based on Transition Matrix (TM) [5] predicted location according to the ability could occur transition "cell-to-cell" of a mobile user is calculated by the previous move. Relying on this basis, the allocation of resources is done in k cells most likely in the neighboring cell. The parameter k is a parameter defined by the user.

In [6], Katsaros et al. used for discovering user mobility patterns from collections of recorded mobile trajectories, and then these patterns are used for the prediction of location and dynamic allocation of resources.

In [7], Yavas et al. proposed an algorithm for predicting the next inter-cell movement of mobile user in PCSs.

The UMPMining algorithm in [7] predicts the next location of mobile users using data mining techniques. Yavas et al presented an AprioriAll based sequential pattern mining algorithm to find the frequent sequences and to predict the next location of mobile users. They compared their algorithm's results with Mobility Prediction based on Transition Matrix (TM).

The algorithm in [9] is also the same as [7], but the paths storage file of mobile users is stored in the grid node placed at different locations. Data grid [8] provides a geographic distributing database for computational Grid and executes by an algorithm called KMPM (Knowledge Grid Based Mobility Pattern Mining). If the number of nodes increases, the computation time of the algorithm decreases.

In our paper, we propose a method which refines the algorithm of [7] to reduce running time of this algorithm.

4   Implementation

- **Get data from the logs of HLR:**
  The movement of a mobile user from his current cell to another cell will be recorded in a database which is called Home Location Register (HLR). The HLR stores the permanent subscriber information in a mobile network. Every base station keeps a database in which the profiles of the users located in this cell are recorded which is called Visiting Location Register (VLR). The VLR maintains temporary user information like current location for managing requests from subscriber who are out of the home area. The movement history of a mobile user is extracted from the logs on its home location register (Fig. 1).

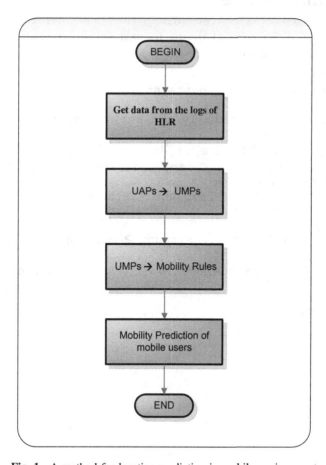

Fig. 1. A method for location prediction in mobile environment

- **Mining the user mobility patterns (UMPs) from user actual paths (UAPs):**
  A user mobility pattern (UMP) is a sequence of neighboring cells in the coverage region network [9]. The consecutive cells of a UMP should be neighbors because the users cannot travel between non neighbor cells. In order to mine the UMPs from user actual paths (UAPs), sequential pattern mining [7] can be used.

Assume that we have UAPs which have form $U = (c_1, c_2, ..., c_n)$. Each c_k denotes the ID number [14] of the k_{th} cell in the coverage region.

Mobility Prediction can be defined as the prediction of a mobile user's next movement where the mobile user is traveling between the cells of a cellular network.

Suppose that there are two UAPs, $A = \{a_1, a_2, ... a_n\}$ and $B = \{b_1, b_2, ... b_m\}$. B is a substring of A, if exist: $1 \le i_1 < ... < i_m \le n$, $b_k = a_{ik}$, $\forall k$, and $1 \le k \le m$.

In addition, B is a substring of A, if all cells of B exist in A (not need sequent in A).

The UMPMining algorithm is a sequence pattern mining algorithm which applied in the movement predict of the cellular networks [7, 9].

UMPMining algorithm

```
Input:   UAPs of database D, min_supp, graph G
Output:  L(UMPs)


 1. C₁ ← the length-1 patterns
 2. k = 1
 3. L = ∅       // initially the set is empty
 4. while Cₖ ≠ ∅
 5.     for each (UAP a ∈ D) do
 6.         S = {s | s ∈ Cₖ and s is subsequence of a}
 7.         for each s ∈ S do
 8.             s.count = s.count + s.suppInc
 9.         endfor
10.     endfor
11.     Lₖ = {s | s ∈ Cₖ, s.count ≥ min_supp }
12.     L = L ∪ Lₖ
13.     Cₖ₊₁←CandidateGeneration(Lₖ,G),∀c∈Cₖ₊₁,, c.count=0
14.     k = k + 1
15. endwhile
16. return L
```

At line 13, the CandidateGeneration () function is written as follows:

CandidateGeneration()

```
Input:   Length-k large pattern, L_k
         Coverage Region Graph, G
Output: Length-(k + 1) candidate patterns, Candidates
```

```
1. Candidates = Ø //Initially the candidates set is empty
2. For each L = (l_1, l_2, ..., l_k), L ∈ L_k {
3.         {N⁺ = {v | there is an edge in G such as l_k → v}
4.         //for each of these neighbor cells, v generate
           a candidate by attaching v to end of L
5.         For each v ∈ N⁺ (l_k ) {
6.              C' = (l_1, l_2, ..., l_k, v)
7.              // Add C' to the candidates' set
8.              Candidates ← Candidates ∪ C'
9.         }
10.    }
11. Return Candidates
```

The above algorithm is a candidate generation algorithm which proposes in [7] and our algorithm as follows (CandidateGeneration_New) is refined in order to decrease running time of candidate patterns.

CandidateGeneration_New()

```
Input:   Length-k large pattern, L_k
         Coverage Region Graph, G
Output: Length-(k + 1) candidate patterns, Candidates
```

Rule: set of length(k) is not large which cannot be subset of large(k+1).

```
1. Candidates = Ø
2. For each L = (l_1, l_2, ..., l_k), L ∈ L_k {
3.   N⁺={v |there is an edge in G such as l_k → v and v∈L}
4.   For each v ∈ N⁺ (l_k) {
5.        C' = (l_1, l_2, ..., l_k, v)
6.        Candidates ← Candidates ∪ C'
7.   }
8. }
9. return Candidates
```

At line 8 of the UMPMining algorithm, value 's' is calculated as follows.

For instance, consider UAPs (4, 6, 8, 0, 5), (2, 4, 8, 0, 6) and (1, 2, 4, 6) where the number 4 represents location of mobile user. The support count of the subsequence (4, 6) can be calculated: s.count = s.count + suppInc and suppInc = $\frac{1}{1+totdis}$ where totdis is number of location between 4 and 6. s.count value is 2 because it appears in 1st and 3rd UAP. In 2nd UAP, there are two locations between 4 and 6. Therefore the support value for 4 and 6 is (4, 6).count = $2 + \frac{1}{1+2}$ = 2.33. It will increase the accuracy of the support counting.

Result with the actual database as follows (Table 1):

Table 1. Result with the actual database

Cn = 2 CANDIDATE	SUPPORT	Ln = 2 PATTERN	SUPPORT
1,7	15.5	1,7	15.5
1,12	15.75	1,12	15.75
1,16	1	1,17	33.5
1,17	33.5	2,21	3
1,18	0.83	3,5	10.34
2,15	0.5	3,17	8.46
2,21	3	3,26	27.67
2,24	0	4,9	20.62
2,45	0	4,23	5
2,47	1.5	4,24	4.5
3,5	10.34	4,25	4.83
3,17	8.46	5,3	11
3,26	27.67	5,16	8.33
4,9	20.62	7,1	11
4,22	0	7,17	3
4,23	5	8,18	6.33
4,24	4.5	8,41	30.33
4,25	4.83	9,4	19
5,3	11	9,21	3.58
5,6	0	10,12	6.98
5,16	8.33	12,1	13.33
5,17	0	12,10	11.83

....

Cn = 3 CANDIDATE	SUPPORT	Ln = 3 PATTERN	SUPPORT
1,7,1	3	1,7,1	3
1,7,17	0	1,12,1	5.83
1,12,1	5.83	1,17,1	10.83
1,12,10	0	3,5,3	2.83
1,12,16	0	3,17,3	1.38
1,17,1	10.83	3,17,26	1.5
1,17,3	0.33	3,26,3	7.5
1,17,7	0.5	4,9,4	5.58
1,17,21	0	4,9,21	1.75
1,17,26	1	4,23,4	2.5
2,21,2	1	4,24,4	2.5
2,21,9	1	4,25,4	1.33
2,21,11	0	5,3,5	3.2
2,21,15	1	5,16,5	4.08
2,21,17	0	7,1,7	5.08
3,5,3	2.83	7,17,7	1.5
3,5,16	0	8,18,8	1.58

....

- **Generation of mobility rules:**

  We can now produce the set of the mobility rules from these UMPs [15]. Assume that we have a UMP C = (c_1, c_2, ..., c_k), where k > 1. All the possible mobility rules which can be derived from such a pattern are:

$$(c_1) \rightarrow (c_2, \ldots, c_k)$$
$$(c_1, c_2) \rightarrow (c_3, \ldots, c_k)$$
$$\ldots$$
$$(c_1, c_2, \ldots, c_{k-1}) \rightarrow (c_k)$$

For example, we have a form UMP is (3, 4, 5). The mobility rules as follows:

$$(3) \rightarrow (4, 5)$$
$$(3, 4) \rightarrow (5)$$

For a mobility rule, we call the part of the rule before the arrow the *head* of the rule, and the part after the arrow the *tail* of the rule. Moreover, when these rules are generated, a confidence value is calculated for each rule. For a mobility rule $R: (c_1, c_2, \ldots, c_{i-1}) \rightarrow (c_i, c_{i+1}, \ldots, c_k)$, the confidence is determined by using the following formula:

$$\text{Confidence (R)} = \frac{(c_1, c_2, \ldots, c_k) \cdot count}{(c_1, c_2, \ldots, c_{i-1}) \cdot count} \times 100$$

By using the mined UMPs, all possible mobility rules are generated and their confidence values are calculated. Then the rules which have a confidence higher than a predefined confidence threshold (min_conf) are selected [15, 16].

we have the results table from actual data as follows (min_conf = 5%):

Table 2. The rules result

The rules: SN	Head	Tail	Confidence
0	1	7	11.8
1	1	12	18.8
2	1	17	36.6
3	3	5	10.5
4	3	17	7.3
5	3	26	25.3
6	4	9	28.5
7	4	23	6.6
8	5	3	13.9
9	5	16	12.1
10	7	1	19.4
11	7	17	8.9
....			
917	53,61	88	9.6
918	53,66	52	75.8
919	54,63	56	6.5
920	54,63	59	5.4
921	54,63	79	36.1
922	54,63	88	8.9
923	54,65	69	12.5
924	54,79	63	64.7
925	56,63	54	64.6
926	56,63	88	50.2
927	56,64	54	99.3
928	57	99,85	6.5

- **The movement prediction of mobile users:**
  From the above rules results (set of mobility rules R), we find out the set of predicted cells as follows (in our work [16]):

Pre_Mov algorithm

```
Input: Current movement of the user: P = (c₁, c₂, ..., cᵢ)
       Set of mobility rules: R.
Output: Set of predicted cells: Pre_Cells.


1. Pre_Cells = Ø    // assign set Pre_Cells = Ø
2. n = 1            // n: cardinal number of Rule_Array
3. For each r: (i₁, i₂,..., iⱼ)→(iⱼ₊₁,..., iₖ)∈ R do
4.     if (i₁, i₂, ..., iⱼ) ⊆ P and iⱼ = cᵢ then
5.         Pre_Rule ← r
6.         Rule_Array[n] ← (Pre_Rule, confidence value)
7.         n = n + 1
8.     endif
9. Endfor
   // in descending order with respect to confidence
   value.
10. Sort (Rule_Array)
11. for i = 1 to n do
       //get the first cell that is on the right side of
         each rule in Rule_Array
12.     Pre_Cells ← Right_cell
13.     n = n + 1
14. Endfor
15. Return Pre_Cells
```

In this part, the next movement of user is predicted. Suppose that the movement of a user (up to now) is $P = (64, 56, 63)$. Current this user is being cell 63 of the coverage region. The algorithm finds out the rules as follows: $(56, 63) \rightarrow (54)$ and $(56, 63) \rightarrow (88)$ (line 925 and 926 of Table 2). The set of predicted cells is {54, 88} (both cell 54 and cell 88 are selected). The cell 54 is selected first because it has the confidence value more than the confidence value of the cell 88 (64.6 and 50.2) (Fig. 3).

5   Experimental Results

We extracted some of data of logs from HLR and the data is:

- The total number of base stations is: 351.
- The total number of user actual paths (UAPs) is: 31415.

C_n, L_n	unrefined		refined	
	quantity	running time	quantity	running time
C_1, L_1	352, 347	27	352, 347	25
C_2, L_2	1493, 1028	125	1489, 1028	69
C_3, L_3	5170, 894	384	4310, 894	184
C_4, L_4	4488, 402	195	1265, 402	56
C_5, L_5	2036, 189	85	487, 189	23
C_6, L_6	931, 64	39	174, 64	9
C_7, L_7	311, 25	13	56, 25	4
C_8, L_8	118, 15	6	21, 15	1
C_9, L_9	74, 9	3	13, 9	1
C_{10}, L_{10}	42, 6	2	7, 6	0
C_{11}, L_{11}	27, 4	1	7, 4	1
C_{12}, L_{12}	20, 2	1	3, 2	0
C_{13}, L_{13}	10, 2	1	3, 2	1
C_{14}, L_{14}	10, 2	0	3, 2	0
C_{15}, L_{15}	10, 0	1	3, 0	0
Total number of running time		883		374

Fig. 2. Experimental results

Where:

- C_1: set of length-1 candidate patterns.
- L_1: set of length-1 large patterns.
- ....
- C_n: set of length-n candidate patterns.
- L_n: set of length-n large patterns.

Time comparing chart:

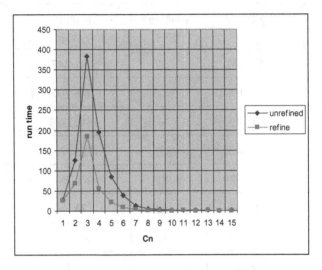

Fig. 3. Comparing time of two algorithms

Our result as follow:

– The number of candidate patterns is reduced:

$C_2 = 1493 - 1489 = 4$
$C_3 = 5170 - 4310 = 860$
$C_4 = 4488 - 1265 = 3223$
$C_5 = 2036 - 487 = 1549$
$C_6 = 931 - 174 = 757$
$C_7 = 311 - 56 = 255$
$C_8 = 118 - 21 = 97$
$C_9 = 74 - 13 = 61$
$C_{10} = 42 - 7 = 35$
$C_{11} = 27 - 7 = 20$
$C_{12} = 20 - 3 = 17$
$C_{13} = 10 - 3 = 7$
$C_{14} = 10 - 3 = 7$
$C_{15} = 10 - 3 = 7$

The total number of candidate patterns is reduced from $C_2 \div C_{15}$: 6899.

– $L_1, L_2, L_3, L_4, L_5, \ldots, L_{15}$ of two algorithms are equal (Fig. 2)
– The total number of running time our algorithm is reduced as follow:

The total number of running time of the algorithm in [7]: 883 s.
The total number of running time of our algorithm: 374 s.
The total number of time reduced: 509 s (57.64%).

6   Conclusion

In this paper, we propose a method which decreases the executing time of the algorithm [7]. In our experimental results, we get data from HLR with 351 base stations and 31415 records of user actual paths (UAPs). The total number of running time of algorithm [7] is 883 s and the total number of running time of our algorithm is 374 s (reduce 57.64%).

References

1. Gok, G., Ulusoy, O.: Transmission of continuous query results in mobile computing sysyems. Inform. Sci. **125**(1–4), 37–63 (2000)
2. Mohan, S., Jain, R.: Two user location strategies for personal communication systems. IEEE Pers. Commun. Mag. **1**, 42–50 (1994)
3. Nanopoulos, A., Katsaros, D., Manolopoulos, Y.: Effective prediction of web user accesses: a data mining approach. In: Proceedings of the WebKDD Workshop (WebKDD 2001) (2001)
4. Nanopoulos, A., Katsaros, D., Manolopoulos, Y.: A data mining algorithm for generalized web prefetching. IEEE Trans. Knowl. Data Eng. **15**(5), 1155–1169 (2003)
5. Rajagopal, S., Srinivasan, R.B., Narayan, R.B., Petit, X.B.C.: GPS-based predictive resource allocation in cellular networks. In: Proceedings of the IEEE International Conference on Networks (IEEE ICON 2002), pp. 229–234 (2002)
6. Katsaros, D., Nanopoulos, A., Karakaya, M., Yavas, G., Ulusoy, Ö., Manolopoulos, Y.: Clustering mobile trajectories for resource allocation in mobile environments. In: R. Berthold, M., Lenz, H.-J., Bradley, E., Kruse, R., Borgelt, C. (eds.) IDA 2003. LNCS, vol. 2810, pp. 319–329. Springer, Heidelberg (2003). doi:10.1007/978-3-540-45231-7_30
7. Yavas, G., Katsaros, D., Ulusoy, O.: A data mining approach for location prediction in mobile environments. Data Knowl. Eng. **54**, 121–146 (2005)
8. Sakthi, U., Hemalatha, R., Bhuvaneswaran, R.S.: Parallel and distributed mining of association rule on knowledge grid. World Acad. Sci. Eng. Technol. **42**, 316–320 (2008)
9. Sakthi, U., Bhuvaneswaran, R.S.: Mobility prediction of mobile users in mobile environment using knowledge grid. J. Comput. Sci. Netw. Secur. **9**(1), 303–309 (2009)
10. Wu, C.-F., et al.: A novel call admission control policy using mobility prediction and throttle mechanism for supporting QoS in wireless cellular networks. J. Control Sci. Eng. **2011**, 21–31 (2011)
11. Nadembega, A., et al.: An integrated predictive mobile-oriented bandwidth-reservation framework to support mobile multimedia streaming. IEEE Trans. Wireless Commun. **13**(12), 6863–6875 (2014)
12. Aljadhai, A., Znaiti, T.: Predictive mobility support for QoS provisioning in mobile wireless environments. IEEE J. Select. Area Commun. **19**(10), 1915–1930 (2001)

13. Jeong, B., Shin, S., Jang, I., Sung, N.W., Yoon, H.: A smart handover decision algorithm using location prediction for hierarchical macro/femto-cell networks. In: 2011 IEEE 74th Vehicular Conference (VTC Fall), San Francisco, CA, September 2011, pp. 1–5 (2011)
14. Manh, L., Duc G.-M.: Transactions in mobile communication. In: Sixth International Conference on Information Technology for Education and Research in HCM City, pp. 120–126 (2010)
15. Duc, G.M., Manh, L., Tuan, D.H.: A novel location prediction algorithm of mobile users for cellular networks. J. Inf. Commun. Technol. (Res. Dev. Inf. Commun. Technol.) E-3, **8**(12), 58–66 (2015)
16. Duc, G.M., Manh, L., Tuan, D.H.: Mobility patterns mining algorithms with fast speed. Trans. Context Aware Syst. Appl. **2**(6), e2 (2015). http://dx.doi.org/10.4108/eai.5-11-2015.150603

Author Index

Printed in the United States
By Bookmasters